THE FINAL VICTORY: THE YEAR 2000

THE FINAL VICTORY: THE YEAR 2000

Marvin Byers

Today, among true Believers, more doctrinal confusion exists regarding what will transpire in the last days than in any other area of truth. God has dedicated more Scripture to this matter than to any other single subject. Therefore, it is evident that God wants us to understand the last days but that Satan, the spirit of error, does not. Why?

© Copyright 1994 — Marvin Byers

All rights reserved. This book is protected under the copyright laws of the United States of America. This book may not be copied or reprinted for commercial gain or profit. The use of short quotations or occasional page copying for personal or group study is permitted and encouraged. Permission will be granted upon request. Unless otherwise identified, Scripture quotations are from the King James Version of the Bible. Emphasis within Scripture is the author's own.

Treasure House

An Imprint of

Destiny Image
P.O. Box 310
Shippensburg, PA 17257

"For where your treasure is
there will your heart be also." Matthew 6:21

ISBN 1-56043-824-X

For Worldwide Distribution
Printed in the U.S.A.

1-800-LAST-DAY
(1-800-527-8329)

First Edition: 1991
Second Edition: 1994

Treasure House books are available through these fine distributors outside the United States:

Christian Growth, Inc.
Jalan Kilang-Timor, Singapore 0315

Lifestream
Nottingham, England

Rhema Ministries Trading
Randburg, South Africa

Salvation Book Centre
Petaling, Jaya, Malaysia

Successful Christian Living
Capetown, Rep. of South Africa

Vision Resources
Ponsonby, Auckland, New Zealand

WA Buchanan Company
Geebung, Queensland, Australia

Word Alive
Niverville, Manitoba, Canada

Inside the U.S., call toll free to order:
1-800-722-6774

Acknowledgments

I am what I am by the grace of God, and anything worthwhile found in this book belongs to Him, and came from Him. These are His truths, and not my discoveries. Anything found here that came from me is less than worthless.

I am where I am by the grace of God that has come to me through my wife, Barb. I recognize that the Lord has used her as a channel to bless and prosper my life spiritually. As a vessel, she is as much a part of this book as I am.

I would also like to thank the many people who were willing to invest a great number of hours in proofreading and correcting the manuscript for this book. I know that they did it with a heart of love for the truth, and for me personally.

Bible Version Abbreviations

AMP .... Amplified Bible
ASV .... American Standard Version
KJV .... King James Version
NAS .... New American Standard
NIV .... New International Version
NKJV .... New King James Version
NRSV .... New Revised Standard
RSV .... Revised Standard Version

Contents

Foreword

When I first read this book in its 1991 edition, I was skeptical. The year 2000 seemed so immediate. Furthermore, a Tribulation of only three and a half years preceding was a radical departure from all I had ever been taught or read. Moreover, asserting specific years aroused my cynicism.

Yet, as I read page after page, a case was emerging from Scripture that was difficult to ignore. Still, I had many questions. During this time, I had occasion to visit Guatemala as the guest of Hebron Ministries of which Marvin Byers is the director.

By Providence, the Lord arranged for us to be able to discuss for several hours each day for a week all of my concerns and questions. As a result, I have come to incorporate the scriptural case made in this book into my everyday thinking and expectation.

Almost 20 centuries ago, learned people missed the main event because they were locked into conventional and preconceived scriptural understanding. It may well be that the contents of this book represent a fresh insight and revelation as we come down to the close of this age.

I can only hope that the reader openly considers not only the urgent timetable explained herein, but also lay hold of the perspective offered regarding Israel and the Jewish people. To me, the biblical saga concerning Israel is awaiting the concluding chapters which will report how all the events concerning the ancient people and promises have all come to pass.

Kings, prophets, and priests have looked forward to the days in which we live. It would make sense, as in the past, that God would whisper revealing words as we approach the nearness of His Coming. May His light shine upon us.

Paul Liberman
Messianic Jewish leader and
author of *The Fig Tree Blossoms*

Introduction

Sir Isaac Newton, considered by many to be the greatest scientist that ever lived, revealed the time of Christ's Second Coming over 250 years ago, basing his prediction on a future restoration of the nation of Israel and Daniel's Seventy Weeks. However, neither his generation nor any other has been given the privilege that is ours today of personally witnessing the ultimate fulfillment of God's prophetic Word. Almost three years after the first edition of this book was published in 1991, I had the privilege of reading, for the first time, a copy of Newton's book entitled, *Observations Upon the Prophecies of Daniel.*[1]

Twenty-four years ago I first came to understand the message that is presented in this book. Since then, I have been asked frequently if anyone else in the Body of Christ has confirmed this message concerning the time of Christ's coming and the interpretation of Daniel's Seventy Weeks given here. In fact, most or all of the various aspects of these truths have been confirmed by other believers we have met along the way, but it was an extremely humbling experience to learn that Sir Isaac Newton saw these things long before I came along. So then, regarding some of the key thoughts in this book, instead of saying that others have confirmed what I have seen, I must confess that I am merely one more person who has been permitted to confirm the revelation of others who have gone before, including Sir Isaac Newton. In addition to being a great scientist, a dedicated Believer, and a lover of the Bible, he was an expert in Hebrew and Greek. He obviously had certain advantages in his search for truth that most of us will never have.

---

1. Library of Congress Catalogue Card Number 91-074116.

However, I feel that there is a certain tragedy in all this. Consider that on September 13, 1993, exactly two years after the first edition of this book was published, the greatest gathering of international dignitaries in the history of the United States took place on the White House lawn in Washington, D.C. They were there for the signing of a peace agreement, referred to by the President as "the first time in history that Ishmael and Isaac have made peace." It was actually hailed as one of the most important events in human history. Consider also that for many decades the Church has preached that Israel would sign a peace treaty with her enemies seven years before the end. Coincidentally, that treaty was signed seven years before the year 2000, the year we carefully examine in this book. In fact, the exact date on which the treaty was signed is precisely 2,300 days before the first day of the new millennium, January 1, 2000! We will see in this book the tremendous significance that the prophet Daniel gives to a 2,300 day period in the last days, and that this treaty is most certainly related to the fulfillment of Daniel's prophecy.

So why is all this tragic? Because the Church, in great measure, is still fast asleep regarding the day in which she is living, and in many ways continues to discount the tremendous events that are taking place in the world and in Israel at this very moment. If even the unbelieving world considers these events to be some of the most important events in human history, what will it take to awaken the Church to the lateness of the hour? The Scriptures are being fulfilled with astonishing precision and at an amazing pace right now, and yet many Believers somehow discount the things that are happening right under their noses, just because it doesn't line up exactly with what *they* believe will happen in the last days. *This* is tragic!

I am aware of the many predictions that have been made regarding the time of Christ's return. A number have asked me, "But what about the many others who have set dates, and have been wrong? Don't you think you are doing the same?" First, according to the English Dictionary, a "date" is a day, month, and year. Therefore, **we are not setting a date**. We are merely considering the biblical evidence that points to a specific year in God's calendar. During my own lifetime I have been aware of a good number of predictions that the passing of time has proven false regarding the Second Coming. Why did this happen? In most cases the predictions simply were not based on a true scriptural foundation, but rather on a series of calculations and speculations that often seemed very interesting indeed, though incorrect. However, in at least one case (which we will consider), the problem was not the date, but rather the interpretation of what was supposed to happen on that date. If, after you have read this book, you do not feel that there is an abundance of very solid scriptural evidence for the things we share, then simply reject this message. Even if you do not agree with the general timing presented in this book, one thing is very clear—Jesus is coming soon, and it is time to seek the Lord!

Marvin Byers

PART I

Keys to Understanding the Last Days

Introduction

Before we look at the details of the last days, we want to consider a few guidelines, or keys, that will help us correctly interpret the Scriptures related to the last days, thus avoiding doctrinal error. Since we will refer to these guidelines throughout the book, we want to establish them from the very beginning.

Chapter 1

God's Desire

The voice of the air traffic controller crackled in my headphones. His words were muffled because we were still two hundred miles from shore, over the Gulf of Mexico. We were on a direct flight from Guatemala, Central America, to Houston, Texas. I listened in disbelief as I tried to decipher his words and the gravity of his report. He asked, "Have you been advised of Sigmet Charlie?" In aviation, the word "Sigmet" is short for "significant meteorological conditions." In simple English it means "bad weather," *real* bad. So bad, in fact, that airliners will either detour around it or ground it. It was just a little too late for us to consider either option. We were over water, and so low on fuel that even a small detour was out of the question!

My wife and I, along with our passengers, were flying at 18,000 feet in a beautiful pressurized twin-engine airplane. We found ourselves in this very dangerous situation because my pre-flight briefer had been mistaken on two important points. He said we would have a tail wind along the entire route of flight, and that Houston had good weather. He couldn't have been more wrong! There was a solid line of huge thunderstorms between our position and the Houston International Airport. And due to a continual en route head wind, we were still one hour out of Houston, with fuel remaining for only one hour and fifteen minutes of flight. Normally, pilots plan to land with at least one hour of fuel remaining. We would have reserves of only fifteen minutes.

To make matters worse, there was an unbroken layer of clouds over Houston. It began at just three hundred feet above the ground. This meant that, if we survived the horrendous experience of passing through a thunderstorm, we would have to do an instrument approach in heavy air traffic. Under *normal* conditions, this can involve a landing delay of up to one hour. The minimum delay is usually twenty minutes, just five minutes longer than our fuel reserve! We knew that even if the controller would show us great kindness and bring us straight in, giving us priority over the other flights, we faced still another grave problem. We could *not* do a missed approach. Our first attempt to land in low clouds would be our only attempt, because we didn't have enough fuel to try it again!

Every loose object in the cabin literally hit the ceiling of the aircraft as we passed through, what appeared to be, the weakest thunderstorm on our radar screen. We learned there is no such thing as a weak thunderstorm. For the last half hour of our flight the only scenery we saw was the inside of clouds, but God showed us great mercy. We safely overcame the first hurdle—the line of thunderstorms! I informed the controller that we were low on fuel. Again God showed us mercy; the controller gave us direct routing to the final approach course. Once again the Lord helped, because I was able to "keep the needles centered," as pilots say, on the instrument landing system. Therefore, one approach to landing was all we needed. That day I saw one of the most beautiful sights ever during my years of flying: Houston's runway indicator lights, as we broke out of the clouds at three hundred feet above the ground!

Statistics show that *the* two principal causes of aviation accidents are bad weather and fuel exhaustion. We faced them both on one flight! What went wrong? Why did we find ourselves in one of the most dangerous situations possible in aviation? There were two very clear reasons: **One, we did not know what was ahead; and two, we had been misinformed.**

Do you know what is ahead? Is there any possibility that you have been misinformed as to what you will encounter in these last days? Misinformation can result in serious consequences for every one of us. None of us are exempt from this fact of life. Though my briefer was *completely* sincere, and honestly believed what he told me that day, that did not change the facts. Neither the weather nor the wind were even slightly altered because of his sincerity or because of my ill-founded confidence. Maybe your "spiritual briefer" has encouraged you, with complete sincerity, that clear skies are ahead. How can you be sure this information is correct? Or, maybe the "voices" coming through are giving conflicting reports. Possibly you are flying without *any* "pre-flight briefer." What are your chances of having a safe landing?

God's Desire Is That We Know What Is Coming

The Scriptures leave little doubt that God is more interested in speaking to us about the future than we are in hearing about it. Some people actually do not believe that God is still in the business of revealing the future. Others simply believe that having an interest in understanding the last days, and asking God to speak to us about it, is probably a waste of time and very possibly displeasing to the Lord since He wants us to be concerned about more important matters in life.

It is very true that there are many more important things that we need to understand in life. For me, one of those more important matters is the subject of how to enter a deeper love relationship with the Lord Jesus Christ. That intimacy with Christ will cause many others to become hungry for what we have and to bow at the feet of the One we love. However, what will happen if someday I find myself right in the middle of a spiritual thunderstorm that I am not expecting and am not prepared to handle? What will become of my "more important things" in life if I crash spiritually before attaining them? As we will see in this chapter and others, we run a very real risk of crashing if we don't understand what is coming so that we can make the necessary preparations.

God longs to speak to us about the last days if we are willing to listen. Knowing that this is God's desire is actually a vital key to understanding the last days. Unless we are thoroughly convinced of this, then we will only half-heartedly seek for understanding, as so many do today. Among the *many* biblical proofs that can be given to show that God *really* wants us to understand the future, I would like to share just a few in the following list:

1. At least one third of the Bible is directly related to the events of the last days. If God does not really want us to be interested in this area of truth, then why did He spend so much time talking to us about it in the Scriptures? Do we really believe that, when He recorded these things in the Bible, His desire was that we would skip over these truths and assume that we don't really need them? Or, that He was saying to us, "Don't listen to Me. What I am saying here really isn't important?" The answer seems self-evident.

2. Jesus tells His disciples, "...when he, the Spirit of truth, is come, he will guide you into all truth...and he **will show you things to come**" (Jn. 16:13). Not only has He dedicated enormous amounts of Scripture to this subject, but He has also given us the Holy Spirit to reveal what is coming in our future. Let us not take lightly this most precious aspect of the ministry of His Spirit.

3. Amos 3:7 tells us that "the Lord God will do nothing, but he revealeth his secret unto his servants the prophets." Man was created

in God's likeness. Therefore, we know that many of our likes and dislikes are a reflection of God's desires also. Just about everyone loves to share his latest secret with his closest friends. God is no different. He enjoys telling His closest friends what He is about to do. We find Him doing this very thing with His friend Abraham. He asks, "Shall I hide from Abraham that thing which I do?" (Gen. 18:17)

Maybe one of our problems is that we don't have enough time to be one of the Lord's close friends who is granted the joy of hearing His secrets. Some people think that they can find out the secrets by listening to others. Unfortunately, regarding secrets, another aspect of God is very much like us. When we tell someone a secret, we often say to them, "But please don't tell anyone else." What we are really saying is, "Don't tell anyone else, because *I* want to tell them all: one by one!" God reserves the right to *personally* share His secrets with each of His friends: one by one. So there are some things that you and I will never know unless we spend time alone with Him as a friend, sitting at His feet, listening to His voice.

4. Most people have a great interest in understanding the future. This is proven by the great number of people who turn to spiritist mediums, fortune-tellers, and palm readers. Obviously true Believers choose another way. Most of us, at one time or another, have sought to understand the future by reading some of the multitude of Bible-based teachings and writings found in the Church today. Is this desire in man's heart to know the future another example of man being created in the likeness of God, or is this deep desire in man's heart a perverse thing that came with his Fall in the Garden? Is it nothing more than carnal curiosity?

The fact that God Himself speaks to man so frequently about the future in the Bible indicates to us that God Himself has planted this interest in man's heart. We know that God is not sadistic. He never seeks to arouse carnal curiosity in us regarding what lies ahead, only to tell us that we shouldn't even think about these things! In Matthew 24 the disciples of Jesus asked Him about the future, after He had aroused their interest in that theme by speaking specifically about the future. Note that the answer Jesus gave was not the typical "Oh, it's not all that important! Just be ready for whatever. You don't really need to understand those things." To the contrary, He entered one of the longest and most detailed discourses of His entire ministry. He undoubtedly wants us to understand the truth about the end!

Is There Any Area of Truth More Confused Today?

I have asked many Believers what area of truth in the Church today they would consider to be the most confused. The response has almost always been immediate and close to unanimous, "Teaching concerning the end." What does this tell us? Does this degree of confusion exist because God simply doesn't care whether or not we understand these truths, and therefore isn't making it clear? As we have shown above, this is highly unlikely. The answer surely has something to do with the first thing Jesus said to His disciples when they asked Him to explain the future to them. He said, "Take heed that no man deceive you" (Mt. 24:4b). Jesus knew that a tremendous spirit of error would bring deception to His people, specifically in this area.

Where does error come from? First John 4:6 tells us that there is a "spirit of error." Therefore, instead of arriving at the false assumption that all the confusion regarding the events of the end is positive proof that we don't really need to know, and that it is probably impossible to know anyway, maybe we should ask ourselves another question. Why would Satan, *the* spirit of error, invest so much time and effort in this one particular area of truth? Confusion doesn't come from God. Satan is the author of confusion. So we can conclude that he is the one who has brought the myriad of false doctrines that exist in this area today. Certainly a good number of these doctrines are false, simply because they are contradictory.

The answer to why the spirit of error has worked feverishly in this area is found in Ephesians 2:20, where we are told that the Church is "built upon the **foundation of the apostles and prophets.**" So then, the prophetic ministry is foundational to the Church. Satan understands the message of the psalmist when he asks, "If the foundations be destroyed, what can the righteous do?" (Ps. 11:3) Basically, Satan is saying to us, "I really don't care how high you build the Church. You can build it one hundred stories high. But if the foundation is destroyed, it is all going to come crashing down."

We are seeing just how effective Satan's efforts are proving to be this very hour in the Church. We are also seeing just how subtle his tactic of muddying the waters of the prophetic message really is. As mentioned in the Introduction, in September of 1993 Israel signed a peace treaty with her enemies, hailed as one of the most important events of human history. It occurred, coincidentally, seven years before the year 2000. It is amazing to see Believers today discount and disregard one historic event after another, saying that these events couldn't possibly be significant because the last seven years have not yet started. What if they have? Has not Satan succeeded in blinding many hearts? It doesn't require a lot of imagination to see how many foundations could be shaken severely in this hour.

For years so much deception has bombarded the Church that even many leaders have come to take these precious truths lightly. Some even speak as if it were impossible to know the truth about the end. I heard one well-known teacher jokingly say, "I used to teach a lot about the last days, but I lost all my charts!" He gave us the impression that the study of the end wasn't worth the effort to find his charts. Maybe he had honest and sincere doubts about the validity of those charts, and simply did not want to lead God's people in a wrong way. That desire would be honorable. However, the very best desire would be to seek God for *new* and *correct* "charts."

Why He Wants Us to Understand the Future

1. Protection. First, we find in Proverbs 22:3, "A prudent man foreseeth the evil, and hideth himself: but the simple pass on, and are punished." If God revealed that a nuclear bomb was going to completely destroy my city tomorrow, I doubt that I would continue making appointments for the next day. I would definitely pray earnestly about leaving! In these days of tremendous chaos and upheaval, "filled with violence,"[1] we desperately need to understand what is coming. Then we can hide ourselves as does the prudent man of Proverbs.

Some years ago a friend of ours was sent to prison for a serious crime (committed before his glorious conversion). While he was serving his time in Jackson State Penitentiary in Jackson, Michigan, severe prison riots broke out. He was housed at that time in a low-security area with wooden buildings. For several days the prisoners burned and destroyed everything in their path.

One day, while outside, he saw a large gang of prisoners coming toward his area. His first thought was that they were going to burn his building also. Dashing inside, he went straight to his room to get his belongings. As he frantically gathered his Bible, notes, and clothing, the Lord told him to drop everything and run for his life. He obeyed instantly, and as he reached the door a fire bomb came through the window and exploded in his room. His life was saved because he heard the voice of the Lord and responded immediately.

---

1. Compare Genesis 6:11 and Matthew 24:37.

God wants to give us this type of guidance in these last days so that we will be able to survive what is coming. In addition to manifesting divine protection, this sort of guidance will also be a testimony to God's greatness, because only He can reveal the future. He frequently declares this in Isaiah (Isa. 44:6-7; 46:9-10). As we learn to receive revelation concerning the future from Him, we will also learn how He wants us to hide ourselves.

2. Vision. In Proverbs 29:18a we learn another important reason why God *wants* us to understand the end. "Where there is no vision, the people perish." This word "vision" means "revelation."[2] In addition to an understanding of the future in general, we need an understanding of our own immediate future in God. Without such a vision we are probably perishing spiritually, or at least growing cold! Few people continue to run when there is no longer a goal set before them to run toward. If you aren't seeking the Lord with all your heart, maybe you need a fresh revelation of what is coming to your own life and to the earth. The Lord refers to the power of a vision in Habakkuk 2:2. He commands the prophet to "Write the vision, and make it plain upon tables, that he may run that readeth it." The man with a vision is the man who will run.

3. Intercession. God has many reasons why He wants us to understand the end, but we want to consider just one more. In Genesis 18, God reveals one of His secrets to His friend Abraham: Sodom and Gomorrah would be destroyed the very next day. Upon learning of this future event Abraham enters one of the greatest depths of intercession found anywhere in the Word of God. It seems that those who have a clear revelation of what is coming also receive a true spiritual burden for the world, and a spirit of intercession not understood by others. Ezekiel 9 tells us that in the last days those who are sighing and crying because of the sins of His people will be preserved. Obviously they are crying because of the sin they see, but also because of the grave consequences that are soon to come because of those sins. May God grant us enough prophetic insight to enable us to earnestly intercede for the Body of Christ.

2. See *Strong's Hebrew Dictionary*, #2377.

Chapter 2

Daniel's Secret

Years ago our little boy, while sitting on my lap, looked up and asked a simple question: "Daddy, why aren't *we* rich?" As the question echoed in my mind, I realized it was a question the Lord Himself wanted me to consider. I thought of my career as a chemist, and how God had granted me a measure of success in a research laboratory of a large corporation in the United States. I thought of what they had offered me in the way of financial prosperity, position, and prestige (as a result of certain discoveries that the Lord had allowed me to make), and of their offer to make me the director of one of their research laboratories.

However, I felt that the Lord wanted me to leave that place of security to go into business on my own, in spite of the uncertainty in my own heart. Could I even make a living for my family? I remembered how the Lord had financially blessed that business in a wonderful way, and I remembered the large sum of money I was making when I sold it to begin my missionary work in the Philippine jungles.

I was in those jungles with my precious wife and four small children. We were fifty miles away from the nearest road, without telephones, mail, doctors, newspapers, and many other things that are often considered necessities. As I meditated, I realized that if I had chosen the business over the Lord's call, I might have attained great financial success. Then, as my son waited for my answer, my thoughts turned to the wonderful truths that God had opened to us along the way. We considered them very precious treasures.

Finally, I responded to my son, "It's because we have paid a lot of money for the wonderful truths that God has shared with us from His

Word. Do you think it was worth it? Was it a good investment?" His positive response warmed my heart. There are many adults who never come to this understanding in life. They can only think of material gain and this world's goods, pleasures, and comforts, and yet they wonder why God never shares deeper truths with them. Yes, friend, "Buy the truth, and sell it not," as Proverbs 23:23 counsels us. If we choose truth over all other riches, as Solomon counsels, then **He will show us mercy and open His secrets to us.** These things are eternal, but our money and the pleasures of life are temporal. Let us weigh very carefully the daily decisions we make in the light of this reality. If we please Him, He will grant us mercy to understand the end and other truths, just as He granted to Daniel.

Daniel had **tremendous** understanding of the future, attained by trusting in a simple key. In Daniel 2:18 he and his friends sought "**mercies of the God of heaven**" so that a very important secret regarding the future would be revealed to them. They urgently needed to understand that secret so that they would not perish with the rest of the wise men of Babylon. Revelation 17 and 18 show that Babylon plays an important role in the last days. This passage is certainly speaking of Satan's world system in the end. Could it be that some "wise men" will perish in *spiritual* Babylon in these days, because they have not received mercy to understand His secrets concerning the end? Perhaps a lack of clarity in the Church today has discouraged them. As a result of confusion, they have concluded that the end really cannot be understood. So they have conveniently "lost their charts!" Or, perhaps they have become lifted up in pride due to the *partial* understanding they have received, thereby shutting the door to further revelation.

Mercy Through Humility

Receiving mercy is surely *the* greatest key to understanding any truth, especially truth related to the future, but **mercy is given to the humble** (Jas. 4:6). The Lord has precious secrets He shares only with His friends, and His ability to hide the truth far outshines our ability to discover the truth! (Pro. 25:2) However, the only friends God has ever had are the humble and lowly ones. Isaiah 57:15 declares, "For thus saith the high and lofty One that inhabiteth eternity, whose name is Holy; I dwell in the high and holy place, with him also that is of a contrite and humble spirit..." Thus, it behooves us to humble ourselves before Him if we desire to understand His ways in any area of truth.

Almost twenty-eight years ago the Lord spoke to my wife and me and told us that He would open our understanding concerning the events of the last days. Since then, I have not studied the Bible with the intent of delving into end-time secrets, trying to discover the truth for myself. Rather, from time to time, the Lord has dropped little truths into my heart. They have become keys for understanding certain aspects of the last days. These keys have been given at the most unexpected times and places, and usually when I felt least deserving of them. In those moments I would cry out, "Lord, I know, and You know, that I do not deserve this precious truth, and that I have done nothing to merit it. I thank You for Your kindness in opening the eyes of the blind to see Your plan for these last days." This repeated experience of receiving light when I didn't deserve light has taught me that **the mercy of God is the greatest key of all** to understanding truth.

Some time after He had spoken to us about His desire to give us understanding of the last days, we went to the Philippines as missionaries. One day, while there, the Lord spoke very clearly to me, "If you want to understand the truth concerning the last days, lay aside all your preconceived ideas and doctrines of which you are so certain. Then come to Me in humility, and ask, 'Lord, what do *You* say, and what does Your *Word* say?' " As human beings we are, by nature, very full of pride, and pride blinds us. The only answer to this pride is a daily work of Calvary's humility in our hearts. In sharing this, I am challenged afresh to obey the Lord and come to Him in humility, recognizing that I really haven't received anything yet. I trust that you feel the same urgency in your heart.

Few, if any, men have known the heights of glory that Moses knew. Imagine the understanding of God's ways that he had after walking with Him for eighty years, even before he experienced the glory of the burning bush. Imagine the glory of God that rested upon him as God used him to bring destruction to Egypt, the greatest nation on earth, and then the glory he experienced as he divided the Red Sea. Imagine the glory of spending forty days on the mountain, talking with God face to face, something that no other man has ever experienced (Deut. 34:10). After descending from the mountain and bringing Israel back to their God, he ascended to spend another forty days with the Lord.

During that second period of forty days, Moses asked the Lord for something that should bring our spiritual pride down to the dust. He prayed, "I beseech thee, show me thy glory" (Ex. 33:18). God could have responded, "Moses, haven't you seen enough? Aren't you content with what you have already received?" But Moses' heart cried out, "Lord, I know that You are so wonderful and Your glory so great that I have barely begun to see what You are. Please bring me closer to Your heart!" Is it any wonder that, in the Church today, we have so little from God, when we are so content with our little measure of His glory and truth, and even get puffed up over what we already know? Let's ask God to so clothe us in His humility, that He would be delighted to walk with us in a new way and show us a greater revelation of His truth and secrets than ever before.

One of the best-known evangelical leaders in the United States once said to my brother and his pastor with total confidence, "Our denomination already has all the truth there is!" Apparently blinded by spiritual pride, he overlooked what Paul said: "And if any man think that he knoweth any thing, he knoweth nothing yet as he ought to know" (1 Cor. 8:2). That leader was confronted with revelation he had never heard before, and it would have cost him dearly to accept it. His reaction was proof that we must pay a price to humble ourselves before the Lord and man and admit that we aren't experts in anything. Let's pay the price to do so, and by His mercy He will be faithful to grant us an ever deeper understanding of His truth!

Chapter 3

The Beginning and Ending

Is it merely a coincidence that when Jesus was born there was a Joseph, a Mary, a Herod, and a Simeon all related to His birth, and then, thirty-three years later, when He died, there was a different Joseph, a different Mary, a different Herod, and a different Simeon all related to His death?[1] Is it significant that the very **first act** of Christ's earthly ministry was to serve wine (Jn. 2:1-11), and that the **last act** of His earthly ministry was to serve wine? (Mk.14:23-26) Is it by chance that the name of David was the very first human name recorded in the New Testament, and also the very last? (Mt. 1:1; Rev. 22:16) Why are these beginnings and endings so clearly related? Is the Lord trying to show us something?

Next to humbling ourselves to receive mercy and grace, the greatest key to understanding the end is to understand the relationship that exists between the beginning and ending of all God's works. Some years ago the Lord spoke to me that He had purposely arranged the sixty-six books of the Bible like chapters in a book. Newborn Believers often want to go directly to the Book of Revelation. However, if they don't start at the first "chapter" (Genesis), they probably won't understand the last "chapter" (Revelation). The Lord said to me, "The degree to which you understand the first sixty-five books will be the degree to which you understand the last book, The Revelation." He made it clear that He based all He said in the Book of Revelation on what He recorded in the Bible from the beginning onward. Revelation is simply a summary of all He said before.

---

1. Note that Simeon and Simon are the same name in the Hebrew. See *Strong's Greek Dictionary*, #4826.

Therefore, in any study of the last days, it is essential to compare the Book of Revelation with other books and passages from the Bible. (A few of these comparisons may be found in the Appendices of this book.)

Some time later, as I was reading the Book of Revelation, my understanding was opened to the extreme importance of the very first words Jesus spoke to John in the book. By nature, the Lord speaks no vain or idle words.[2] I have often jokingly told Latin-American congregations that Jesus wasn't a Latin, because He never used the Latin way of greeting people. When we went to Latin America as missionaries, we faced the monumental task of learning another language and adapting to a foreign culture. From the beginning, one of our difficulties was to learn the proper way to say "hello" and "good-bye." That really shouldn't seem difficult, but Latin greetings can last two or three minutes using different expressions, and good-byes can last another two or three minutes. Sometimes, after five minutes of conversation, very little has been said.

The Lord is not that way. He gets right to the point, and never wastes His words. In John 3, Nicodemus came to Jesus with a "Latin" salutation, saying, "Rabbi, we know that thou art a teacher come from God: for no man can do these miracles that thou doest, except God be with him" (Jn. 3:2). Jesus didn't say, "Good evening, Nicodemus. It is a pleasure to meet you. Please come in. Won't you have a seat? It's a nice evening, isn't it? How's the family? I understand that you have three sons? Would you like something to drink?" Rather, Jesus went right to the point. His very first statement was the most important issue in the life of Nicodemus; it was a matter of eternal life or death! He began by saying, "Verily, verily, I say unto thee, Except a man be born again, he cannot see the kingdom of God" (Jn. 3:3).[3]

Indeed, God's nature is to go straight to the point. An awareness of this fact is a vital key to discovering the theme of each book of the Bible. The theme can almost always be found in the first verse, or verses, of the book. Unfortunately, we often read those verses as merely a salutation, a short historical introduction, or maybe just something to satisfy our curiosity about the setting or the people involved. They often contain names and places that seem boring to anyone who isn't interested in history or geography. However, if we study the meanings of those names and places in the Greek or Hebrew, or if we carefully consider what the author is saying

---

2. In fact, we will be judged for every idle word we speak (Mt. 12:36-37).
3. I'm not suggesting here that we abandon all the niceties of our culture—at least not yet!

in the first verses, we will find a key thought to understand the message or theme of the book.

Therefore, in Revelation, the very first statement of Christ Himself is an extremely important key for understanding the entire book. He says that He is "*the beginning* and *the ending*" (Rev. 1:8). At this very moment John is about to receive a revelation of the end. Jesus, at the outset of that revelation, makes it clear that He *is* the end! Since the Book of Revelation is a revelation of **the end,** it is no wonder that Revelation 1:1 declares that the book is a revelation of Christ, who is **the End.** Note: Jesus doesn't say that He is simply *in* the end, or a *part* of the end. Rather He testifies that He *is* the End, and that He *is* the Beginning, and we know that He never changes. Hebrews 13:8 declares, "Jesus Christ the same yesterday, and to day, and for ever." Therefore, **the beginning and the ending must be the same!** The fact that the Lord repeats this key thought six times in the book shows how very important it is. It appears four times at the beginning and twice at the end.[4]

Therefore, to better understand the end, which is a revelation of the One who *is* the End, we must go to Genesis and receive a revelation of the One who is the Beginning! The first book of the Bible is as much a revelation of the last days as the Book of Revelation itself. Both are a revelation of the person, nature, ministry, and ways of Christ. We are given a revelation of Christ in Genesis, with the same associated details that are found in Revelation, confirming that the One who is the Beginning is also the Ending.

Genesis Is a Revelation of Christ, the End

In Genesis, the accounts of the lives and works of one man of faith after another are really a revelation of Christ's life and works. This begins with Adam, who is called "the son of God" in Luke 3. Although he was not deceived by Satan into sinning, he was willing to be identified with his wife in her sin and experience the death she had been overtaken by. Did Christ not do the same for His Bride? It is understandable why Paul said that Adam was a foreshadow of Christ (Rom. 5:14). Then came Abel, who not only offered a lamb on the altar as a symbol of *the* Lamb slain from the foundation of the earth, but in one sense Abel himself became a lamb when wicked Cain, his own brother, arose and slew him. Hebrews 12:24 compares the shedding of Abel's blood with the shedding of Christ's blood. Hebrews declares that Christ's blood is far better, most

4. Compare Revelation 1:8,11,17; 2:8; 21:6; and 22:13.

assuredly, because whereas Abel's blood cried from the ground for vengeance on his brother, Christ's blood cries from the ground for forgiveness on His brethren who killed Him.

We can also see Christ in Noah, the one who built the ark of safety, in which his whole family was saved from destruction. His father Lamech said that he would bring them into rest. It is Christ who has built an Ark of safety for His Wife and Children, and who brings us into spiritual rest. The revelation of Christ in Genesis goes on and on and is a beautiful study. Only a brief summary is presented here. We see Christ in Isaac, the one who was offered on the altar by his own father. We see Christ in Jacob, the one who pastored sheep in order to obtain a wife, just as the Good Shepherd is doing today to gain a Bride, the Church. Finally, we see Christ in Joseph, the one who went down into the suffering of Egypt and paid the price so that he could save his own brethren from death, the same ones who had sold him for twenty pieces of silver. He suffered to be able to feed them with bread. After his suffering he was exalted to the throne of Egypt. Christ, too, went down into Egypt at the beginning of His life to escape from Herod, and then went down again at the end of His life when He was crucified in "spiritual Egypt" (see Rev. 11:8). He was sold for thirty pieces of silver by one of those closest to Him, and suffered so that His brethren could be saved from death. He suffered to give us the Bread of Life. There is a wonderful ending to this story also. Christ, too, has ascended to the Throne that will forever govern this world!

Not only is Christ, the End, revealed through the lives of the men of faith in Genesis at mankind's *beginnings*, but the word "Genesis" actually means "the beginnings." Ancient manuscripts divided the book into ten sections where each began with "these are the beginnings." Each of those ten sections is a tremendous revelation of the endtime and the Book of Revelation. Although a detailed study on this topic is outside the scope of this book, I will share a few examples from the first of those ten sections only.

The words "these are the beginnings" first appear in Genesis 2:4, translated as "these are the generations" in the King James Version. Genesis 2:4 through 5:1 contain many details revealed also in Revelation. First, a new Heaven and a new earth are seen in Genesis 2 as well as in Revelation 21:1-6. In Genesis 2:7 man comes forth from the dust of the earth, and the same will happen in the end, at the Resurrection. (Compare Dan. 12:2 and Rev. 20:6.) Furthermore, in Genesis 2:8 God plants a garden. From that garden flows a river of life, and in that garden is the tree of life (Gen. 2:9-10). Revelation 22:1-2 also reveals a garden with a river of life and a tree of life.

The relationship between the beginning and ending becomes even clearer as we progress in the comparison between Genesis and Revelation. In Genesis 2:18-25 we find the first marriage between a man and a woman, and in Revelation 19:7, 21:9 and 22:17 we find the last marriage between a Man and a Woman. First Corinthians 15:45 even tells us that the heavenly Bridegroom of Revelation is the last Adam, linking Him to the Adam found in Genesis!

Genesis 3 introduces the serpent and the deceiver. God then promises that the "seed of the woman" will bruise the head of the serpent. In Revelation 13:14 that same deceiver is at work, and he "deceiveth them that dwell on the earth." In Revelation 12:1-11 a woman gives birth to a child (her seed) who crushes the head of the "old serpent."

In Genesis 3:21 the Lord gave man clothing, or a covering. In Revelation 19:8 God gives a covering: "And to her was granted that she should be arrayed in fine linen, clean and white."

The Prophets and Wise Men Understood This Truth

The prophet Isaiah also knew that the beginning is the key to the end. In Isaiah 46:9-10 he counsels us, "Remember the former things of old: for I am God...and there is none like me, declaring the end from the beginning." Since the world began, God has been revealing Himself to humanity through the men of faith and through the events surrounding their lives. Isaiah confirms that what He revealed about Himself in the beginning will be the same as what He reveals to man in the end, because He *is* the beginning and the ending, and He never changes.

Solomon, the man to whom God granted great wisdom, gives us further understanding of this same truth in Ecclesiastes 1:9-10, where he says, "The thing that hath been, it is that which shall be; and that which is done is that which shall be done: and there is no new thing under the sun. Is there any thing whereof it may be said, See, this is new? It hath been already of old time, which was before us." Therefore, true doctrine concerning the end will not contain anything that cannot be found in the beginning also. Solomon assures us that we will never be able to say there is something new under the sun! Everything that happens in the end in Revelation is something that happened in the beginning. There is *nothing* new. Some might bring to mind the Rapture[5] and affirm, "Surely *that* will

5. See the introduction to Part II if you do not understand the use of the word "Rapture."

be new." However, in Genesis 5 Enoch had that experience in the beginning. So even the Rapture is not new, and Solomon's wisdom is again confirmed.

In the light of the Lord's declaration that He is the Beginning and the Ending, the saying "history repeats itself" becomes clear. "History" is really "His story." He sovereignly and providentially controls the events that occur on the face of this earth. As Nebuchadnezzar learned in Daniel 4:17, "The most High ruleth in the kingdom of men."

However, "His story" always begins and ends in the same way. This is true regarding any event of history, whether a work of blessing or a work of judgment. We can understand, then, why not only Christ's life, but also His ministry, **began and ended** in the same way. Although I mentioned just one similarity that links the beginning of His ministry with the end of His ministry (the serving of wine), there are many others (too many, however, to include in this study).

An extraordinary modern example of history repeating itself in the beginning and ending is found in the presidential support given to the civil rights movement for black people in the United States. Presidential support for that movement began with President Lincoln and the abolition of slavery, and it ended with the death of President Kennedy. Let's briefly compare the events of the beginning and ending of that support.

Lincoln was elected in the year 1860, and Kennedy was elected in 1960. Both were killed on a Friday, and in the presence of their wives. Both were shot in the head. Both vice-presidents succeeding them were surnamed Johnson. Both Johnsons came from the South, and both had been senators before becoming vice-presidents. Andrew Johnson was born in 1808 and Lyndon Johnson was born in 1908. John Wilkes Booth, the assassin of Lincoln, was born in 1839, and Lee Harvey Oswald, who was accused of assassinating Kennedy, was born in 1939. Both of these men were assassinated themselves before going to trial. The wife of Lincoln, as well as the wife of Kennedy, experienced the premature death of a child while living in the White House. The secretary of Lincoln, whose name was Kennedy, warned Lincoln not to go to the theater. The secretary of Kennedy, whose name was Lincoln, warned Kennedy not to go to Dallas. John Wilkes Booth shot Lincoln in a theater and then ran to a warehouse. Lee Harvey Oswald shot from a warehouse and then ran to a theater. Could all this be mere coincidence, or is this an example of the intimate relationship that exists between the beginning and the ending of "His Story," that is, of the events on this earth that He sovereignly controls? Because the One who declares Himself to be the Beginning and the Ending controls history, history repeats itself, whether it be modern or ancient!

Chapter 4

Israel, the Church, and the Forsaken Root

Unfortunately, many Gentile Believers have not really understood the relationship between God's people Israel and the so-called Gentile Church. The result is that many heretical and damaging doctrines have entered into the gospel that is preached around the world today. Two common errors that are often propagated by Believers are that (1) Israel and the Church are two different peoples and (2) the Gentile Church has taken the place of Israel, God's chosen people, because Israel rejected their Messiah. This is known as Replacement Theology. These ideas are not only in total contradiction to New Testament doctrine, but they also give birth to some very strange ideas about the events of the last days and what God is going to do in the world and in the Church. Let's consider the gradual doctrinal changes in these areas that occurred in the early Church. These changes actually brought the Church into the death, destruction, and sorrow of the Dark Ages.

The Early Church Was Strictly Jewish

When Jesus, a Jew, began to preach the gospel of the Kingdom, He gathered around Himself twelve Jewish disciples. He said that He was not sent to anyone but the lost sheep of the house of Israel (Mt. 15:24). Furthermore, when He sent out the disciples, He told them that they were not sent to the Gentiles either, but rather to the lost sheep of the house of Israel only (Mt. 10:5-6). In John 4:22 He even went so far as to say that "salvation is of the Jews," to show the "Jewishness" of His work. After the cross, on the Day of Pentecost the only Believers that were involved in the outpouring of the Holy Spirit in the upper room were Jewish. Afterward, three thousand, and then five thousand, Jews were added to the Church.

For approximately eight to ten years after the cross, the only true Church was strictly a Jewish Church. In fact, they preached the gospel *only* to Jews (Acts 11:19). They were simply obeying the Lord's original commandment to not go to the Gentiles, but rather only to the lost sheep of the house of Israel. It is very understandable, therefore, why these same leaders and apostles got quite upset with Peter for going to the Gentiles and preaching the gospel to them (Acts 11:1-3). However, once Peter explained to them what had happened, they came to an amazing and absolutely revolutionary conclusion. We are told that "when they heard these things, they held their peace, and glorified God, saying, Then hath God also to the Gentiles granted repentance unto life" (Acts 11:18). Imagine their utter surprise when they realized that God was actually going to include the Gentiles in His Israelite Church! As Paul later explained in Romans 11:17, the Lord was allowing the Gentiles to be grafted into that enormous body of Jewish Believers, called "the Church" (Acts 2:47). But consider who that "Church" was. It was composed of Israelites, who, through the new birth, had been changed from a strictly natural people of Israel into a spiritual people of Israel. They were, in reality, descendants of Abraham who could say, at long last, that they had really entered into the blessings that the Lord had promised to His people Israel, and that they were now actually "completed Jews."

Jews Approve of Gentiles Not Keeping the Law

At this point, tremendous doctrinal problems began to surface in the early Church. Imagine the consternation of these thousands of "completed Jews," when thousands of Gentiles suddenly appeared on the scene! *All* of those Jews were zealous in keeping the Old Testament sacrificial law, as Acts 21:20 clearly declares, even many years after the cross. But those new Gentile Believers did not have the slightest notion of the difference between one sacrifice and another—sacrifices that continued to be offered in the temple, where the early Church often met. They didn't even know how to properly observe the Sabbath, much less what circumcision was all about. So it was, that some Jews arose and began to tell the Gentiles that if they did not keep the law of Moses they couldn't be saved (Acts 15:1,5). In order to resolve the problem, the famous council of Acts 15 was held. The principal leaders of the Church gathered to pray about this matter. In that council, the Jewish Church concluded that the Holy Spirit was not requiring the Gentiles to keep the law. The Gentiles were then given just four essential laws to keep, if they were to be considered true

Believers (Acts 15:28-29). In short, the Gentiles were given permission to disregard the law.

Jewish Believers Continue to Keep the Law

The problems for the Jewish Believers did not end here, however, because the Gentile sector of the Body of Christ began to increase dramatically. Soon the Jews were far outnumbered. The Gentiles began to wonder, "Why in the world do the Jewish Believers continue to observe the many sacrificial laws?" They just couldn't understand that, for a Jew, the law was part of their national and spiritual inheritance, as Romans 9:4-5 reveals. Even more perplexing to the Gentiles, in the light of Christ's sacrifice on the cross, was why believing Jews should want to continue offering blood sacrifices in a physical temple, as Paul did in Acts 21:26? Some of us may not have noticed that in Acts 21:20-27, Paul was in the temple to show the many believing Jews that he too kept the law.

Some have concluded that, in this situation, the Apostle Paul simply compromised with legalistic Jewish brethren, and that if he hadn't made this mistake, then he would never have been taken prisoner. However, I find it difficult to accept this sort of explanation for the life of this great Apostle. Remember, he was declared by Scripture itself to be an example to those who would believe afterward (1 Tim. 1:16), and he was the one who rebuked Peter for having a double standard concerning his fellowship with the Gentiles (Gal. 2:11-12). He also withstood the proponents of the law in Jerusalem before the whole church (Gal. 2:1-7). To believe that he would now compromise on his own convictions and buckle under the pressure of the Jewish brethren is a bit much to accept. Rather, Paul was being perfectly consistent with his convictions and way of life here. He said, "And unto the Jews I became as a Jew, that I might gain the Jews; to them that are under the law, as under the law, that I might gain them that are under the law, to them that are without law, as without law, (being not without law to God, but under the law to Christ,) that I might gain them that are without law. To the weak became I as weak, that I might gain the weak: I am made all things to all men, that I might by all means save some" (1 Cor. 9:20-22).

If Paul kept the law to gain those that were under the law, then he also had to offer blood sacrifices in the temple, as did the rest of the Jews, or he wasn't really keeping the law. So we find him doing precisely that in Acts 21:24-26. There, Paul and four other men entered the temple and shaved their heads to show that their days of purification had ended, so that an offering could be offered for them. Of course, this was not the first time that Paul shaved his head in the keeping of a vow and as a rite of purification in accordance to the law (see Acts 18:18). Note also that this rite of purification was related to a seven day period (Acts 21:27). We find the prescribed manner of fulfilling this rite in Leviticus 14:8-10. The person who was purifying himself had to offer three lambs as a sacrifice. No wonder the Church leaders in Jerusalem asked Paul to "pay the expenses" of the men who were purifying themselves (Acts 21:24 NKJV). It was clearly a very costly ritual!

So then, how could the same Apostle who wrote so eloquently to the Galatians that they should not trust in the law to bring them into perfection, turn around and keep the law himself? Either Paul was a weak, compromising man pleaser, or else we are missing part of the message of Paul's teaching regarding the law. To understand what was happening here, consider for a moment a ritual that the Church participates in to this very day—the Lord's Supper. For most Believers, the bread and wine that are used for this ceremony are nothing more than symbols of the body and blood of Christ who was sacrificed for us. When we partake of them, we are simply remembering what the Lamb of Calvary did for us on the cross. We do these things because the Lord commanded us to do them, but our faith is centered in Him, and not in this ritual. However, there are many religious people today who actually believe that the bread and wine are transformed into the *literal* flesh and blood of Jesus. This is the very well-known doctrine of transubstantiation. They believe that their very salvation and continued favor with God depend on keeping this ritual. However, most Believers know that this is not the case. If we combine Paul's teaching regarding the ritual of the law with his personal, continued, observance of that law, we discover that the crux of what he was opposing was the false confidence that some placed in the rituals. This same false confidence is expressed today in the doctrine of transubstantiation. The heart of man tends to continue making the same mistakes!

Paul tells the Galatians that if they are trusting in the outward rituals of the law to either save them or to perfect them, then they have fallen from grace (Gal. 3:1-5; 5:4). In reality, this was *always* the case with the true men of faith in the Old Testament Age. All those who understood God's promise to send a Redeemer, the Lamb slain from the foundation of the world, knew that it was not the blood of natural bulls and goats that brought them salvation. They understood that offering those sacrifices was simply an act of obedience to God's commandments, and that their works of obedience proved they had real faith (Heb. 10:4; Jas. 2:20-26). It was faith and not sacrifices that justified Abraham, and it was faith that justified *all* the men of faith. When Abraham and his descendants offered blood sacrifices, they were simply looking ahead to the offering of *the*

Lamb on the cross. Was it sinful or wicked to offer those animals? Was it actually a *lack* of faith that caused them to offer them? Obviously, the answer is "no."

So then, *after* the cross, would it have been sinful, wicked, or an indication of unbelief if a "completed Jew" chose to offer a blood sacrifice in the temple? Would it have been sinful even if he weren't looking at it as a source of forgiveness or salvation, but as a time to *look back* at what Christ had already accomplished on the cross, much as we do during the Lord's Supper? Again, the obvious answer is "no." The only problem with offering sacrifices would have been if the confidence and hope of the worshiper were placed in those sacrifices instead of in the Lord's sacrifice. There was nothing wrong with using sacrifices to look *back* to the cross, just as the Old Testament saints used sacrifices to look *forward* to the cross. This is the crux of Paul's teaching and living example concerning the ritual of the law.

Gentiles Disapprove of Jews Keeping the Law

Somehow, the Gentile Believers never seemed to understand these things. The Holy Spirit had freed them from keeping all the rituals that Jewish Believers chose to keep, but after about three hundred years the whole concept was turned around. During the Council of Nicaea in A.D. 325, the Gentile Church issued a doctrinal statement that strictly forbade any Jewish Believer to observe the law. The Church told the Jews that if they were going to be followers of their Messiah (that is, the Jews' Messiah), they would have to live like the Gentiles and become part of the Gentile Church. Imagine this. In the beginning, the Church was strictly Jewish, but the Jews and the Holy Spirit graciously permitted the Gentiles to be grafted in among the natural olive branches, giving them permission to *not observe the law* that the Jews continued to observe. Now, just a few years later, the Gentiles inform the Jews that they will no longer be granted permission to keep their own precious law! Although Paul said that there is neither Jew nor Gentile in Christ, somehow the Gentiles came to believe that a Jew must become a Gentile to be saved. They forgot that they had actually been given special *permission* to ignore the law. They somehow carried that permission to the other extreme and came to the erroneous conclusion that by *not* keeping the law a person was somehow more spiritual or pleasing to the very God who had given the law on Mount Sinai. While the Jewish council in Acts 15 manifested compassion and understanding, the Gentile council of A.D. 325 manifested inflexibility and a *lack* of understanding.

Notice that in Romans 11:17 Paul does *not* say that the wild olive branches (the Gentiles) were grafted into the root *in place of* the natural branches (the Jews). Rather, he says that *some* of the natural branches were broken off (not all), and that the Gentiles were grafted *in among* the natural branches. He goes on to say that the Gentile branches do not bear the root, this "root" being the fathers, or life-source, of the Jewish race. Rather, it is the root that bears the Gentiles. Jews and Gentiles alike are blessed as a result of God's promises and blessings on the fathers, just as Paul makes clear in Galatians 3:7-8: "Therefore know that only those who are of faith are sons of Abraham. And the Scripture, foreseeing that God would justify the Gentiles by faith, preached the gospel to Abraham beforehand, saying, 'In you all the nations shall be blessed' " (NKJV). This is the root that bears and blesses us—father Abraham and his descendants! At the beginning of Romans 11 Paul clearly states that God has *never* rejected Israel, the descendants of Abraham. He says that he is living proof of that fact, being an Israelite himself from the tribe of Benjamin. Paul declared that God has always had, and always will have, a remnant of believing Jews. Two thousand years of Church history have proven that God has always had that remnant.

The Lord assures us that His covenant with the people of Israel will never be annulled as long as day and night exist: "Thus saith the Lord; If ye can break my covenant of the day, and my covenant of the night... that there should not be day and night in their season...**Then will I cast away the seed of Jacob...for I will cause their captivity to return,** and have mercy on them" (Jer. 33:20-26). Therefore, unless day and night cease God will never reject the seed of Jacob. If there is any doubt as to whom the "seed of Jacob" refers, they are clearly defined in this passage as the ones who have gone into captivity and have been caused to return to their land.

The Gentile Church Cut Itself Off From the Root

Sadly enough, what happened to the "Gentile Church" after it arrogantly forbade the Jews from being Jews any longer, is testimony enough to the truth of what Paul tells us in Romans 11:17 (NIV). There he declares that the Gentiles are partakers of the "nourishing sap from the olive root." When the Gentiles cut themselves off from that root, they lost the life of the tree, and it is therefore little wonder that the Church and the world entered the spiritual darkness, death and destruction of the Dark Ages. Even sadder is the history of many fanatical groups of so-called "Christians," who, with a sword in one hand and a cross in the other, killed literally millions of God's chosen people down through the ages. Is it any wonder that today such a Church continues to be divided and weak? In Christ's eyes it is a Church that is "wretched, miserable, poor, blind, and naked" (Rev. 3:17). And yet, she is so greatly puffed up and very sure of all that she says and does. She rarely sees any need whatsoever to re-examine or change her doctrine. In fact, I have heard some boast that they have never had to change any aspect of their doctrine even once during their entire ministry. During the Dark Ages, the Crusaders were also very sure of all that they said and did. They were so sure of themselves and their doctrine that they could march through Europe in the name of Christ crying, "Kill a Jew and save your soul," without even flinching!

Anti-Semitism was birthed in the Gentile Church shortly after the death of the early Church fathers, and has continued to this very day among many. The slaughter of Hitler's Holocaust was nothing more than the fruit of the Church's very grave doctrinal error. Hitler even quoted Martin Luther to justify his death camps. Although Luther was used by God to restore the basic truth of justification by faith, there were *many* areas of truth that he did *not* restore to God's people. When Luther said that the only good Jew is a dead Jew, he obviously did not yet understand the tragedy of being cut off from the root and source of blessing that comes on all the world through Abraham's seed! Fortunately for all, God is restoring this area of truth to the Body of Christ in these last days. In this last hour, He will again manifest the wonderful work of the cross that made both peoples (Jews and Gentiles) to be one new man, or one **living and growing Church** (Eph. 2:11-15,21). When God finally restores His last-day Church to an even greater glory than that of the early Church, the Jew will once again have the liberty to observe his feasts and ordinances, and the Gentile will continue to have the liberty to disregard the law of Moses. It was this way during the first years of the Church Age, and it will be that way during the last. In recent years, the Lord has been opening the eyes of many Jewish people to see that Jesus really is their Messiah. The result has been the entrance of approximately 100,000 Jewish Believers into the Body of Christ, more than all the Jews who entered during almost 2,000 years since the cross. The faithful remnant is growing again, and they now know that they are still free to be Jewish!

Israel's Old Testament History Is a Parable

We are told that Jesus never spoke to the multitudes unless He did so with a parable (Mt. 13:34). **A parable is a natural, earthly story** that involves people, places, or things, but the story has a **heavenly or spiritual meaning**. The story may be actual history or it may be fiction. The use of natural things to represent spiritual truths is not only called a parable, but also a "type" in Greek. When Jesus came using parables, He was not using a new teaching technique that He had developed especially for His earthly ministry. Rather, parables are part of His divine nature, and Christ's use of parables was a continuation of the method He used in the Creation of Heaven and earth, and then throughout the Old Testament Age.[1] In fact, Romans 1:20 tells us that mankind is able to understand the Godhead Himself by considering the things that He made in the Creation. By using natural, everyday stories and objects, the Lord, in His wisdom decided to teach man His deep, spiritual secrets through the use of simple object lessons that are easily understood. Carnal man can see, hear, smell, touch, and taste the natural creation. These experiences give him an understanding of the world in which he lives, but, if he considers them well, they also give him an understanding of God's world and the spiritual realms. In this way God's task of teaching an earthly man His spiritual truths is greatly simplified.

Solomon was a man who considered well the creation around him and could see wisdom and understanding in all of God's works. "And he spake of trees, from the cedar tree that is in Lebanon even unto the hyssop that springeth out of the wall: he spake also of beasts, and of fowl, and of creeping things, and of fishes. And **there came of all people to hear the wisdom of Solomon**" (1 Kings 4:33-34a). Solomon found heavenly wisdom hidden in all of these things, great and small. May God open our eyes also, that we may learn spiritual lessons from the natural things that surround us. How blind we are at times!

Of all the parables that God has given to man, the greatest and longest parable found in the Bible is the story of Israel, in this case, a true story. Almost all of the Old Testament revolves around that story. In what I believe to be one of the most important verses in the New Testament, the Apostle Paul tells us that the events in Israel's Old Testament history are really parables or types for the spiritual nation of Israel in the New Testament. Concerning events in the Old Testament history of Israel, we are told that "Now *all these things happened to them as examples,* and they were written for our admonition, upon whom the ends of the ages have come" (1 Cor. 10:11 NKJV). The word translated as "examples" here is really "tupos" or "types" in the Greek, and in addition to meaning an object that prefigures something else, this Greek word also means a "mold." When something is made from a mold, the details found in the mold are reproduced in the final product. Paul says that Old Testament Israel was literally a "mold" from which God's New Testament Israel, or people, were taken. An awareness of this fact is essential for properly interpreting

1. E.g., Psalms 49:4; 78:2 and Ezekiel 17:2; 24:3.

many New Testament passages. Therefore, Israel and her history have spiritual meanings or lessons for all New Testament Believers, and history (His story) will indeed repeat itself in His spiritual people during the New Testament Age.

In other words, God first dealt with the nation of Israel on a natural, earthly level and then later on a spiritual, heavenly level. This is one of the key thoughts in the Book of Hebrews, which was written to help the Hebrew, or Israelite Believer, make the transition between the Old Testament Age and the New Testament Age. Hebrews explains that in the Old Testament, Israel was a natural people on a natural journey from a natural Egypt to a natural Canaan, through a natural wilderness (Heb. 3–4), and they were given a natural priesthood (Heb. 7), with a natural, physical tabernacle (Heb. 8–9) where natural sacrifices (Heb. 10:1-4) were offered on a natural altar (Heb. 13:10). Hebrews explains that in the New Testament Age the Lord has brought the nation of Israel into a spiritual realm. Now all believing Israelites have become a spiritual people who are on a spiritual journey from a spiritual Egypt to a spiritual Canaan, through a spiritual wilderness, and they have been given an eternal, spiritual priesthood after the order of Melchisedek, in order to minister in a spiritual, heavenly Tabernacle (Heb. 8:1-5) where spiritual sacrifices are offered on a spiritual altar (Heb 13:10,15). In other words, the Old Testament Age can actually be superimposed on the New Testament Age, and we will see that it is, indeed, a very precise "mold" from which the New Testament, spiritual Israel, is taken. Throughout the Church Age, the Old Testament history of Israel has, most surely, been repeating itself, but on a spiritual level. Now, at the end of the Church Age He is uniting natural Israel and spiritual Israel once again, bringing them back to their own land. Israel lived in Canaan at the beginning of this Age, and that is where they will be at the end!

By making the nation of Israel a natural people first in the Old Testament and then later a spiritual people in the New Testament, God revealed the order of events in the life of every individual Believer. We are first born as a natural, earthly man, and then, as the life of Christ begins to be formed in us at our "second birth" (or new birth), we become a spiritual, heavenly man. Paul mentions this order of events in First Corinthians 15:46-49: "Howbeit that was not first which is spiritual, but that which is natural; and afterward that which is spiritual. The first man is of the earth, earthy: the second man is the Lord from heaven. As is the earthy, such are they also that are earthy: and as is the heavenly, such are they also that are heavenly. And as we have borne the image of the earthy, we shall also bear the image of the heavenly." Remember that in Genesis 22:17 God promised Abraham that his children would be as the sand of the sea (an earthly people), and *also* as the stars of Heaven (a heavenly people).

Conclusion

So then, the only true Church, from the very beginning until today, is the Church composed of all the Israelites who have believed along with all the Gentiles who have been grafted into that olive tree through faith in Christ. Even in Old Testament times, God made provision for any Gentile, who so desired, to become an Israelite by converting as did Ruth, Rahab, and other Gentiles (see Ezek. 47:21-22). That provision has simply never changed. Any Gentile who is willing to convert to the Jewish Messiah, and become a member of the only true Church whose owner and master is forever Jewish, will be accepted as a citizen of God's true Israel. He becomes a true Jew and a "fellow *citizen* with God's people," Israel (Eph. 2:19 NIV). But this does *not* mean that a natural born Jew ceases to be a Jew just because he believes in the Jewish Messiah and the everlasting Kingdom of David. God has clearly declared that His covenant with the house of Jacob is everlasting and unchanging (Jer. 33:20-26). Paul says that the unbelief of some of Jacob's children does not void the covenant in any way (Rom. 3:3). So then, Israel is the Church and the Church is Israel. All Gentiles are invited to become a citizen of Israel today, and in God's eyes, that's what they are if they have come under the lordship and government of the King of the Jews!

Consider how an understanding of this fact greatly simplifies the study of Scripture. For many years some theologians have tried to decide which Scriptures apply to Israel and which apply to the Church. The very attempt to make this distinction at all is proof that such a person has been influenced by either Replacement Theology, or else what I call "Division Theology." Division Theology considers the Church and Israel to be two different entities, something that never was, nor ever will be, the case. This theology attempts to divide something that God Himself has never divided, and consequently becomes quite complex indeed. Israel was the Church in the Old Testament, and Israel is the Church in the New Testament (compare Acts 2:47 and 7:38). Therefore, our study of Scripture becomes much easier. We can simply do what the early Church did, and that was to recognize that *all* Scriptures relating to God's people were written *to* His chosen people and *for* His chosen people—Israel with all her ingrafted Gentiles.

Chapter 5

The Beginning and Ending of the Old Testament Age

"Quick, hide the baby! They're knocking at the door! Someone must have told them your mother gave birth yesterday. I know that you love baby Joshua with all your heart. But if you don't hurry, Elizabeth, you will never see your baby brother again! He will be cast into the river with all the other babies born this year!"

This heartrending scene must have been repeated over and over as the Old Testament Age began. Can we even begin to imagine the tears of anguish and the cries for mercy as newborn babes were snatched from loving arms and cruelly cast into the river by the servants of Pharaoh? This was a daily occurrence when little Moses was born. He was to be the mediator of the Old Testament,[1] and the author of its first five books. Pharaoh desperately sought to destroy the deliverer before he would have the opportunity to set Israel free from their slavery.

As the enemy sought his next innocent victim, there was one place he didn't think to look—in the river! Yes, the parents of Moses had already "cast" him into the river, after lovingly preparing him an ark of bulrushes. What wisdom on the part of his parents! It seems their action is related to the Words of Jesus: "For whosoever will save his life shall lose it: and whosoever will lose his life...shall find it" (Mt. 16:25). Moses' life was "found" by Pharaoh's daughter as she bathed in the river. The deliverer

1. "Testament" and "Covenant" are the same words. The Old Covenant was actually given by God through Moses. The Old Testament Age, therefore, began with the birth of Moses.

was then hidden, and raised, in an even more secure place—in Pharaoh's own house. The enemy never thought to look for the deliverer in his own house! He even paid to raise the one who would later destroy him![2] (Note: If we daily embrace the suffering and death of the cross, we will continually find that our loving Father has already prepared an "ark of bulrushes" to uphold and save us from many disastrous situations. Furthermore, He will cause everything to work for our good!)

The Old Testament Age began with the slaughter of infants. However, the heartrending scene of a cruel king destroying little lives was repeated at the end of the Old Testament Age, with the birth of Jesus Christ. Herod, having heard that the Deliverer was born, ordered all the babies of Bethlehem to be killed. But the Lord once again protected His Deliverer by directing the parents with divine wisdom, and they took the babe to Egypt to save Him.[3] Later, He was raised in Nazareth, a most unlikely place, where sin abounded.[4]

Many Details Link the Beginning and Ending of the Old Testament Age

The Old Testament Age began and ended with a birth and with the slaughter of innocents. However, there are many other details that link the beginning and ending of that Age.

1. It began and ended with a Moses. The first Moses said, "The Lord thy God will raise up unto thee a Prophet from the midst of thee, of thy brethren, like unto me; unto him ye shall hearken" (Deut. 18:15,18). Just as the Bible reveals a "first Adam" and a "second Adam" (Christ),[5] so too, it reveals a "first Moses" and a "second Moses" (Christ).

2. It began and ended with the coming of a deliverer. The first Moses is called a "deliverer" in Acts 7:35. Christ is also called the "Deliverer" in Romans 11:26.

2. I speak of "Pharaoh" as an office, or as the title of the national leader. The Pharaoh that Moses actually destroyed was not the same one who raised him.
3. Note that Egypt speaks of the world and death in the Bible (Rev. 11:8). Even today, one of the principal reasons that tourists visit Egypt is to see the tombs of past kings (the pyramids, for example).
4. See John 1:46 and Isaiah 53:2. He grew up as a root out of a "dry ground." Spiritually speaking, Nazareth had little or no spiritual blessing upon it. The kind of people found there is revealed by their attempts to kill the Lord when He later returned to visit them.
5. First Corinthians 15:45-47 and Romans 5:14 (the first Adam is called a "figure of Him that was to come").

3. It began and ended with a Passover. Moses gave Israel the Passover of Exodus 12, which saved them from death and brought them out of the bondage of Egypt. Christ gave His people the Passover that saved us from death and brought us out of the bondage of a spiritual "Egypt," the world (1 Cor. 5:7).

4. It began and ended with a wilderness "journey." Moses and Israel had a wilderness experience of forty years. Christ had a wilderness experience of forty days (Mt. 4:1-2).

5. It began and ended with the giving of a priesthood. Moses gave a priesthood to God's people, and Christ did also (Heb. 7:5,11,14,22).

6. It began and ended with the giving of a tabernacle. Moses gave God's people a tabernacle, and Christ gave us a better Tabernacle (Heb. 9:1-2,21-24).

7. It began and ended with the giving of sacrifices. Moses showed Israel how to offer sacrifices acceptable to God, at the beginning of the Old Testament Age, and Christ showed Israel how to offer sacrifices acceptable to God at the end of the Old Testament Age (1 Pet. 2:5; Heb. 13:15-16; 9:23-24).

8. It began and ended with the giving of an altar. Moses gave Israel an altar on which to offer their sacrifices. Since Hebrews tells us that Jesus gave us "better sacrifices," we also should expect that we have a better altar. It is found in Hebrews 13:10.

9. It began and ended with the giving of a law. Moses is called the mediator of the Old Covenant, the "lawgiver." Christ is called the Mediator of the New Covenant. He, too, is called the "lawgiver" (Isa. 33:22; Jas. 4:12). Moses gave the Old Testament law of ritual, while Jesus gave the New Testament law of righteousness. Hebrews 7:12,22 tells us that Jesus changed the law. He did that in Matthew 5–7 when He "went up into a mountain" (Mt. 5:1), just as Moses gave the Old Testament law from a mountain. Six times in Matthew 5 Jesus says, "You have heard it said" and He then quotes what the law of Moses said. However, in each case He goes on to say, "But I say unto thee." He then raises the standard of the law from outward rituals, which deal with the outer man, to inner righteousness, which deals with the inner man. This is why He begins with, "Think not that I am come to destroy the law...but to fulfill...except your righteousness shall exceed the righteousness of the scribes and Pharisees, ye shall in no case enter into the kingdom of heaven" (Mt. 5:17,20). The New Testament law is much higher than the Old. "He that despised Moses' law died without mercy under two or three witnesses: of how much sorer punishment, suppose ye, shall he be thought worthy, who hath trodden under foot the Son of God?" (Heb. 10:28-29)

10. It began and ended with a visible manifestation of the Lord. During the days of Moses the Lord appeared in a visible form. The people experienced a visible manifestation of His glory in the cloud, in the pillar of fire, and finally, at Mount Sinai, where the elders "saw God" (Ex. 24:11). The same thing happened when Jesus Christ came to earth. "And we beheld his glory, the glory as of the only begotten of the Father" (Jn. 1:14).

11. It began and ended with supernatural bread in the wilderness. God supernaturally fed His people with manna in a physical wilderness. In Matthew 14:15 Jesus also supernaturally fed His people, in a physical wilderness, with the "bread from heaven." (See John 6:32, where He links this miracle with Moses and manna.)

In conclusion, the beginning and the ending of the Old Testament Age are intimately related. However, since God's people of that Age are a "parable" for His people in the New Testament Age, shouldn't we expect that the beginning and the ending of the New Testament Age will also be related? This we will see in the next chapter.

Chapter 6

The Beginning and Ending of the New Testament Age

An Ending a Beginning, a Beginning an Ending

Birth is the end of life in the womb, but at the same time it is the beginning of life on the earth. Death is the end of earthly life, but it is also the beginning of one's eternal existence in God.[1] The very instant one day ends the new day begins. The instant the old year ends the new year begins. That "instant" in time is both an ending and a beginning. Life teaches us that endings can also be beginnings, and that beginnings can be endings.

The New Testament Age Also Begins and Ends With a Birth

At the moment Christ came, He was **ending** the Old Testament Age, and He was **beginning** the New Testament Age. So then, that ending was also a beginning. This is one more example of why He can call Himself "the beginning and the ending." In fact, since He alone controls our present and our future, we need to see Him in our hour of trial as the only One who can bring an end to our present situation and begin a new day for us. In His coming, He revealed both a beginning and an ending at the same moment. Going one step further, we conclude that He will also

1. That is, of course, if we are redeemed by the blood of Christ.

begin and end the New Testament Age with the same events as the Old Testament Age, because (1) He is the beginning and ending of the New Testament Age as well and (2) Old Testament Israel is our pattern or "parable," and their Age began and ended in the same way—with a birth. Remember, a parable is a story with a spiritual application. Therefore, we should fully expect *our* Age to begin and end with a birth. Let's consider whether this will be the case.

The New Testament Age begins in Matthew 1 with a virgin being found with child by the Holy Spirit before her wedding. Revelation 12 reveals that the New Testament Age will end the same way! There we find a virgin, found with child by the Holy Spirit, before the wedding, which takes place in Revelation 19. That woman is the Church of the last days. (We will see the scriptural reasons for this in Chapter 17.) Therefore, just as the Old Testament Age began and ended with a birth, so also will the New Testament Age begin and end with a birth.

At this point, you may not understand our next statement, or you may reject it outright, but please wait until you have first considered all the biblical evidence before you pass judgment. **Christ came the first time with a birth, and He will come the second time with a birth.** The difference between these two births is that the first birth was a physical birth, coming through a physical Israel, while the second birth will be a spiritual birth, coming through a spiritual Israel, the Israel we considered in Chapter 4. This is one more example of how every jot and tittle written about our "parable," Old Testament Israel, will be fulfilled in the New Testament Age, and of how history repeats itself. Throughout this book we will repeatedly come back to the thought of Christ coming through a spiritual birth, referred to by Paul as, "Christ *in* you, the hope of glory" (Col. 1:27). I want to emphasize here that I am *not* ignoring or eliminating the physical coming of the Lord at the end. Rather, I am saying that He will first come *in* His people (Mal. 3:1-4;[2] Col. 1:27), then He will come *for* His people (1 Thess. 4:16-18), and finally He will come *with* His people (Rev. 19:13-14).

2. Note the context of Malachi 3:1-4. This cannot refer primarily to Christ's First Coming and the ministry of John the Baptist because the fruit of the coming referred to in Malachi 3 is that "then shall the offering of Judah and Jerusalem be pleasant unto the Lord, as in the days of old." This did not happen after the First Coming. Rather, He was rejected. Therefore, just as Malachi 4:5-6 and Matthew 17:10-13 reveal that there will be a more complete fulfillment of Elijah's coming to prepare His way for the Second Coming, likewise, Malachi 3 was partially fulfilled in John the Baptist, but will find a complete fulfillment in the Second Coming. We are told that the Lord will come to His Temple, which is the Church. However, He will only come to those who are seeking Him and expecting Him to come in that way, something that many are not expecting today.

One of the reasons that Israel did not understand or accept the coming of Christ the first time is that they did not perceive that He would come in more than one stage. First, His coming was announced by the angels at His birth in Bethlehem, when they said that the Christ had come that night (Lk. 2:8-14). Then He was revealed in the temple at the age of twelve (Lk. 2:46). Later, He was revealed as the Christ at the baptism of John (Jn. 1:29-34). Finally, after He was crucified, He came back to His people again as the glorified Christ (Acts 1:3). At the end of the Old Testament Age, most of Israel did not foresee any of these stages and this was one reason they missed Him altogether. Is it possible that we are making a similar mistake at the end of our Age? Will this tragic aspect of history repeat itself also?

Regarding the thought of Christ coming in us and through us by means of a spiritual birthing, He shows us that we can all become His "mother" in Mark 3:35: "For whosoever shall do the will of God, the same is my...mother." He is, without doubt, speaking here about spiritual things, not natural things. But what is a "mother"? We are given insight through the life of Mary, His first mother. Christ, as the eternal Son of God, was with the Father since before the foundation of the world, long before Mary existed. Therefore, Mary simply became a channel through which He was brought forth to a needy world. Mary was a pattern mother, but there will be many other "mothers," or channels, through which His life will flow freely to a needy world.

Some may ask, "But hasn't Christ already been in us ever since our new birth?" Yes, the babe born in that dirty manger of Bethlehem was willing to be born in *our* "manger" also—in an unclean and undesirable place like the human heart. When His life was born in us we became "babes in Christ." However, the Apostle Paul speaks often about coming to the place where it is no longer the Babe of the manger, nor the young Man of the carpenter shop, who is living in us and manifesting Himself through us, but rather the full-grown Son of God. He speaks of growing up until we reach the "measure of the stature of the fulness of Christ" (Eph. 4:13-15). We wait for a revelation of *that* Man, longed for by this world and so desperately needed by all of us. This should be the goal of every Christian.

Paul was one of those channels. He too travailed, confirming that the Church will also give birth. "My little children, of whom I **travail in birth again** until Christ be formed in you" (Gal. 4:19). This travailing and *birth* are much deeper experiences than the new birth of the Believer. The Galatian Believers, his "little children," were already born-again, but the fullness of Christ's life had not yet been formed in them. For that reason Paul "travailed in birth" for them.

In this same context, Paul says that the Church, the heavenly Jerusalem, is the woman referred to in Isaiah 54:1. "Sing, O barren, thou that didst not bear; break forth into singing, and cry aloud, thou that didst not *travail* with child: for more are the children of the desolate than the children of the married wife, saith the Lord." Therefore, we know that the Church *will* travail. A travailing woman is seen in many Scriptures throughout the Bible. Could she be the same as the woman travailing at the end of the Church Age in Revelation 12? This question will be answered here and in later chapters.

They Are Killing the Babies Again!

Herod killed dozens of babies in Bethlehem. Pharaoh killed hundreds or perhaps thousands in Egypt. Today abortion kills millions of little lives before they even have a chance to cry out for help! The Old Testament Age began and ended with babies being murdered, and the New Testament Age began, and is now ending, the same way. In the days of Moses only the little nation of Israel suffered. During Christ's day it happened only in Bethlehem. However, in these last days the enemy is revealing his barbaric nature on a worldwide scale, because the revelation of the Deliverer will be worldwide also and not limited to one nation. All flesh shall see the glory of the Lord, and *everyone* who calls upon the name of the Lord shall be delivered (Isa. 40:5; Joel 2:32).

We Will See Christ Again When the Church Travails

Jesus spoke an extremely difficult riddle to His disciples in John 16:16-24. This riddle was related to the travail and "birth" of Revelation 12. It reveals that Christ will come and be revealed again in the last days, first through a spiritual birth in the Church, *before* He comes physically during the Rapture. His riddle is, "A little while, and ye shall not see me: and again, a little while, and ye shall see me, because I go to the Father" (Jn. 16:16).

The first part of this statement was quite easy for them to understand. In a short time they were no longer going to see Him. They understood that part only too well, because He had just told them He was going away, and returning to the Father (Jn. 16:5-6). It was the second part of the riddle that did not make sense.

If He had said, "And again, a little while, and ye shall see me **because I come,**" they would have understood this perfectly. They would have understood that they were going to see Him again, after a little while, because He would return for them. However, He didn't say that they would see Him again in a little while because He would come. Rather He said, "again, a little while, and ye shall see me, **because I go...**" (Jn. 16:16).

This was such a difficult, yet important riddle that between verses 16 and 19 this thought is repeated four times. He has made it quite redundant, because He wanted it to catch our attention. He leaves no room for doubt concerning His desire for us to think on this matter, and to seek Him for understanding.

He explains in verses 20 through 23 that we shall weep and lament, but that our sorrow will be turned to joy. He tells us that "a woman when she is in *travail* hath sorrow, because her hour is come: but as soon as she is delivered of the child, she remembereth no more the anguish, for joy that a man is born into the world" (Jn. 16:21). He then applies this thought of spiritual "travail" directly to His disciples by saying, "*And ye now therefore have sorrow*" (Jn. 16:22). A woman travailing to bring forth a son is compared to us, His people! The reason we are going to see Him after another "little while" is because there will be travail and a birth, not because of a Rapture.

The Disciples and the Early Church Travailed

Why was His going, or departure, a key to their seeing Him again? In what way did the disciples travail in the beginning of the Church Age, and what was the final result? We should consider this carefully, because the end of the Church Age will surely be the same.

Imagine what was taking place in the hearts of those eleven faithful followers of the Lamb, as He prepared to leave them. We often look at the disciples as men who just couldn't seem to understand spiritual truths. We may have seen them with just one ambition in life—to sit on thrones and occupy the first place in the Kingdom. However, these men had forsaken houses and lands, fathers, mothers, brothers, sisters, wives, and children, to wander all over the country for three and a half years with the Carpenter of Nazareth! They had made a tremendous commitment to Him, one that few of us have even considered making. After walking with Him for more than three years, it is very doubtful that their only goal in life was to satisfy their own carnal ambitions. It is highly unlikely that any *sincere* person, as the eleven were, could walk for so long with the Creator without experiencing a mighty transformation of the desires in his heart.

These men's hearts had often burned as they came to understand, by experience, that their Messiah was the answer to every need of fallen man. Imagine what they felt the day they drew near to the village of Nain, where sadness was filling many hearts (Lk. 7:11-15). A poor widow lived there. She accompanied the funeral procession of her only son with weeping, believing that she would never have the joy of being with him again in his life. He had also been a key to her sustenance, but had now died. She faced hunger, and an even deeper poverty than she had known before. Who would ever help her? Most of Israel struggled with poverty in those days, living under the heavy hand of Rome. They couldn't help the poor, because they were *all* poor! Now she was the poorest of the poor. In a few moments she would leave her son's graveside to face life completely alone.

But Jesus came! Everyone watched as He stopped the procession to comfort that poor soul. "He is *so* kind," onlookers surely thought, as He drew near to the casket to pay his final respects to the deceased. But no! Something much more glorious was happening. The young man was rising from the dead and being presented back to his weeping mother, who was now ecstatic with joy! Oh, how the hearts of those disciples must have burned with the brokenness and joy of that moment.

Imagine also their emotion that day when the Greeks came and said, "Sir, we would see Jesus!" (Jn. 12:21) They could just envision that now this wonderful outpouring of Heaven's glory would come to all the nations of the earth. Even the Greeks, those world-renowned philosophers, had heard of His glory, and they would soon recognize what His disciples already knew, that Jesus was everything that man could ever ask for or need.

The disciples, in spite of their false motives and personal ambitions, by now had much less interest in self than ever before, having been touched by His glory and presence. They longed for the whole world to see, hear, and touch what they had witnessed. They longed for others to see Jesus, too. They wanted the world to know that the Savior had come, and that all the sick, the dying, the poor, and the discouraged could find their answer in His presence. Yes, Jesus was the fulfillment of all their hopes and dreams as true Israelites. To them, He was everything they had ever lived or longed for!

But there was one great sorrow filling their hearts. Jesus had just told them He was leaving, and that they would see Him no more. He was returning to the Father and Heaven. At that darkest hour, they were surely saying to Him, "Lord, this can't be true. Just when we realize that You are everything to us, and that You are what the world needs, You tell us it is all over! Just when this visitation is beginning to touch other nations, You tell us You are leaving. Doesn't it matter to You, Lord, that there are still untold thousands who need You in Israel and in the world?"

Imagine what was in their hearts when they saw Him for the last time on the day of His Ascension. These same disciples had spent over three years trying to decide who was the greatest among them. At that moment John might have questioned, "Peter, what are we going to do now? Neither the Greeks nor the world will ever see what we have seen during these wonderful years. The Word was made flesh and dwelt among us, and we beheld His glory, the glory as of the only begotten of the Father, full of grace and truth. But will anyone else ever receive that blessing?"

Peter's response could have been, "I don't know, John, but suddenly it doesn't matter who is number one among us. I just feel a deep longing to find a place to pray, and to pour out my heart before Him."

Imagine how they wept, prayed, interceded, and travailed in those days as the cry of the Greeks echoed in their ears, "Sir, we would see Jesus." They knew that no one would ever see Him again. Unless...unless that sorrow and travail Jesus had spoken of would cause them to be so transformed that maybe, just maybe, the world would someday see Jesus through **them**. Maybe they *would* give birth to His life, the life of the Son of promise. Maybe they *would* see Him again after a "little while." Maybe they *would* become channels, prepared vessels, through which He would meet the needs of the world. Could it be that they too would become His "mother"?

The life of the Lamb was indeed birthed in John through travail, the travail of intercession to which Paul refers.[3] Christ's life was formed in him to such an extent that, writing many years later, he could say, "That which we have heard, which we have seen with our eyes, which we have looked upon, and our hands have handled, of the Word of life...that is the very same Life which we have revealed to you, that is the Life which you have seen in us. He has come to you through us, so that you can see what we saw, and hear what we heard, and know the precious communion with the Father and the Son that we have experienced" (1 Jn. 1:1-3 paraphrased).

Yes, that travail had indeed caused His life to be birthed in them, and the early Church saw Him again, not in the Rapture, but in His Body. They saw Him again after a "little while" because He *went away*. Such a mighty travail, sorrow, and burden fell upon the disciples that they completely forgot about personal ambition, and soon after He had returned to His Father the world saw Him again, through them. When they stood before the council in Jerusalem, those hypocritical Pharisees had to acknowledge

3. Romans 8:26 and Galatians 4:19.

that they had been with Jesus! The world saw Jesus through those travailing Jews.

I wonder if the cry of the "Greeks" has entered our hearts in these last days? Have we spent enough time alone with Jesus to be profoundly convinced in our hearts that others would be deeply grateful for the opportunity to see what we have seen in that secret place? Have *we* seen the depths of despair and anguish that grip the hearts of millions in the earth today? Have we been so moved with the needs of the sick and the dying, on the one hand, and with the glory of His presence on the other, that a spiritual travail has begun to grip our hearts? Does a cry ascend from our hearts that will cause His life to be birthed in us so that others will see Him?

There is one thing of which we can be very sure. There will be no Rapture until this concern grips the heart and soul of His Bride. The world needs to see the beauty that the Church itself *should* be seeing every day in the intimacy of the King's chambers of love. He *will* be birthed in the Church, and His gospel of the Kingdom *will* be preached in all the world for a witness, and then shall the end come. As we gain understanding of these things, we will begin to discern the difference between the truth and the myths that have bombarded the Church concerning the last days.

Other Similarities Between the Beginning and Ending of the New Testament Age

Israel longed for deliverance from Rome and for the Kingdom. When Christ came the first time, there were two principal desires in the hearts of God's people. They expected their Messiah to fulfill those desires when He came, and if He couldn't or wouldn't then they weren't prepared to accept Him. First, they wanted to be delivered from Rome. Second, they wanted to receive the Kingdom. Today there are two principal things that Believers expect to receive through the coming of the Messiah. First, we see the old Roman Empire on the rise again as the European nations unite. This appears to be part of the foundation of the "New World Order" and future world government. As Believers, we long for Him to come to save us from this "Rome," through the Rapture. And second, one of the principal messages of the Church today is the message of the Kingdom. His answer to these two desires is the same at His Second Coming as it was at His First Coming. Yes, the Messiah is coming. But rather than delivering us from the hand of Rome through a Rapture, He will give us the power to *conquer* Rome, through the glory of the Lord, just as He did in the First Coming.[4]

To those who longed for the Kingdom, the Messiah came and offered the cross. Peter wanted the Kingdom, but he couldn't make the connection between choosing the death of the cross and inheriting the Kingdom. For that reason Peter, the one who was truly willing to die for Him, who proved it by pulling out his sword and risking his life to protect Him, ended up denying Him. It was not because he no longer desired the Kingdom, nor because he lost his willingness to fight for it, but because he didn't understand the way to get there—the way of the cross. He didn't understand that the Lord was calling him and all Believers to follow the Lamb to the cross and to die with Him in meekness as lambs. He didn't understand that afterwards the Father would raise *the* Lamb from the dead, along with *every* lamb, and set them on the throne.[5] Let's not continue making the same mistakes that Israel made in His First Coming. Let's choose the way of the cross, the way to really conquer Rome. The cross also conquers the "Rome" that is in every one of us—that is, the flesh.

There were many denominations. Another similarity between the beginning and ending of the Church Age is a very sad one. Then, just as now, the people of God were divided into many conflicting and rivaling denominations. There were the Pharisees, the Sadducees, the Herodians, the Essenes, and so on. Each wanted to protect its turf and obtain more proselytes. But as a group, none of them actually received the blessing that accompanied the First Coming. Most of them rejected the Lord because they couldn't recognize Him when He came. They were too engrossed in seeking ministerial success and position, bigger congregations in their synagogues, the honor of man, more tithes, and more of this world's goods. They didn't love the presence of the One who had created them and had called them into the ministry. Oh, yes, they loved the ministry, but they didn't really love *Him*. They faithfully protected their congregations from doctrinal heresies, not because of a love for the truth, but because of a love for the tithes of the sheep they risked losing.

One day a river of His presence began to flow in Israel as "the voice of one" was heard in the wilderness. John the Baptist came with an anointing that couldn't be resisted, and all their sheep went out into the wilderness

---

4. The Church finally conquered Rome and the Gentile world in A.D. 313, under Constantine, at least in the name of Christianity, though not in its spirit.
5. See Revelation 3:21. When we refer to the "dead" here we aren't referring only to physical death, but rather to the daily work of the cross in our lives.

to be immersed in that precious river of life. They ended up calling John a heretic. They called him a heretic, not because of what he taught, but because he emptied their synagogues. They had held the people under their ministries for a long time without paying the price to feed them with the "Bread of His Presence." They chose comfort, pleasures, cares, the things of this world, and their own fleshly ways and lusts. They had forsaken the fountain of living waters and hewn out for themselves broken cisterns that could hold no water. They refused to give their lives to prayer, fasting, and seeking the Lord with an honest and humble heart and an upright life.

When the river of life began to flow, and the Bread of His Presence began to be manifested, the hungry and the thirsty souls, who had been crying for the reality of Heaven and His presence, left the comfort, position, and prestige of the synagogues in droves. They identified themselves first with that wild man in the desert, and later with the Messiah Himself, from whose life flowed the waters they had lacked, but had so longed for year after year. They didn't care any more if they lost their eldership. They didn't care if they were removed from being the church treasurer. It didn't matter if they were expelled from the synagogue, as long as they were never again expelled from His glorious presence, and never again fed with the dry sawdust of dead sermons!

The religious leaders of that day, leaders of God's only true people, couldn't accept the loss of the things they wanted in life. If only there had been a desire in their hearts for the One they had been called to know and make known, they would have gladly laid down everything and would have run after His presence along with their sheep. Then they wouldn't have lost their sheep. Rather, they would have been among the many spiritual leaders whom the Chief Shepherd placed over His flock after the cross. Jesus reiterated this truth by saying that if we lose our life for His sake we will *always* end up saving it.

The reaction of the religious leaders of Christ's day is often seen today. Not long ago a pastor was afraid of losing some of his key members to another work that was feeding them the Bread of Life. Rather than seeking God for a fresh anointing on his own ministry, he forbade his leaders to visit there, saying the other work had dangerous false doctrines. When the supposed heretical pastor, for the sake of unity, offered to meet with the accusing pastor and change any of his doctrine that was unscriptural, the offer was refused, because a love of the truth was not the real issue. Because of his lack of love for truth, and fear of losing his sheep, it is doubtful he will end up keeping the **hungry** hearts when that Voice once again resonates in the earth and all flesh sees His glory.

The Lord of glory is going to visit His people again. He is going to come *in* His Temple before He comes *for* His Temple in the Rapture. He is coming for a glorious Church without spot, or wrinkle, or any such thing (Eph. 5:27). The only way for that to become a reality today is for Christ Jesus Himself to be brought forth in its members. And when that happens there will be many leaders of the true people of God whose lack of relationship with the Lord will be revealed by their lack of living water also. In many cases, just as in the First Coming, those leaders will attack the King of Glory, Who will be manifested in and through His people. Instead of yielding in repentance, and choosing the way of the cross, the way to an **eternal** Kingdom, they will place *Him* on the cross, spiritually speaking, so they can continue with their spiritual games and build their earthly kingdoms. Yes, the beginning and the ending of the Church Age will be both wonderfully, and yet tragically, the same. What side will we be on in that day?

Chapter 7

The Chronology of Revelation

And he saith unto me, Seal not the sayings of the prophecy of this book: for the time is at hand (Revelation 22:10).

John is instructed by the angel not to seal the Book of Revelation, because the Lord wants us to understand its message. The Lord was not trying to hide the truth here, but rather reveal it. In the first verse of the book, He tells us that His whole purpose in giving us this Revelation is to clearly show us the future. This book should be easy to understand, but it seems that man and the enemy have managed to make it confusing! It is not full of tricky wording, or what Solomon would refer to as "dark sayings" with hidden meanings. Confusion has entered the Church through spirits of error. There is a tendency to use Revelation to prove what is already considered to be "established doctrine." This provides fertile ground for those spirits of error. The way of wisdom is to come with a child's simplicity, asking, "Lord, what do You say in this book?"

If It Is Easy, Then Where Are the Seven Years in the End?

When the Lord spoke to me in the Philippines about understanding the end, He said, "If you want to understand the truth concerning the last days, lay aside all your preconceived ideas and doctrines of which you are so certain. Then come to Me in humility, and ask, 'Lord, what do *You* say, and what does Your *Word* say?' " After saying that, He concluded with a challenge: "For example, you are so sure there will be seven years of tribulation in the end. Show Me just one verse in the Bible saying that." That challenge brought a shocking discovery. Tradition, teachings, and doctrines of men can so subtly brainwash us that we don't even realize it has happened. I am still searching futilely for that verse!

During my first twenty years as a Christian I had been taught, and had also shared with others, the popular end-time theology of the Church today. When the Lord gave me this challenge I immediately thought of the well-known "last week" of Daniel's Seventy Weeks as a proof text. Invariably, this is the text that is given to prove that there will be a seven-year period of tribulation in the end. But I realized I could not base an entire doctrine on one verse, much less on man's interpretation of that one verse. There *had* to be another one![1]

Consider the Number Seven

Before further discussion of a possible seven-year period in the last days and the time period that is actually found in the Book of Revelation, consider how the Lord uses the number seven in the Bible. In the Hebrew language the word "seven"is intimately linked with the concept of a covenant or an oath. The number seven is not just a number that *represents* the covenant, but the root of this word actually means "to make a covenant" or "to make an oath."[2] The scriptural use of the number seven is very interesting in the light of the relationship that exists between the beginning and ending, and between Genesis and Revelation. The Hebrew word translated as "seven" appears in Genesis fifty-nine times, **many** more times than in most other books, with only one exception—the Book of Revelation, where the Greek word translated as "seven" appears fifty-four times!

Consider these facts:

1. God wants us to understand the future, and especially the message of Revelation because it brings us blessing (Rev. 1:3).
2. God has intimately linked the messages of Genesis and Revelation.
3. He uses the number seven more extensively in those two books than in any other book of the Bible.
4. Never once is a seven-year period ever mentioned in the Book of Revelation.

---

1. This "last week of Daniel" will be discussed at length in Part III.
2. Compare *Strong's Hebrew Dictionary*, #7650 and #7651.

The above facts are amazing for at least three reasons:

1. If there will be a special seven-year period in the end, why doesn't God ever mention it in Revelation, since this book in particular is God's attempt to make the message clear? Wouldn't it be logical to speak of the seven years since the number seven is used extensively anyway?

2. Although a seven-year period never appears in Revelation, a specific time period of three and a half years, or forty-two months, or 1,260 days, or "time, times, and half a time," is often mentioned.

3. Since the beginning and ending are the same, it is important to note that, biblically speaking, the Church Age did not begin with a special seven-year period, but rather with a three-and-a-half-year period.[3] The ministry of Christ, as revealed in the Gospels, lasted three and a half years.[4] When the Lord refers exclusively to a three-and-a-half-year period before the Second Coming in Revelation, is He trying to show us that indeed the Church Age begins and ends with a three-and-a-half-year period, instead of beginning with a three-and-a-half-year period and ending with a seven-year period? We will see that this is precisely the case.

Seven Years?

From where, then, do theologians find **seven years** in the Book of Revelation? A period of **three and a half years** is found in **each** of chapters 11, 12, and 13. Some have simply made the decision to *add* two of these periods to arrive at seven years. What scriptural authorization is there for doing that? Just as I did, when the Lord spoke to me in the Philippines, some would turn to Daniel's Seventy Weeks for their justification. This is an example of approaching Revelation with a desire to prove a preconceived idea. Why not add the three-and-a-half-year period found in all

---

3. I am aware that some say there was, in fact, a special seven-year period of ministry to the Jews after the cross, but this is based on interpretation and not on facts given in the Bible.

4. See Tenney, Merrill C., ed., *The Zondervan Pictorial Encyclopedia of the Bible,* Zondervan Publishing House, Grand Rapids, Michigan, 1975, p. 820. This encyclopedia refers to Eusebius of Caesarea, Ecclesiastical History, A.D. 300, Hist. I. x. 39,40. Eusebius states that Christ ministered for three and a half years. He quotes Melito, who wrote in A.D. 165 that Christ's ministry spanned three years.
Thompson, Frank, Charles, *Thompson Chain-Reference Bible,* B.B. Kirkbride Bible Co., Inc., Indianapolis, Indiana, "Harmony of the Gospels," pp. 269-272. This shows Christ's three-and-a-half-year ministry.
Halley, H., *Halley's Bible Handbook,* Zondervan Publishing House, Grand Rapids, Michigan, 1965, pp. 459-460.

three of those chapters? The answer: a ten-and-a-half-year total would result, which would be contrary to the preconceived idea of seven years. There is as much scriptural justification for adding three periods as there is for adding two periods—none!

Revelation consistently reveals only one specific period of time throughout the book. Chapters 11, 12, and 13 all show the *same* period of three and a half years, only from three different perspectives: in chapter 11 from the perspective of the two witnesses; in chapter 12 from the Church's perspective; in chapter 13 from the world's perspective.

Three and a Half Years

For more light on this period of three and a half years, we allow the Bible to interpret itself. The revelation of the end was given to Jesus Christ by the Father (Rev. 1:1). We do not know exactly when the Father gave Him this revelation concerning the last days. However, we *do* know that it was before His discourse on the last days found in Matthew 24, because He could not have given His disciples that revelation had He not already received it from His Father.[5] Matthew 24, therefore, must be precisely the same revelation of the end that Christ gives to His Church in the Book of Revelation, because this is the one true revelation concerning the last days. In fact, Matthew 24 and Revelation are so similar that even the order of events is the same. The similarities between the two are so clear that we could actually call Matthew 22:41 through 24:35 a miniature Book of Revelation. (See Appendix C, where this comparison is made.)

Comparing Matthew 24 with the Book of Revelation, it quickly becomes apparent that the Lord speaks of only one specific period of time in the last days. He calls that the time of "great tribulation" (v. 21). According to His revelation of the last days, that tribulation begins with the "abomination of desolation, spoken of by Daniel the prophet" (v. 15). Daniel reveals that from the abomination of desolation to the end there will be a period of 1,290 days, or three and a half years (Dan. 12:11). Basically, all evangelical theologians believe that the Great Tribulation lasts for three and a half years, as revealed by comparing Matthew 24:15 and

5. Remember, when Jesus became a man, He "emptied Himself" of His divinity. Luke 2:52 tells us He "increased in wisdom and stature." He couldn't have grown in wisdom if He already knew everything, nor would there have been any need for His Father to give Him the revelation if He already knew all things. Finally, Jesus said that He only shared with His disciples the things that He had heard from His Father (Jn. 7:16-18; 15:15).

Daniel 12:11. However, many of them also believe that there will be seven years of general tribulation, but that only the last half of that period will be the Great Tribulation. However, if we limit ourselves to Christ's revelation of the last days, we will never find any specific period of time related to the end other than three and a half years.

What is the biblical basis for believing that there will be two classes of tribulation in the last days, that is, a seven-year period divided into three and a half years of tribulation, followed by three and a half years of Great Tribulation? We will see in later chapters that this is strictly speculation with no biblical foundation whatsoever. Jesus gives us a "promise" in John 16:33: "In the world ye shall have tribulation." This, coupled with our own daily experience, makes us recognize that "general" tribulation will last throughout the entire Church Age, ending with three and a half years of Great Tribulation. These are the only two types of tribulation that Jesus ever refers to in the Bible. One lasts for many centuries, and the other lasts for three and a half years. Isn't it remarkable that even though our Teacher and Example doesn't ever mention seven years of tribulation in any of His teachings, yet *we* do? Maybe He wasn't aware of our revelation!

The Chronology of the Book of Revelation

Most of those who have seriously studied Revelation realize that the chronology of events seems difficult. Some have finally concluded that those events are not in chronological order. I believe that the chronology is quite simple if we receive one little key.

"In the mouth of two or three witnesses shall every word be established."[6] This is a principle we must believe and live by. Any revelation must be confirmed by at least two or three witnesses who say the same thing. (We should not accept it until there is confirmation.) An example of this is seen in Revelation 11, where God sends two witnesses, not just one. Didn't John the Apostle also need a witness to confirm his "Revelation"?

Where, then, is the other mouth that confirms the message of Revelation? The book itself gives us the answer, showing that two messengers do, in fact, speak forth the message of the book. In Revelation 1:1 we find the first messenger (or "angel")[7] who gives The Revelation. His message actually revolves around a "little book." John is caught up into heavenly places in chapter 4, and then in chapter 5 he sees a little book that is sealed

6. Second Corinthians 13:1 is one of the places in which this principle appears.
7. "Angel" also means "messenger" in the Greek. See *Strong's Greek Dictionary*, #32.

with seven seals. No one is found worthy to open those seals except the Lamb that was slain. The message of the little book unfolds in chapters 6–10. There is a progressive revelation of its message as the seals are opened one after another, the seventh seal disclosing seven trumpets. In chapter 10 we come to the very end, as seen in verses 6 and 7. There the angel declares that there shall be "time," or delay, no longer, and the seventh and last trumpet is blown, which brings us to the end,[8] and to the consummation of the message of that little book.

Afterward, John again sees that little book, now open.[9] He is told to eat it. Eating the Word carries with it the thought of assimilating that Word so that it actually becomes part of our very life and message (Jer. 15:16). After being told to eat the book, the angel said to John, "Thou must prophesy again" (Rev. 10:11). The message of the little book now becomes part of John, and he speaks forth prophetically that same message again. The repetition of that message appears in subsequent chapters of the Book of Revelation. There John repeats, in his own words, the same revelation and message given by the messenger in the first part of the book. Thus, it is confirmed in the mouth of two witnesses: first by the messenger who was sent to John (chapters 4-10), and afterwards by John himself as he spoke it forth under a prophetic anointing (chapters 14-19). Is this purely speculation or a private interpretation? See Appendix A, which shows that forty-two of the details found in the first half of the book are repeated in the second half, in almost the identical order!

So then, is the Book of Revelation in chronological order or not? The answer is "yes," if we take into account the divisions that exist in the book.[10] Therefore, the book is chronological, which is also logical since He wants to make the message clear to us. And the only specific time period that is found in Revelation, or referred to in Matthew 24 is that of three and a half years.

---

8. Refer here to Part II ("When Does the Rapture Occur, Before or After the Great Tribulation?"). See especially Chapters 9 and 10, which deal with the seventh trumpet.
9. If the Greek text itself is compared here it will be observed that the "little book" of Revelation 10:8 and the "book" of Revelation 5:1-9 is the same Greek word in these passages. *Strong's Greek Dictionary* has an error here (#974 should be #975).
10. In other words, we must understand that the message of Revelation 4–10 is repeated in Revelation 14–19, and that in between those two sections the details of the last three and a half years are given in Revelation 11–13. Read Appendix A for the details.

What Have We Learned So Far?

(Summary Part I)

In Part I we saw that God wants us to understand the end, and He has actually placed the desire to know in our hearts. This is so we can have protection, a vision that keeps us running, and a heart for intercession. Next, we discussed two keys for understanding the end: (1) mercy obtained through humility and (2) Christ is the Beginning and Ending.

We also learned that Old Testament Israel is a parable that will be fulfilled by New Testament Israel. With this understanding we discovered that the beginning and ending of the Old Testament Age are the same as the beginning and ending of the New Testament Age.

Finally, we concluded with two insights from Revelation: (1) There is no seven-year period in Revelation, but rather a three-and-a-half-year period seen from three different viewpoints in chapters 11, 12, and 13 respectively and (2) Revelation is chronological but is repeated twice, first by the angel, and then by John.

PART II

When Does the Rapture Occur, Before or After the Great Tribulation?

Introduction

There are two thoughts I would like to encourage you to keep in mind while reading this part: (1) there isn't necessarily any direct link between one chapter and the next, except that each presents evidence showing when the Rapture will take place, before or after the Great Tribulation and (2) regardless of our doctrinal persuasion on any subject, it is important to always come to the Lord and His Word with an open heart. The Rapture is such an important subject for the Church living today that all of us should carefully consider the biblical evidence on both sides of the Rapture question with an honest and sincere heart.

Note: The word "Rapture" is used to refer to the supernatural "catching up" of the Believers in the last days in accordance to First Thessalonians 4:16-17. (As seen there, a resurrection of the dead saints immediately precedes that "catching up.") Some people argue that "Rapture" is not a biblical term. That's true, but remember that the Bible was written primarily in Hebrew and Greek. Therefore *none* of the words in our translations are really "biblical" in the strictest sense. "Rapture" comes from the Latin word "raptus," which was used in the Latin Bible to translate the Greek word that is translated as "caught up" in the King James Version of the Bible. Therefore, those who use "Rapture" have as much right to do so as those who use "caught up," because neither term is Greek. Therefore, instead of discussing our choice of words, let's understand that although the word "rapture" does not appear in our translation of the Bible, the *concept* of a "Rapture" is a biblical concept.

Chapter 8

Encouraged to Pray and Study

Many years ago my wife, Barb, had a dream that confirmed the fresh biblical light the Lord was beginning to shed on our end-time doctrine. It should be emphasized here that we cannot base doctrine on a dream, but a dream *can* cause us to reconsider our doctrine. In this case, we were encouraged to pray and study more regarding what the Bible had to say on this subject.

In the dream Barb was standing before a large ship. Though she knew that her very salvation depended upon being able to board that ship, she couldn't find the way. As she desperately searched, a man dressed in white appeared and showed her a narrow plank leading to an entrance. She had to kneel, and crawl on her hands and knees, to board. However, she was so grateful to find the way that she didn't mind the humiliation at all, and very shortly was safe inside.

To her utter amazement, she discovered that three groups of people were actually leaving the ship. Those in the first group were saying, "Well, none of my friends are on board, and I prefer to be with my friends!" Another group was leaving because they didn't like the kind of people they found there. They were saying, "This ship is full of hypocrites, adulterers, murderers, liars, and sinners of every sort. We're leaving!" The third group that was leaving were people offended and angry that the ship hadn't departed at the time they were told it would depart. When she shared this dream with me, I had a strong feeling that the Lord was trying to speak to us. After all, this isn't exactly the kind of dream that a person has every night!

Interpretation

The ship is the Church, the Ark of safety. The first two groups reveal what has been happening throughout the Church Age.

Many people do go back into the world. They are not willing to pay the price to walk with God as Abraham did. They prefer to stay in "Ur of the Chaldees" rather than leave it behind. Being with their old friends, who are part of the world and their past life, is more important than their eternal salvation.

The second group of people leave because they don't like the company. They see only the faults and failures of other Believers. They just don't understand that Jesus is *still* willing to eat with publicans and sinners. A hypocrite is someone who preaches one message but lives another. Therefore, in their eyes, most of us are considered "hypocrites" to one degree or another, because our walk falls short of our talk. However, this is because we preach a vision for which we do not yet have the grace to fully live. After all, if the only things we preach are things we have already attained, then why preach them? And where is the vision that we encourage people to run after? Those who are quick to criticize forget that one day by His grace, all sincere Believers will have the strength and character to live what they preach! They also forget that besides all the "hypocrites" in the Church, one other Person is present—the Lord Jesus Christ Himself. Their very salvation and eternal destiny depend on their relationship with Him. All those "hypocrites" who stay in the "ship" are going to be changed, and one day soon they will no longer be hypocrites. To the eternal sorrow of those who leave, they may one day find themselves in hell. Then, with nowhere to flee, their *only* companions would be the real hypocrites of this world—those who couldn't help seeing the reality of God's existence through the creation but pretended like He wasn't real. Those who continue to allow hypocrites to offend them would do well to remember the old saying—"If there is a hypocrite standing between you and God, then he is closer to God than you are."

We began to consider the significance of the third group in the dream. Multitudes of Believers have been solemnly assured for many years that they will definitely escape the Great Tribulation through a Rapture. What would happen to them if they were to find themselves right in the middle of the Great Tribulation? What would happen to their "saving faith" in Christ? After all, the only gospel they have heard intimately links their faith in Christ with a pre-tribulation Rapture. Would they reach the conclusion that since one part of the message had proven to be wrong, perhaps the other part was wrong also?

Examples

1. A missionary. An experience of H. A. Baker,[1] a missionary to China for many years, gives us some indication of what might happen. He was the only pastor in his city who taught his church that they would have to suffer, and even pass through, the Great Tribulation. He told them they would *not* escape. The other pastors told their people they would not face tribulation. On the night the communists took over, some Believers accused their pastors, saying, "You lied to us. You preached a false message to us. What you taught us was not true, and we reject you and your gospel." They lost out with God. Some of Pastor Baker's flock came with words of appreciation. They said, "Brother Baker, what you taught us was true. We are ready to go through whatever fire He asks us to face. We are ready to die for the One who died for us. Thank you for preparing us for this hour!"

Pastor, leader, or teacher, what would *your* sheep say to you if one day they found themselves here with the world falling apart, ready to swallow them up? Some will answer, "Well *that* will never happen, because I *know* that we won't be here during the Tribulation." Linking that extreme confidence in a pre-tribulation Rapture to our gospel message is precisely what my wife's dream seemed to be warning against.

2. An evangelist. One very well-known evangelist said not long ago, "If anyone teaches that the Church will be here for the Great Tribulation, I doubt if that person is even born-again." That sort of declaration intimately links a pre-tribulation Rapture with a saving faith in Christ. As this man has done, many have made a pre-tribulation Rapture an integral part of their gospel. If they are wrong, many lives could be lost. Just as happened in China, many will become embittered and abandon the ship because it didn't leave when they thought it would. If any doubt exists in our hearts on this subject, it is wiser to prepare for the worst and hope for the best! Because if those who teach that the Church *will* go through the Tribulation are wrong, then their followers have a delightful surprise awaiting them. They are going to escape a hard time that they were earnestly preparing for, and they won't mind admitting their doctrine was wrong! But what if it's the other way around?

3. The children of Israel. The children of Israel reveal how many would react to the pressures of a Great Tribulation if they had been told to expect only blessing and Heaven. In the Book of Exodus, Moses promised Israel a land of milk and honey if they would just leave Egypt behind and

---

1. Author of *Visions Beyond the Veil*, Whitaker House, Springdale, Pennsylvania, 1973.

follow their God. However, to their amazement and sorrow, a terrible wilderness lay between them and the fulfillment of that promise. They began to face the unexpected trials and pressures of that wilderness experience. Bitterness against God and Moses soon filled their hearts, and they soon had just one desire—a longing for the Egypt they had left behind. In the last days many will surely return to the world if they face a furnace of affliction they were not expecting. Bitterness and unbelief will overwhelm them if their hearts are prepared to receive only blessing. This is not an opinion or mere conjecture: this is human nature.

Paul's message was, "We must **through much tribulation** enter into the kingdom of God" (Acts 14:22). We all want to enter the Kingdom of God in these last days, but we must accept the path that will lead us there. It will be a path that leads through much tribulation. Let's consider what the Bible says about when the Rapture will occur.

Chapter 9

Three Rapture Keys

I once heard a whole message on the radio dedicated to proving that the "last trump" mentioned by Paul in First Corinthians 15:52 is not *really* the last trump after all. The preacher's goal was to prove that after the "last trumpet" there will still be other trumpets. He stated that in the end there will be different types or classes of trumpets, each class of trumpet having a different purpose. He concluded that Paul's "last trump" was really only the final one in a particular series. Supposedly, other series of trumpets could follow for other purposes. Ever since the Lord gave us His discourse concerning the end in Matthew 24, and the Book of Revelation, He has wanted His people to understand the end, but it seems that man has complicated it.

I have heard others going into long discourses of what this Greek word "last" really means, and that it doesn't really mean "last" as we understand it in English. (Unfortunately no Greek expert involved in any translation yet has been aware of this "fact.") However, a quick survey of the forty-nine times this word is used in the New Testament quickly dispels any doubt as to its meaning. One clear usage of this word appears in Revelation 1:11 where Jesus declares to John, "I am Alpha and Omega, the first and **the last**." Alpha is the first letter in the Greek alphabet, and Omega is the last. In Greek there are no more letters after Omega, and never will be. Therefore, we can be sure that no one will either outlast, or come *after* the Lord Jesus Christ. He was here first, before anyone else, and He will survive as the last One, when all others have passed away! Only those who are "in Christ" and have become one with Him will remain in the end (Jn. 14:20; 17:21). Can there be any doubt then, that "the last" is "the last"?

The Bible was written by one Author, the Holy Spirit. Therefore, we can be sure that His use of words and concepts is consistent throughout the Scriptures.[1] For example, the Book of Hebrews tells us that the "sword" represents the Word of God (Heb. 4:12). Therefore, we cannot interpret the "sword" that proceeds out of the Lord's mouth in Revelation 1:16 to represent something entirely different. If this is not the case, then there is no hope of ever allowing the Bible to interpret itself. We would be hopelessly abandoned to the personal interpretation, opinion, and revelation of men, something that is endemic in the cults. Comparing Scripture with Scripture is essential for sound biblical interpretation. We want to do so in this chapter with regard to when the Rapture of the Church will take place in the last days.

Is the Last Trump Really the Last Trump?

During the Great Tribulation seven different trumpets will sound. Therefore, it is vitally important for any teacher of a pre-tribulation Rapture to prove, at least in his own mind, that the last trumpet is not *really* the last trumpet. This is what the radio preacher was attempting to do, because otherwise, the pre-tribulation Rapture doctrine cannot possibly be correct. If no other trumpets can sound after the *last* trumpet (which is what the word "last" means in Greek and English), then the Rapture at the last trumpet cannot occur before the seventh, or last, trumpet of Revelation.[2]

However, let us assume for a moment that what the radio preacher said was totally true. Suppose there will be different types of trumpets, and that each of those types is blown for a different purpose. The question then becomes, "Regardless of whether they are long trumpets or short trumpets, fat trumpets or skinny trumpets, silver trumpets or gold trumpets, trumpets of judgment or trumpets of blessing, aren't they all still trumpets?" They certainly aren't violins or harps. So, no matter how many kinds of trumpets we find in the New Testament, or for what purpose they are blown, they still continue to be the same musical instrument—trumpets. Let's remember that the words and concepts used in one book of the Bible mean the same thing when they are found in other books. In light of this, could it be that the "last trump" of First Corinthians is referring

1. We are referring here to the words of the original Hebrew and Greek texts and not to a translation.
2. In other words if the "last trump," which sounds at the Rapture, is blown before *any* of the seven trumpets found in Revelation, then it can no longer be called the "last trump."

to the seventh and last trump found in Revelation? If so, the Church will not be raptured before the seven trumpets of Revelation and the Great Tribulation. We find the answer in Paul's writings.

Three Details Given By Paul

Comparing Scripture with Scripture we discover three concepts that Paul associates directly with the Rapture of the Church. In First Corinthians 15:51-52 we find this statement: "Behold, I show you a **mystery**; We shall not all sleep, but we shall all be changed, in a moment, in the twinkling of an eye, at the **last trump**: for the trumpet shall sound, and the dead shall be raised incorruptible, and we shall be changed." Here there are two concepts that Paul associates with the Resurrection and Rapture: (1) the **"last trumpet"** and (2) a **"mystery."**

Later, in Chapter 9, we will consider exactly what the "mystery" is that Paul often refers to, but knowing that it is associated with the Rapture is sufficient for our purposes at the moment. Returning again to the "mystery," in Ephesians 3:3-5 Paul writes, "...by revelation he made known unto me the mystery; (as I wrote afore in few words...) Which in other ages was not made known unto the sons of men, as it is now revealed unto his holy apostles and prophets by the Spirit." Here we learn something else about this mystery—that it was revealed to the apostles and prophets. We find, therefore, in these passages three concepts that Paul associates with the Rapture: (1) it will occur at the last trumpet, (2) it is related to a mystery and (3) that mystery has been revealed to the prophets (and of course, to the apostles also).

The Seven Trumpets of Revelation

Obviously, the seventh trumpet found in Revelation is the last trumpet mentioned in the Bible. Paul's reference to a "last trump" in the last days clearly implies that more than one trumpet is related to the events of the last days. Therefore, it comes as no surprise that trumpets appear in Revelation in the context of the end. Remember that the Holy Spirit is consistent with His use of words and concepts in Scripture. Can we honestly feel comfortable with the teaching of some Believers that the Holy Spirit's reference to trumpets in the last days, found in Paul's writings, has nothing to do with His reference to trumpets in the last days, found in Revelation? If we have any doubt, the Word of God clearly brings both references together for us in Revelation 10:7: "...In the days of the voice of the **seventh angel**, when he shall begin to sound, the **mystery** of God should be finished, as he hath declared to his servants **the prophets.**" Here, associated with the seventh or last trumpet found in God's Word, we find precisely the same three concepts that Paul tells us are related to the Rapture (the last trumpet, a mystery, and a mystery revealed to the prophets). Few today doubt that these seven trumpets are blown during the Great Tribulation, just before Christ returns. So if the Rapture of the Believers takes place at the seventh, or last trumpet, the Believers must obviously go into at least part of that Great Tribulation.[3]

3. If we lightly ignore scriptural connections of this nature existing between passages when the conclusions don't confirm our doctrine, then, to be honest, we have no right to resort to the principle of proving our interpretation of one Scripture by using another when it is convenient for us to do so (when it confirms our doctrine). This type of biblical interpretation would be hypocritical, and could possibly be labeled as "handling the word of God deceitfully" (2 Cor. 4:2).

Chapter 10

The Great Trumpet

Christ's doctrinal position concerning the events of the last days is found in Matthew 24. In verse 15 He refers to the "abomination of desolation." Daniel tells us there will be a period of three and a half years following that abomination (Dan. 12:11-12). The Lord continues by saying, "For then shall be great tribulation, such as was not since the beginning of the world to this time, no, nor ever shall be" (Mt. 24:21). This is called the **Great** Tribulation because of the uniqueness of its severity, *not* because man has never suffered before.

Matthew 24:29 further states, "**Immediately** ***after*** **the tribulation of those days** shall the sun be darkened, and the moon shall not give her light, and the stars shall fall from heaven." He has just told us that this is the *Great* Tribulation. Next He is seen coming in the clouds (v. 30). First Thessalonians 4:16-17 associates His coming in the clouds with the Rapture, at which time He will gather His elect. He is seen doing this in Matthew 24:31. "And he shall send his angels with **a great sound of a trumpet**, and they shall gather together his elect from the four winds, from one end of heaven to the other." Here we find a trumpet when the elect from Heaven and earth are being gathered to Him.[1] Saints, both dead and alive, will be gathered to Him at this moment when He comes in the clouds. Therefore, according to Christ's own words we find a trumpet sounding immediately **after** the Great Tribulation. So then, the Rapture,

---

1. Mark 13:24-37 quotes this same discourse of Christ concerning the last days, and in verse 27 we are told that the elect are gathered "from the uttermost part of the earth to the uttermost part of heaven." So these are saints that are both dead and alive being gathered here.

which occurs at the **last trumpet**, could not have taken place previous to this trumpet.

In Matthew 24, *after* the Great Tribulation, we have found:

1. He comes in the clouds.
2. He gathers His elect from Heaven and earth.
3. The angels are involved in this coming.
4. This all takes place at the sound of a trumpet.

Comparing Scripture with Scripture, in First Thessalonians 4:15-17 we find every one of these details in the context of the Rapture. We dare not ignore the similarities between these two passages, or presume that there is no connection. The Lord leaves no doubt in Matthew 24 that these four events, associated with the Rapture, occur *after* the Great Tribulation.

Chapter 11

The Supersaints

How long can a person be faithful to the Lord without the help of the Holy Spirit? I have often presented this question to those attending our seminars. There is always unanimous agreement that without the Spirit of grace we cannot be faithful to Him at all—not even for a second. In Romans 8:9b (NKJV) Paul tells us, "Now if anyone does not have the Spirit of Christ, he is not His." So a person who does not have the Holy Spirit doesn't even belong to Christ; he isn't a Christian; he isn't saved.

The Problem

One of the popular doctrinal positions today states that the Holy Spirit will be taken out of the world after the Rapture. Supposedly, He will have little or no influence on earth for the last seven years.[1] Rather, He will hand the entire world over to Satan for that seven-year period. One isolated verse has become the doctrinal foundation for this whole concept: "For the mystery of lawlessness is already at work; only He who now restrains will do so until He is taken out of the way" (2 Thess. 2:7 NKJV).

We know that the Lord, through the Holy Spirit, has restrained or hindered Satan for many centuries from reaching one of his primary goals, to unite his kingdom. Jesus said, "Every kingdom divided against itself...shall not stand" (Mt. 12:25b). Satan's kingdom is divided into many rivaling factions throughout the earth. It obviously will not stand.

---

1. I am aware that not all the Church believes that the Holy Spirit will be taken out of the earth. I mention this here only for the sake of those who are in agreement with this belief.

Throughout history Satan has sought to put an end to this division. He has used many conquerors who have attempted to unite the entire world under their own personal leadership. Certainly Satan has been promoting that goal, but has never achieved it.

Second Thessalonians 2:7 (NKJV) declares that He who has been restraining will be "taken out of the way." Satan will finally achieve what *appears* to be success in uniting his kingdom. However, Daniel explains that the apparent unity of the Antichrist empire will be like iron mixed with clay. It will prove to be a false unity, with more division and turmoil than true unity and peace between the members. Daniel 2:41-42 says it this way, "And whereas thou sawest the feet and toes, part of potters' clay, and part of iron, the kingdom shall be divided . . . so the kingdom shall be partly strong, and partly broken."

Those who believe that the Holy Spirit will be taken from the earth have a problem explaining Matthew 24:21-22: "For then shall be great tribulation, such as was not since the beginning of the world to this time, no, nor ever shall be...but **for the elect's sake** those days shall be shortened." Therefore, at least some "elect" are on the earth during the Great Tribulation.[2] Who are these "elect"? Some say they are people who have heard and rejected the gospel during their lives.[3] We are told that upon seeing the Believers raptured and the Holy Spirit taken out of the earth, they decide to follow the Lord faithfully during the Tribulation. Those of us living today cannot be faithful to Him without the Holy Spirit for even one second in the very **best** of times. However, here we would have a company of people who supposedly are going to be faithful to the Lord without the Holy Spirit for seven years in the very **worst** of times! They would indeed be "**supersaints,**" invalidating Romans 8:9 (which was quoted in the first paragraph of this chapter).

The root reason for this doctrinal error is much more serious than a simple misunderstanding of God's Word. This doctrine actually exists because of a problem in the human heart, a problem that can destroy our spiritual lives. It is confidence in the flesh. If we reduce this doctrine to its essence, we discover that it is a declaration of the ability and strength of man. Supposedly these "elect" have rejected God's grace, and now see the results of going their own way. They then say to Christ

2. If the "elect" mentioned here were already in Heaven, it wouldn't matter to them whether the days of the Great Tribulation were shortened or not. Therefore, we conclude that they are still on earth.
3. We want to avoid this type of pure speculation, which so often enters an interpretation when it doesn't have sufficient scriptural basis.

(not with words, but with actions), "Lord, I didn't accept You when You were willing to help me, but now I will show You that I can live for You *without* Your help!"

God has sought to teach man a simple lesson for thousands of years. Throughout the Bible, He has shown that the arm of flesh cannot save us. Using one living example after another, He has shown that our own works and faithfulness are insufficient. Only by grace will we ever be saved. And that grace comes through the "Spirit of grace." No, this doctrinal error is not merely a misunderstanding of Scripture. Rather, it is the fruit of a deep-seated root that exists in man's heart, a root of pride and confidence in his own ability. This doctrine is not just a mistake, but rather it is an abomination and an affront to God and His Word![4]

The Answer

Second Thessalonians 2:7 says the Holy Spirit[5] will "be taken out of the way," *not* out of the world. There is a tremendous difference between these two thoughts. Rather than abandoning the world, the One who hinders will simply step aside and give Satan a degree of freedom to move ahead with his plans. Before the cross, Satan offered to Jesus the kingdoms of this world if He would just bow down and give Satan worship. The Lord refused to accept that shortcut to the Kingdom, and chose the way of the cross to reach the throne. He **purchased** the kingdoms of this world with His own blood. He took those kingdoms, and the keys, from Satan by entering Satan's own territory and defeating him. The kingdoms of this world now belong to the Savior. He will never again deliver them over to Satan, not even for a moment, much less for seven years.[6] He has

4. I am not saying here that everyone who has ever believed this doctrine necessarily has deep-rooted pride working in his own life. Rather, I am saying that the source of this doctrine is pride, manifested as confidence in the flesh. Many of those who have believed it simply may not have considered these implications.
5. Or any other agent the Lord may be using to restrain the wicked one in his plans. Note that some have assumed that this verse refers to the Holy Spirit as the agent who restrains Satan. We shouldn't be too dogmatic on this point because the context in the Greek does not make it clear who is actually restraining Satan. See Marshall, Alfred, *The R.S.V. Interlinear Greek-English New Testament,* Zondervan Publishing House, Grand Rapids, Michigan, 1970.
6. Some may point to Revelation 13:5,7 where we are told that Satan will have power over all the earth for forty-two months. However, notice what Revelation 13 really reveals. We are told "there was *given* unto him a mouth" (v. 5), and "it was *given* unto him to make war," and "power was *given* him" (v. 7). The Antichrist will obviously have nothing that is not given to him. Therefore, this passage reveals that there is someone higher than the Antichrist giving him authority. We may think that these things are given by the dragon, seen in Revelation 13:1-2.

promised that He will never leave or forsake anyone who can be called "elect." According to Jesus in Matthew 24:22, there will be "elect" ones on the earth during the Great Tribulation. We already saw in Chapter 10 of this book that Jesus goes on to declare that those "elect" ones will be gathered to Him, in the Rapture, "immediately after the tribulation of those days" (Mt. 24:29-31).

However, Jesus says, "All power is given unto me in heaven and in earth" (Mt. 28:18). So the power that is "given" to the Antichrist, or the dragon as well, must come from Christ, since all power now belongs to Him. Likewise, Second Thessalonians 2:9-11 says that the Antichrist will come and deceive, but God Himself is the One who sends him! (v. 11) Therefore, in reality even this glorifies the Lord and reveals who is, in fact, reigning sovereignly over all! This is exactly what God did with Pharaoh. Romans 9:17 tells us that this was God's purpose in raising up Pharaoh also—to glorify Himself, revealing who was really ruling in the earth.

Chapter 12

The Plagues

In Part I we established two keys to help us understand the truth about the end: (1) natural Israel of the Old Testament is a parable, or mold, from which spiritual Israel in the New Testament is taken and (2) the beginning and the ending are the same in God; history repeats itself. Now let's use these keys to help us understand **when the Rapture will occur**, before or after the Great Tribulation.

In the beginning of Israel's history, father Abraham journeyed to a foreign country during a time of famine to find food. While there, he was greatly multiplied in both people and riches (Gen. 12:16). But one serious problem arose, Pharaoh took control of his wife. God responded by sending "great plagues" on the house of Pharaoh to set Abraham's wife free (Gen. 12:17). Abraham then departed from Egypt with many riches and returned to Canaan.

Many years later, Jacob, a descendant of Abraham, also faced a time of grave famine. He, too, descended into Egypt for food and was greatly multiplied in people and material wealth, becoming the mighty nation of Israel (Gen. 46). One serious problem arose for them also. They found themselves under the complete control of Pharaoh. (In this case Israel, the **Lord's** wife, was oppressed by Pharaoh. See Jer. 3:20 and Isa. 54:5-7.) Once again the Lord's answer was to send great plagues on Pharaoh to set a wife free. The Israelites departed from Egypt with many riches and returned to Canaan in the Book of Exodus.[1]

---

1. Some have questioned whether or not Abraham did the right thing in going down into Egypt, but since every detail is repeated in his descendants, and since God clearly tells Jacob that it is His will for him to descend into Egypt (Gen. 46:3), we

How does this give us a key for knowing when the Rapture of the Church will take place? The answer lies in the fact that precisely the same plagues found in the beginning, in Exodus, also appear in Revelation. In the case of Abraham, and also of Israel, the plagues were sent to set a wife free from Egypt. Since Israel is our "parable," and since father Abraham is the pattern for all his sons, and since the beginning and ending are the same, we conclude that the plagues of Revelation are also sent to set a wife free from Egypt. Furthermore, it was the Lord's wife, Israel, who was set free in the beginning. Therefore, it will be the Lord's wife, the Church, who will be set free in the end. She will be set free from "Egypt," or the world. So then, when those plagues are poured out on the world ("Egypt"), the Bride will still be on earth, oppressed by Pharaoh (the Antichrist). The Rapture, when the Lord's Wife will be set free, will not take place *before* the plagues, but rather *after*.

Consider two other details concerning those plagues. First, they were actually brought by the people of God, through Moses, the deliverer. And second, none of the plagues came upon God's people except the first three. They were sent to judge the **world**, not His people. In Revelation 11 we find two witnesses in the **end** who can smite the earth with plagues as often as they choose, as Moses did in the **beginning** to set God's people free. So the plagues of the end will definitely be brought and controlled by the servants of the Lord. Thus, the Church will still be here during the Tribulation, being used to bring Pharaoh's kingdom to its knees, and to place all enemies under the Lord's feet.

---

can safely assume that it was also God's will for Abraham to descend there. Otherwise we wouldn't see the pattern in father and son that God wanted to reveal there. Furthermore, the Lord said, "Out of Egypt have I called my son" (Hos. 11:1). Therefore, the father also had to go into Egypt!

Chapter 13

Christ Seated Until...

In the Garden of Eden **man chose**, by an act of his will, to place himself under the dominion of Satan. Satan injected his poison and death into the human race. Once man was under Satan's control, he experienced the bondage and chains of a cruel taskmaster. From then on, man's own strength and determination were not sufficient to liberate him. But Jesus came and all that was changed!

However, the concept that Jesus comes and just snatches us out from under the control of Satan is not the idea given in the New Testament. Nor would this kind of "salvation" bring the glory to Him that will be seen in His "so great salvation." Rather, the Lord has given to His Church "power...over all the power of the enemy" (Lk. 10:19). Hebrews 10:12-13 (NKJV) tells us that after Christ had offered one sacrifice for sins forever He "sat down at the right hand of God, from that time **waiting till His enemies are made His footstool.**" In answer to the poison and death that Satan injected into humanity, Christ injected His life and power, and now He is waiting for us to use it. **We again have a choice.** By an act of our will we can open our hearts to His life and receive the grace to actually rise above our taskmaster and conquer him through the power of the Lion who has the mind and nature of the Lamb (Rev. 5:5-6). And the wonderful outcome of this provision of grace will bring great glory to God in **the final victory**.

Consider what the Lord is doing in the earth. One third of the angels followed Satan in his rebellion (Rev. 12). Satan succeeded in gaining one third of God's heavenly Kingdom through deception, darkness, lies, pride, hatred, and envy. Just before the Second Coming of Christ, one third of the earth will turn to the Lord (Zech. 13:8-9). So in **the final victory** God will gain one third of Satan's kingdom (this earth) through truth, light, humility, love, and selflessness. Rather than snatching man away from Satan's grasp, the Lord is offering us His life and power so that we can choose whom we want to follow without being coerced by anyone. In this way the same human race that chose to put themselves under Satan's feet will now arise and put Satan under Christ's feet. This will bring Him glory, as mankind reveals who is truly the "desire of nations" (Hag. 2:7). He is seated and "waiting till" this happens.

The Rapture will not take place as long as Christ is seated. He must arise before He can come in the clouds. But He is waiting, and will continue to wait until His enemies have been conquered. But how, and by whom, are His enemies going to be conquered? In the work of His First Coming, Christ finished all that was necessary to bring about the defeat of His enemies. Then, Christ gave to man power over all the power of the enemy, and returned to His place with the Father. He will wait until we have used that power in these last days.

It is evident from First Corinthians 15:25-26,51-54 that there will be no Rapture until all His enemies are placed under His feet. The last enemy that will be conquered is death, and Paul says death is conquered in the Rapture (v. 54). So then, if any enemy remains unconquered by the Church in these days, the moment to conquer death has not yet arrived! Furthermore, the Antichrist is an enemy that must be conquered before the "last enemy" (death), can be conquered in the Rapture.[1] The Church has a work to accomplish, and she will not leave this world until she can say as Christ said, "It is finished!" We will leave "Egypt" when "Pharaoh" and his servants are under the feet of the Church, and not before, just as Moses and Israel left Egypt after obtaining the victory over the Pharaoh of their day.

God's Pattern for Us Is Victory Before the Supper

From Genesis

Through father Abraham's life we receive a revelation of what God will do with the Church, Abraham's children, in the end. In Genesis 14 the

1. Note that every one of the statements we make here is found in First Corinthians 15. Clearly Paul did not see anything contradictory in what he was saying. We are, therefore, given to understand that Christ is seated, and arises to gather His elect in the Rapture, at the moment the Church is ready to conquer the last enemy, death, after all others have been conquered.

kings that governed the territory of ancient Babylon and Assyria[2] allied themselves against Canaan, and carried Lot away after conquering the area of Sodom and Gomorrah. The Scriptures show that these two kings are both a foreshadow of the Antichrist (Isa. 14:4,12,25-26). In fact, Babylon's end-time role occupies two full chapters in the Book of Revelation (Rev. 17–18). The spiritual connection between Babylon and Assyria should not surprise us because the capital cities of both these kings, Babel and Nineveh respectively, even today, are part of the same country, Iraq.

Father Abraham was living in a place called "Hebron" when these kings captured Sodom and Gomorrah, carrying away Lot and his family. The Hebrew word "Hebron" means "seat of association,"[3] and while Abraham was living in Hebron he was walking in unity, or association, with other brethren (Gen. 14:13). Psalm 133:1-2 tells us that when brethren live together in harmony the blessing of God flows. In fact, if we do not walk with others we cannot expect to gain the victory over our enemies. We need the strength, encouragement, and help of other Believers to win this war that we are in.

When Abraham received news of the conquest of the kings of Babylon and Assyria, he arose from that place of fellowship and destroyed the yoke of the Assyrian and Babylonian kings that had been placed over God's land. But note something very important here. Immediately after that battle and victory, we find Melchisedek going out to meet Abraham to serve him bread and wine. Father Abraham is a pattern for us, as the Apostle Paul indicates throughout his writings. Therefore, as Abraham's children, we must first destroy the power of the Antichrist before our High Priest is going to come forth and serve us bread and wine at the Marriage Supper of the Lamb.

To Revelation

Since history repeats itself, it is no wonder the Kingdom of Babylon appears again in Revelation 17–18. Once again Babylon is destroyed. But who destroys it? Again, we must go back to the beginning and to Genesis to find the answer. If Abraham is our father and pattern, then just as the father did, so must the children do. The task of bringing God's enemies into subjection to Him has been given to Abraham's children! There is a war that we must win (Eph. 6:12). Immediately after that victory in Revelation 18 there is a mighty expression of worship in Heaven, and the

2. In Genesis 11:2,9 we see that "Shinar" is Babylon. Genesis 10:9-11 shows that Nimrod was the founder of both these empires (the Babylonian and the Assyrian).
3. See *Strong's Hebrew Dictionary*, #2275.

Church is invited to the Marriage Supper (Rev. 19:1-9). At that Supper our heavenly Melchisedek will be serving bread and wine to all the victors.

In the light of these things, can we continue to believe that we will leave the world before **the final victory** has been gained? The "King of Babylon" and his kingdom will be conquered and placed under *the* King's feet. Christ is seated and waiting for **the final victory** of the Church, where the authority of the Lion will be revealed through those who have the mind and meekness of the Lamb. Until all enemies are under His feet He will not arise, and there will be no Rapture.

Chapter 14

The 144,000 Sealed Ones

The 144,000 who are sealed during the Great Tribulation in Revelation 7 present a grave doctrinal problem if the Believers are raptured out of the earth before the Great Tribulation. There are several theories on what those 144,000 will be doing on the earth during the Tribulation after being sealed. The most popular theory is that they will be used to evangelize the world during that period, experiencing divine protection as a result of God's seal on them. Regardless of what they might possibly do, one thing is certain; they are definitely people that please the Lord, and they will be saved by Him.

Two Problems

1. Why didn't they go in the Rapture? If these people are worthy to be sealed and protected during the Great Tribulation, then why were they not included in the Rapture *if* it has just recently occurred? The obvious answer would be that since these people are still on the earth, they must not have been born-again when the Rapture took place, or supposedly they would have gone in the Rapture. This concept leads us to an even graver problem.

2. How can newborns be leading a great revival? There can be no question that the greatest harvest of souls that mankind has ever witnessed will occur during the Great Tribulation. This is confirmed by many Scriptures, but one of the clearest is found in Zechariah 13:8-14:4. The context of this passage is the Second Coming of Christ, when He will stand upon the Mount of Olives and fight for Israel who will be surrounded by the armies of the world. He will save Israel from her enemies and establish

His Kingdom in Jerusalem. From then on, all the nations of the earth will send representatives to Jerusalem annually to celebrate the Feast of Tabernacles (Zech. 14). We are told that immediately before His coming, two thirds of all the earth will die, but one third will be saved and become His people (Zech. 13:8-9). *This* is a tremendous harvest! Of course, since the Rapture has supposedly already occurred, then the only spiritual leaders available for the two billion souls that will be born again are newborns themselves—the 144,000 who weren't ready for the Rapture.

As with any false doctrine, the arguments required to sustain an error exposed to the light of the Scriptures become increasingly tenuous and twisted. Establishing newborns as leaders is something God will simply not allow, much less promote. First Timothy 3:1-6 tells us that a spiritual leader cannot be a "novice." This Greek word literally means "a new convert," or "one who has recently become a Christian."[1] Therefore, if a group of 144,000 newborns are the leaders of the great end-time harvest, God will be violating His own Word, rather than fulfilling and upholding it as He has promised to do.

Furthermore, this doctrine suggests that 144,000 new Believers, *without* the Holy Spirit, will accomplish in seven years that which the worldwide Body of Christ could not do *with* the Holy Spirit during almost 2,000 years (that is, to take the gospel of the Kingdom to the nations of the world). This would not only be an unfavorable testimony to the dedication of the Church for 2,000 years, but it might also reflect negatively on the power and effectiveness of the Spirit of grace. After all, couldn't the Holy Spirit have evangelized the world with or without the cooperation of His people? If the pre-tribulation Rapture is correct, the Lord is going to do precisely that, anyway, with basically no leaders on earth to help Him.

So Who Are the 144,000 Sealed Ones?

1. Compare Revelation 4–10 with Revelation 14–19. Appendix A of this book shows clearly that the message of Revelation is presented twice in the book. In other words, the message found in chapters 4–10 is repeated in chapters 14–19. It is no wonder, then, that we find reference to the 144,000 again in Revelation 14:1-5 where we are given several clear details to help us understand who these people are.

The "seal" that was placed on their foreheads in Revelation 7 is explained here. It is their Father's name. They are found on Mount Zion, and Hebrews 12:22 says that Mount Zion is the Church, the heavenly

---

1. The *Strong's Greek Dictionary* brings this out (#3504).

Jerusalem. We saw in Chapter 4 that Israel is the Church. In other words, we saw that the Church is the Old Testament chosen people who, in this Age, have been brought into a spiritual realm in God. As always, the Gentiles are permitted to be grafted in among the natural branches. It is understandable then why we are told that the "sealed ones" come from the twelve tribes (Rev. 7). God is still dealing with Israel, as He always has. The 144,000 are virgins, not having been defiled with women (Rev. 14:4). The characteristics described here are obviously spiritual qualifications. This does not mean that married people are excluded. Spiritually speaking, this signifies that they have no other loves. They are not running after other attractions in the world. Rather, they follow the Lamb whithersoever He goes, and since the foundation of the world we always find that the Lamb is headed toward the altar. They embrace the path of the cross and self-denial. They are not living for earthly pleasures and carnal delights. This company of people are without fault—perfected. They are also called **firstfruits**. Firstfruits are grains which have ripened, or reached maturity first, before the general harvest. This tells us that they will be **Believers who have reached maturity first, *not* newborns.**[2]

Yes, these mature Believers will preach the gospel of the Kingdom to all nations during the last three and a half years, and then the end will come, just as Jesus promised in Matthew 24:14. Personally, I do not know whether the number 144,000 is symbolic or literal. But the Lord has made me to understand that no one will be excluded because of a lack of space. There is room for everyone who receives the grace to seek the Lord with his whole heart. The creation earnestly longs for such ones according to Paul in Romans 8:19 (NKJV), where he says, "For the earnest expectation of the creation eagerly waits for the revealing of the sons of God." We will see more about this in Chapter 17.

2. Compare Revelation with Ezekiel. By comparing Ezekiel and Revelation we discover that the two books give the same message. (See Appendix B for the details.) And since both speak about a group of people being marked in their foreheads, we conclude that it is the same event. However, Ezekiel gives us an interesting detail. These people are the ones who are sighing and crying because of all the abominations done by God's people. These people are seeking God in intercession. They are carrying a spiritual burden. They are not just floating through life unconcerned

---

2. This further proves that the Rapture does not take place before the Great Tribulation. If the Rapture had already occurred, mature Christians would be in Heaven and not on the earth.

about others. Interestingly enough, after the 144,000 are sealed in Revelation 7, John sees the incense of prayer and intercession ascending before the Lord at the beginning of Revelation 8. Again, the message from both prophets is clear; it is time to seek the Lord, not only for ourselves, but also for others.

Chapter 15

Resurrection at Restoration

I was standing outside the Holocaust Museum in Jerusalem, Israel, as the tour group that I was guiding gathered around me. I wanted to share with them a few thoughts to prepare their hearts for what they were about to see. After viewing what is displayed in that museum, most normal people will never be quite the same. I have seen mature adults weeping uncontrollably as they stood before blown up photographs of the indescribable anguish and suffering of the Jewish people in Hitler's death camps. I was literally beginning to speak to my group, when something happened that changed my life forever. I was about to repeat what I had heard from Christians for over thirty years when they explained the reason for the suffering of the Holocaust. I was going to say, "What you are about to witness is the result of the fathers of Israel crying out 2,000 years ago, 'Let His blood be upon us and upon our children.' " To my amazement, in the place of those words, something came out that I had personally never heard before. I said, "What you are about to witness is the highest price ever paid for a homeland by any people on the face of the earth. The price was the blood of six million Jews, and if that price hadn't been paid, the world would still be refusing to give the Jewish people a place to live on this earth. The Jewish people would still be wandering as strangers in a strange land, persecuted and reviled throughout the nations of the world."

Yes, at the Trial of the Messiah, the Jews did cry out, "Let His blood be upon us and upon our children" (Mt. 27:25). But when His blood was being poured out, their Messiah prayed, "Father, forgive them, for they know not what they do" (Lk. 23:34). I believe that every prayer that the Lord ever prayed was answered or will be answered. I believe that the

Father forgave them. In fact, that was the whole reason the Lord came to earth and poured out His life—to be able to "save His people from their sins" (Mt. 1:21 NKJV). How many of us, as Believers, have asked the Lord to "cover us with His blood," or let His precious blood be applied to our lives? If that becomes a blessing for us, would not the seeming curse that the Jewish fathers brought on themselves actually become a blessing in their lives and in the lives of their children also? If His blood is upon them, then surely they are a blessed people because His blood speaks of better things than the blood of Abel (Heb. 12:24). Abel's blood cried to the Father for vengeance on his brother, but Christ's blood cries to the Father for forgiveness on His brethren. We should *hope* that His blood is upon them and on their children forever! Their own High Priest, Caiaphas, prophesied that He would die for the nation so that it wouldn't perish. It hasn't perished and never will (Jn. 11:50-51).

Could it be that God has indeed chosen to forgive His people, while the Gentiles refuse to grant forgiveness and continue to falsely accuse the Jewish people of being "Christ killers"? The Jews did not put Christ on the cross. It was my sins and your sins that did that, along with the sins of the whole world, and the Lord confirmed that fact by allowing the Roman Gentiles and the Jews to work together to crucify Him. However, no one took His life from Him. He laid it down, choosing to die for Jew and Gentile alike, a choice He made before the foundation of the world. Can we begin to imagine what would have happened if the Jews had *not* rejected their Messiah? The world may not have been saved if I understand correctly what Paul means when he declares that the Gentiles "have now obtained mercy through their [the Jews'] disobedience" (Rom. 11:30 NKJV).

Could it be that the blood of the Lamb that is sufficient to cleanse and forgive the rest of the world is also able to cleanse and forgive His own people? Maybe the Gentile Church has manifested harshness toward the Jews for their sins due to a spiritual blindness in man's heart that keeps him from seeing his own sinfulness and unworthiness. Are the Jews worse sinners than anyone else because they rejected the Messiah whom all of us are guilty of rejecting in one way or another every day? We go our own way, seek our own will, and run after other desires and loves in this world as He stands at our door day after day, knocking and seeking our love and fellowship. We have all been guilty of breaking His heart by rejecting Him for some other god, such as our stomach or youthful passion. Is it possible that we are still not able to remove the mote that is in the eye of the Jews because we have a beam in our own eye?

Those who have reviled, rejected, and even persecuted the Jews have been guilty of faulty reasoning to justify their own actions. The prophetic ear of Jeremiah could hear the reasoning of Israel's enemies long before the cross. Speaking of their plight, he laments, "All that found them have devoured them: and their adversaries said, **We offend not, because they have sinned against the Lord,** the habitation of justice, even the Lord, the hope of their fathers" (Jer. 50:7). Imagine! They justify themselves for destroying the Jews because the Jews have sinned against the Lord. Haven't we all? But the Word of the Lord through Jeremiah goes on to declare the end of the matter and God's unchanging attitude toward Israel and each one of us. He promises, "In those days and in that time, says the Lord, the iniquity of Israel shall be sought, but there shall be none; and the sins of Judah, but they shall not be found; for I will pardon those whom I preserve" (Jer 50:20 NKJV). If the blood that shall never lose its power is sufficient to atone for the sins of the Gentiles, how much more can it atone for the sins of the chosen people also, preserved by God to this day! Paul said that salvation is brought to the "Jew first and also to the Gentile" (Rom. 1:16).

We well know that Paul rightfully ascribes the source of many blessings to the Jewish race: "...the sonship, the glory, the covenants, the giving of the law, the worship, and the promises; to them belong the patriarchs, and of their race, according to the flesh, is the Christ..." (Rom. 9:4-5 RSV). He goes on to say that God Himself "hath given them...eyes that they should not see," and that God actually permitted them to fall and reject their own Messiah in order to bring salvation to the Gentiles and thereby inspire jealousy in the hearts of the natural-born citizens (Rom. 11:8,11). In fact, Paul says that the Gentiles "have now received mercy as a result of [the Jews'] disobedience" (Rom. 11:30 NIV). So then, far from condemning Israel for having rejected their Messiah, the Gentile Believers should be humbled by the fact that they might not be saved today had Israel not rejected Him. This should inspire compassion rather than condemnation, and brokenness rather than bitterness toward them. He declares that Israel became a source of mercy for the Gentiles in the beginning, and that now the Gentiles must become a source of mercy for Israel in the end (Rom. 11:30-31). The Gentiles most surely have a debt of love to pay to the Jewish race, and many are beginning to recognize that the time has come to pay it.

Has the Gentile Church showed the Jewish people the mercy of the Savior? Have they paid their debt of love? Have they manifested the gentleness, patience, and longsuffering of *the* Jew who died for Jews and Gentiles alike? Can we possibly believe that the answer is "yes" when the Gentile Church, down through the ages, has tortured and killed literally hundreds of thousands of Jews in the name of Christ? In the Crusades, their cry was, "Kill a Jew and save your soul." In the Inquisition, Jews were given the choice of renouncing the law they so loved or be tortured and killed. In the Holocaust, many were deceived into paying for their own train tickets to be carried to the gas chambers. All these atrocities stand as witnesses that the Gentile Church has not paid her debt but rather increased it greatly.

Some may say that the Holocaust, unlike the Crusades and Inquisition, was never done in the name of Christ. But how does the Lord view the Church who knew for several years what Hitler was doing and by her worldwide silence became Hitler's accomplice? Will that Church be those of whom the Lord will say, "For I was an hungred, and ye gave me meat: I was thirsty, and ye gave me drink: I was a stranger, and ye took me in: naked, and ye clothed me: I was sick, and ye visited me: I was in prison, and ye came unto me"? (Mt. 25:35-36). Some would respond, "Yes, but He is speaking there about born-again Believers, not unregenerate Jews." The answer of the Holy Spirit is found in Romans 9:3 where Paul cries, "For I could wish that myself were accursed from Christ **for my brethren,** my kinsmen according to the flesh." Paul, by the Spirit, calls them "brethren." If the infallible Scriptures call the Jews Paul's natural brethren, most surely they continue to be Christ's natural brethren also. The Lord tells us that those who have ministered love and kindness to the "least of these **my brethren**" will inherit the Kingdom. Doesn't this declaration include His natural brethren also? Maybe some would question this. However, I certainly wouldn't want to jeopardize my eternal destiny by cursing Israel instead of blessing her, just because I incorrectly assumed that somehow Jesus Christ lost all the natural affection for His brethren that He often demonstrated openly as He wept for them. How tragic that, whereas Paul wished to be accursed from Christ for their sakes, and Christ laid down His own life for them, some "Christians" have cried, "Kill a Jew and save your soul!" They knew not what spirit they were of.

When we have a love in our hearts for Israel like Paul had, when we show them the kindness and mercy of the Messiah that came through their own Jewish race, when we are willing to lay down *our* lives for them instead of taking *their* lives because of hatred and jealousy, then something is going to happen in the hearts of the Jewish people. Why is it today that a Jew can be an atheist, a Hindu, a Buddhist, an agnostic, or even a spiritist medium, and still be welcomed back to the nation of Israel as a citizen, but if he is a Jew who believes in Messiah Yeshua (Jesus) he is literally excluded from his own land and people by a decision of the Israeli Supreme Court? Is this because they are violent Christ haters? No. They don't hate the "Christ of the Cross." Rather, they hate the Christ that has been revealed through the Gentile Church for centuries, a false Christ. We know precisely what the Jewish race will do one day when they see the great mercy and love of their Yeshua, revealed through true Christians, when they come to realize that He is not their enemy but rather their Lover-Redeemer. Zechariah 12 says that the whole nation will weep bitterly as one weeps for their only begotten son. They don't know who Yeshua really is, and they will *never* know until those who have received mercy *through* them begin to manifest mercy *toward* them.

In what way does all this indicate to us that the Rapture will occur *after* the Great Tribulation? Paul assures us that "all Israel will be saved" (Rom. 11:26). Most theologians know that Israel, as a nation, fully turns back to the Lord at the end of the Great Tribulation (Zech. 12-14; Isa. 25:8-9). However, Paul goes on to show *how* they will be saved: "And so all Israel will be saved, as it is written: The Deliverer will come out of Zion, And He will turn away ungodliness from Jacob" (Rom. 11:26 NKJV). The Bible reveals to us who Zion is: "But you have come to Mount Zion and to the city of the living God...to the general assembly and **church** of the firstborn" (Heb. 12:22-23 NKJV). Zion is the Church, and through the Church the Deliverer will reveal Himself to Israel. The only hope of Israel being saved is if the Church will arise to pay her debt of love to the Jewish race. We have seen that the Church itself is comprised of believing Israelites among whom the Gentile branches were grafted in, but today there are far more Gentile branches in the Church than Jewish branches. However, *every* branch is duty bound to be a part of the river of life and mercy that must flow toward Israel in the end. Not everyone is called to physically move to the land of Israel, but we are *all* called to "pray for the peace of Jerusalem" and to show the love of Yeshua to the Jewish people (Ps. 122:6).

So then, where will the Church be during the Great Tribulation? If the Believers (Jew and Gentile alike) are called to be the channel of mercy through which the Lord saves Israel, and if Israel is not saved until the end of the Great Tribulation, then how can the Believers accomplish their objective if they aren't even on the earth? Some may wonder if our reasoning here is sound. No need to fear. Paul clarifies it for us in Romans 11:15: "For if the casting away of them be the reconciling of the world, what shall the receiving of them be, but **life from the dead**?" There will be no "life from the dead" (Resurrection and Rapture) for the Believers until Israel has been received back by the Lord. The Believers are the ones who hold the key to that happening.

For those who need more proof, please compare First Corinthians 15:52-54, which we know is the Resurrection and Rapture, with Isaiah 25:8-9, which is in the context of the end of the Great Tribulation when the

Lord will fight against the nations that besiege Jerusalem. Paul links the Rapture with Israel's return to their God by quoting from Isaiah 25:8, saying that it is at *this* time that "death is swallowed up in victory." In other words, when Israel returns to the Lord at the end of the Great Tribulation, the Resurrection will take place, because their return will bring life from the dead!

Paul's "Mystery"

The oft-mentioned "mystery" in Paul's writings is related to the unity that will soon come between Jew and Gentile. In Ephesians 1:9-10 he refers to that "mystery" as the "gathering together in one all things in Christ," which he says will happen "in the fullness of times" (that is, in the last days). Then in Ephesians 2:11-22 he expounds on that mystery. There we learn that one of the major works of the cross was to make Jew and Gentile one Body in Christ—this is the "mystery" he referred to in Ephesians 1:10. Finally, he brings it all together in Ephesians 3:3-6. He declares that the "mystery" is that "the Gentiles should be **fellowheirs**, and **of the same body**, and **partakers of his promise** in Christ by the gospel" (Eph. 3:6). This is the same concept he mentioned in Ephesians 2:12,16.

Paul refers to a "mystery" fifteen times in his epistles. With the exception of possibly two or three times, he is speaking about the Jews and Gentiles being brought together in Christ. In fact, in several Scriptures Paul refers to this as the mystery of the gospel message itself (Rom. 16:25; Eph. 3:8-9; 6:19; Col 4:3). We know that he considered the message of Jew and Gentile unity an essential part of his gospel, because he asked the Colossian church to pray that "God would open unto us a door of utterance, **to speak the mystery of Christ, for which I am also in bonds**" (Col 4:3). Paul was a prisoner for just one message—his preaching to the Gentiles telling them that they were one with the Jews in the Kingdom. This is confirmed in Acts 21:19-28 and 22:20-23. There Paul was placed in bonds because the Jews were angry that God had sent him to the Gentiles to tell them they were part of the nation, and the Jews assumed that he had defiled their temple by permitting Gentiles to participate in the worship there.

Consider the tremendous importance of all this. From the scriptural context of the various references that Paul makes to this "mystery," it is obvious that a key part of the gospel message that he carried to the Gentiles was that they were one Body and one Church with the Jews in Christ. Paul laid down his life to carry that message to the Gentiles. I wonder today how many Gentiles are now laying down their lives to carry that same message back to the Jews? Many have seen the Jews and the Gentile

Church as two separate entities. There is only one Church. From the very beginning it was strictly a Jewish Church, and later the Gentile branches were grafted in among the natural branches. The Gentiles ended up cutting themselves off from that Jewish root, and therefore lost the flow of the life-giving sap that only the root can provide.

If anyone thinks that the Gentile Church is really alive today, they need to compare themselves with the glory of the early Church, and then recognize that God promises that the last day Church will be even much more glorious. We should be experiencing resurrections on every hand. The miracles of Christ and His disciples should flow and even "greater works than these" should be done today. Why isn't that resurrection life flowing? Because the Gentiles are not one with the root. When will we see mighty revival again in the earth? When we begin to preach and live once again the gospel that Paul preached—that the Jews and Gentiles are one in Christ. Paul plainly declares that "life from the dead" will only come to the Church and the world when the Jews and Gentiles are one again (Rom. 11:15). If we are longing for a mighty revival in this hour, then it is time to get involved in the *original* gospel instead of our own version!

This glorious work of bringing Jew and Gentile together in one Body was not only a major aspect of Paul's gospel, but also a major aspect of Christ's work on the cross (Eph. 2:11-19). This was clearly something very near and dear to the heart of the Lord. He laid down His life on the cross to accomplish it, and later on, Paul did the same. We will never be part of the glory that will be revealed at Israel's restoration unless we are willing to follow Christ's example and take up *our* cross. If *our* cross is *His* cross, then a major aspect of the work that we will accomplish by bearing that cross will be to unite Jew and Gentile, because this is what *His* cross did, and still does. We must begin to deny ourselves. This means denying our petty jealousy and ambition, and giving of our time, money, and strength in prayer, to see all Israel saved. Israel doesn't really need more "missionaries" right now. In fact, the word "missionary" in Israel is a very bad word! The battle for the souls of God's people is spiritual. The Jews need the help of people who know how to intercede for the peace of Jerusalem, and who will be led by the Spirit to do whatever the Lord tells them to do, regardless of the cost. They don't need to hear more preaching. They need to experience more love.

Chapter 16

The Problem: Pharisaism

A young man was seeking counsel concerning a "heresy" that was entering his local church. He was part of a church that our ministry was closely associated with. This young man obtained an appointment with a leader from one of the largest evangelical denominations in the world. This leader was the second man from the top in the national leadership of that movement, and was considered to be one of their foremost teachers on the last days. The young man was able to meet with him only because of a mutual friend.

The day came for their meeting, and behind closed doors he shared his concern. "I am here because the terrible heresy that says the Church will pass through the Great Tribulation has entered our local church. I would like you to give me a list of Scriptures that prove the Rapture will occur *before* the Tribulation." Keeping in mind that this leader is looked upon as an "expert" in this field, consider his answer. He said, "The truth is, there is not one single Scripture that proves the Church will be raptured before the Great Tribulation. However, there are *many* Scriptures showing that it will, in fact, pass through the Tribulation. But we all know that if we were to teach that in our denomination, it would blow apart. So, we simply don't tell the people."

An entire denomination involving literally hundreds of thousands of lives is being kept in darkness, and at least one of the top leaders knows the truth. This was one of the main problems the Pharisees had. They had far more concern about the loyalty of their followers and the praise of men than they had for receiving and teaching the truth.

Another very well-known teacher of the pre-tribulation Rapture doctrine made this statement before he passed away, "I know that what I teach is full of holes, but I am too old, and have written too many books on the subject, to change now."[1] What a tragedy. He was willing to allow his followers to be misled until the end of his life. He also chose to ignore the light until he stood before the Lord. How much better it is to allow Him to straighten out our doctrine in this life, though it may hurt and be embarrassing. Some would rather wait until they stand before Him and all the universe, suffering the great humiliation of being corrected there instead of in this present life. God's judgment will fall in a severe way upon leaders who knowingly misled their people concerning passing through the Tribulation. Amos 9:10 says, "All the sinners of my people shall die by the sword, which say, The evil shall not overtake nor prevent us."

Jesus says, "Whosoever therefore shall break one of these least commandments, **and shall teach men so,** he shall be called the least in the kingdom of heaven" (Mt. 5:19a). Along the path of life He causes light to shine on our way, in His faithfulness, giving little warning signs when either our lives or our doctrine need to be corrected. But if we love man's praise more than God's praise, as the Pharisees did, we will cover our doctrinal mistakes and pretend to see nothing in the Bible that contradicts us. The result is that our growth in grace will be hindered until we are willing to confess and forsake our faults, and walk in the light we have received. May our love of the truth be so great that there is no longer room in our hearts to love the praise of men!

The Pharisees Love the Praise of Man

Doctrinal heresy is a work of the flesh (Gal. 5:20). It springs out of the heart and is really just a fruit of what we are. One root in us that produces this fruit is loving the praise and approval of man rather than God's approval (Jn. 5:44). This was something the Pharisees never conquered. This evil root in the character of man is far more serious than the doctrinal heresy it produces. Love for the honor of man is a hindrance to faithfully declaring the Word of the Lord. The prophet Jeremiah was called upon to declare that God's people would pass through the fire. In Jeremiah's day, his was the only voice that told Israel they would face tribulation, which made him rather unpopular. Far from receiving the honor and praise of man, Jeremiah was commissioned to bear great reproach and rejection. We are all called to bear the same for Christ's sake and for the sake of truth itself. Incidentally, Jeremiah tells us twice that his message is really directed toward God's people who will be living in the last days (Jer. 23:20; 30:24).

1. MacPherson, Dave, *The Great Rapture Hoax*, New Puritan Library, Fletcher, North Carolina, 1983, p. 86.

Announcing the coming of the Tribulation instead of the Rapture is not popular today either. It will not generally open the doors for a minister to speak in the great "spiritual renewal conferences" of our day. It certainly isn't the type of encouraging and exciting message that Believers want to hear in this time of relative prosperity. But very soon this message will indeed become popular, because once we find ourselves in that Tribulation it will actually be a very comforting message. In difficult times it is always comforting to know that we are in the furnace of affliction because of God's love for us and not because we have failed Him and been rejected. Maybe you are facing very real difficulties at this very moment, and the enemy has come to sow doubts in your heart, telling you that you have lost God's favor. Satan has always used this tactic. However, God's furnace of affliction produces pure gold in our lives. Furthermore, we can be sure that if we are sons who are truly loved by the Lord, then He will not leave us without discipline when we need it. Far from being a sign that God's favor is lost, it actually proves that He still loves us, and that His hand is still on us (Heb. 12:6-12).

Through several prophets God pronounces severe judgment on false teachers who promise God's people freedom from trouble. We should observe here that we never find such a curse pronounced on ministers who mistakenly tell God's people that they will pass through tribulation when, in fact, they will escape it. It is obviously safer to make the mistake of promising tribulation when only blessing awaits us, than of promising blessing when, in fact, tribulation is coming. Therefore, unless we have searched the Scriptures, and have heard from God regarding the Rapture, it would be far better to avoid the subject than to give God's people a false hope.

The Pharisees Do Not See Their Need

"God, I thank thee, that I am not as other men are..." (Lk. 18:11-12). Another characteristic of Pharisaism is revealed in this prayer of the Pharisee, who could only see how well off he was spiritually. The Pharisee can easily discern the great spiritual need of others, but he does not recognize his own. He can enumerate all the areas that need to be corrected in the lives of those around him or under him. It never occurs to him that he might need correction as well.

I feel very uneasy about people who are continually getting clear messages from God for themselves and others, yet are never hearing anything that convicts them of sin, or causes them to cry out to God for mercy. The Pharisee is seldom found saying, "Brother, I realize that I made a grave mistake in the way I dealt with you...or in something that I did.

Please forgive me." He never sees his own need, or if he does, he doesn't confess it.

The Laodicean Church that says it is "rich and has need of nothing" reveals the general spiritual condition of the Church today (Rev. 3:17). In the wealthier nations of the world some have taught that this passage is speaking of possessing natural riches. According to that teaching, the Laodicean Church is said to be rich in material goods, but spiritually poor. In fact, many have called her the "materialistic Church." However, anyone who has spent time ministering in other countries knows that in most places of the world the Church is not rich in material goods—quite the contrary. So this interpretation cannot be given to this passage in those countries. Therefore, we conclude that this passage deals rather with a spiritual wealth. This is an attitude of heart diametrically opposed to being "poor in spirit," and brings a curse just as surely as being poor in spirit brings a blessing (Mt. 5:3).

The Bible does not teach that being rich in material goods is wrong. Abraham was rich, as were many other men of faith in the Old and New Testaments. The problem is not the possession of goods, but rather an incorrect and evil attitude of heart, common to us all. This attitude of being rich even exists in the poorest Believers of the Third World. The same spirit of Pharisaism that pervades the hearts of Believers of the First World also pervades the hearts of the Believers in those countries. Like all of us, without eye salve they fail to see their great spiritual need, seeing only their spiritual riches instead of their spiritual poverty.

There is a tendency in all of us to see only how wonderful we are, and how much revelation and understanding of truth we have.[2] How can anyone dare suggest that our doctrine might need a few adjustments? Is it any wonder that Jesus tells us we are "wretched, and miserable, and poor, and blind, and naked," and we don't know it? In other words, because we think we are rich in spirit, rather than poor in spirit, we continue to live in spiritual poverty. This is similar to what He told the Pharisees, "For judgment I am come into this world, that they which see not might see; and that they which see might be made blind. And some of the Pharisees which were with him...said unto him, Are we blind also? Jesus said unto them...ye say, We see; therefore your sin remaineth" (Jn. 9:39-41).

What does this have to do with the false doctrine of a pre-tribulation Rapture in the Church today? This doctrine is actually a fruit of the

2. Ironically, this is true even though some people live under constant condemnation. One part of their heart condemns them, and the other part exalts them, because pride is deeply rooted in every heart.

Laodicean Church that is rich in spirit. If we were truly poor in spirit, we would see our tremendous spiritual need, and that instead of being dressed for a wedding, we are naked; instead of having great understanding of spiritual truths, we are blind; instead of being ready to enter Heaven and the fellowship of the "spirits of just men made perfect," we are wretched. If we were truly poor in spirit, we would then expect the purifying fires of the Tribulation before the blessing of the Rapture.

"Lord, have mercy on me, a sinner," is an urgent end-time prayer. Some Pharisees in Christ's day came to understand their need for mercy and turned to the Lord. There is hope for any leader who chooses the path of humility in the presence of the Lamb of Calvary. However, anyone who thinks the Bride of Christ is ready for Heaven today desperately needs to heed Christ's counsel to buy eye salve in order to see. Anyone who looks at his own spiritual life and can somehow convince himself that he is already prepared to receive the heavenly Bridegroom, who is coming for a "glorious church, not having spot, or wrinkle, or any such thing," is most likely just as deceived as that Pharisee who thanked the Lord that he was not like other men. One of the reasons that the pre-tribulation Rapture doctrine even exists is because we do not yet see our condition. We desperately need both the fire of God as well as His visitation, both of which will be hallmarks of the last three and a half years that are soon to begin. No, the next step for the Laodicean Church of today is not the Rapture, but rather a revelation of the fact that we are not ready!

Chapter 17

Two Women: Two "Jerusalems"

The following is a true story. The names have been withheld for the sake of suspense. Although the details cannot be verified, they are definitely similar to what actually took place:

"Slave, I want you to do the laundry, wash the dishes, dust all the furniture, remove the garbage, plant these flowers, and give both dogs a bath. And hurry! I want it all done by noon, because I have a few other things that you must do today."

The slave responds to her mistress, "But today is my day off. I planned to wash my own clothes, and do a few other personal things."

"That's too bad," replies the difficult mistress, "and from now on you won't *have* a day off. You're going to work seven days a week, and instead of working twelve hours a day you must now work fourteen hours!"

Anger fills the face of the slave. "Enough is enough! I want you to know that I'm no longer your slave. I will now be called the *wife* of your husband. I will be giving birth to his child, his *only* child, something you haven't been able to accomplish during all your years of marriage to him. So you'll just have to do your *own* work from now on. I'm going to dedicate *my* time to raising his child!"

At that moment a man enters, just in time to hear the slave's declaration. The horrified mistress exclaims, "Now you have heard her with your own ears! What shall I do with her?"

He stands there, bewildered and troubled, staring outside and shaking his head, as though to ask, "Why did it turn out this way?" Finally, as he wearily turns to go, he says, "She's *your* slave. Do with her whatever you want!"

The slave flings herself at his feet, wailing like a child. "I am honorable; I am bearing your child. You don't love your child, or you would never call his mother a slave. You took me as your wife, so how can you leave me under the heel of this woman who can't even give you an heir?"

This is a sample of the turmoil that probably existed in Abraham and Sarah's home after she made the grave mistake of insisting on having children even though God had "restrained her from bearing" (Gen. 16:2). She sought a son through Hagar, the Egyptian slave, and paid dearly for that mistake for many years (Gen. 16). Another fruit of this mistake was that our spiritual father, Abraham, spent many long years with two women living in the same house. They both claimed to be his wife, and they were in continual disagreement. What sorrow it must have brought to that home.

This tremendous conflict between two women living in the same house in the beginning (Gen. 16 and 21) is also seen in the end, where two women are also living in the same house (Rev. 12 and 17). Revelation not only speaks of two women, but also makes a clear connection between the two by giving many related details about both. The Author of Revelation, the Holy Spirit, obviously wants us to see and understand the connection that exists between them. Let's compare the information given about each of these women:

1. **Revelation 12:6**–This woman is in the wilderness.

   Revelation 17:3–This woman is also in the wilderness.

2. **Revelation 12:1**–This woman is clothed with the "sun" (the riches of Heaven, or the Lord Himself, who is called the "Sun of righteousness"[1]).

   Revelation 17:4–This woman is clothed with purple, scarlet, gold, precious stones, pearls (the riches of earth—Lk. 16:19).

3. **Revelation 12:3-5**–The beast that has seven heads and ten horns opposes this woman, and attempts to destroy her seed.

   Revelation 17:7–That same beast carries this woman (i.e., sustains, advances, serves, and upholds her).

4. **Revelation 12:1**–Upon her head is a crown of twelve stars, or apostolic authority and government (a crown speaks of authority and government, and Revelation 21:14 uses the number twelve in the context of the twelve apostles of the Lamb).

1. See Malachi 4:2. Also note that Paul tells us we should be clothed upon with Christ in Romans 13:14. That is what the Greek means there, which is translated as "put on" Christ in the King James Version.

Revelation 17:5,18–Upon her head (forehead) is written "BABYLON THE GREAT..." She, too, has authority because verse eighteen tells us that she "reigneth over the kings of the earth."

5. **Revelation 12:5**–She is a mother, the mother of a "man child" and deliverer who rules all nations and overcomes the Devil (Rev. 12:11).

Revelation 17:5–She is a mother also, the mother of harlots and abominations.

6. **Revelation 12:2**–She has a new life within her, which she brings forth, and which brings joy to Heaven and the saints (Rev. 12:11-12).

Revelation 17:6–She is filled with the blood of the saints. So instead of bringing forth life for others, she has devoured the lives of others. She is filled with their blood (life). She produces death in others.

7. **Revelation 12:5**–This woman carries a king in her womb, and gives birth to that king.

Revelation 17:7,10-11–This woman is carried by a king. (The beast is a king, v. 10-11.)

8. **Revelation 12:10**–Those who are related to this woman receive the everlasting Kingdom of their God.

Revelation 17:12–Those who are related to this woman receive a kingdom for one hour.

9. **Revelation 12:7,11**–Those related to this woman make war with Satan, and with his angels, and overcome them.

Revelation 17:14–Those related to this woman make war with the Lamb and with the saints who are with Him and are overcome by them.

10. **Revelation 12:15-16**–Satan uses water, seeking to destroy this woman.

Revelation 17:1,15–This woman sits upon waters. Verse 15 says that these waters represent the multitudes and nations of the earth. Satan will seek to use his multitudes to destroy the woman of Revelation 12.

11. **Revelation 12:16**–The earth helps this woman.

Revelation 17:16-17–The earth hates this woman.

Both Women Are Cities

In light of these comparisons, we can be sure that these two women are somehow related. Whatever they represent, they are in the same general category. In other words, the Author of Revelation is not comparing apples with oranges here, but rather apples with apples. If the first woman is an apple, then the second woman is also an apple—a very bad apple!

In Revelation 17:18 we are told that the wicked woman is a **city** that rules over the kings of the earth. Since the wicked woman in Revelation 17 is a city, the righteous woman in Revelation 12 must be a city also. In the context of the Book of Revelation we are shown a righteous woman who is also called a **city**: "I John, saw the holy city, the new Jerusalem... prepared as a bride..." (Rev. 21:2).[2] That "city," or woman, is the Bride of Christ, His Church. Unless we conclude that there are really *three* women who are cities in the Book of Revelation (instead of two), then the woman who is a "city" in Revelation 21 must be the same woman found in Revelation 12—the Church.

Continuing our comparison, since the woman in Revelation 12 is a city, which represents **the true Church**, then the woman in Revelation 17, who is called a city, must also be some sort of a church, **a false church**. In other words, they both represent a spiritual people. Again, **our interpretations must be firmly founded on other Scriptures**, allowing the Bible to interpret itself. This is especially true for Revelation, because the end and the beginning are the same, and there is "nothing new under the sun, all can be found in previous Scriptures." Since we are told that these two persons are at the same time **women, mothers**, and **cities**, our search for a similar description in another Scripture should not be difficult since this is a very unusual combination of characteristics. Are there such Scriptures?

Two Women, Two Mothers, and Two Cities Are Found in Paul's Writings

Paul explains who the two women, two mothers, and two cities really are in Galatians 4. He says, "Abraham had two sons, the one by a bondmaid, the other by a freewoman" (v. 22). Both of these women are mothers. Paul goes on to say that these women are "symbolic" of something (v. 24 NKJV). "Hagar...corresponds to the present Jerusalem, for she is in slavery with her children" (v. 25 NAS). Therefore, one woman represents the earthly Jerusalem, a **city**. Finally he says, "But the Jerusalem which is above is free, which is the mother of us all" (v. 26). So the other woman represents the heavenly Jerusalem, which is also a **city**, called the "city of God" (Heb. 12:22-23). She is called a "mother," because she gives

2. Some may note that the woman in Revelation 12 is found on the earth, while in Revelation 21:2 she is descending from Heaven. However, if we follow the sequence of events found in the book, we find that between Revelation 12, where she passes through her "wilderness" experience, and Revelation 21:2, where she comes down from Heaven, we are told that she is taken up to Heaven, and the Marriage Supper, in Revelation 19:7-9. We will see more about this in Chapters 17 and 18.

birth to the sons of God to whom Paul often refers in his epistles. So then, Paul shows that there are **two "Jerusalems,"** the earthly and the heavenly.

Several Men Had Two Wives in the Same House

Both of the women in Genesis 16 lived in the same house. Since Abraham is a pattern for both natural Israel and spiritual Israel, it is understandable that we should find other scriptural examples of two women living in the same house. These two women are always in conflict with one another.

This story was repeated in Jacob's house, where Rachel and Leah were in constant conflict. It was repeated in Elkanah's house also, where Hannah and Peninnah were in conflict. In the Book of Esther we find that King Ahasuerus had two wives, Vashti and Esther.

Could it be that these Old Testament men serve as examples (as Paul tells us), suffering something that Christ Himself would also suffer? Could it be that Revelation is giving us this same message, showing that there are two women in the Lord's house also? Paul's comments in Galatians 4 certainly seem to indicate that this is the case, because there he actually compares Abraham and the two women in his house with Christ Himself. We reach this conclusion because Paul compares Abraham's two women, Sarah and Hagar, with the heavenly and earthly Jerusalems, respectively. But to whom does the heavenly Jerusalem (the Church) belong? To the Lord Himself, and the Church's sons are His sons. But what about the sons born after the flesh" and the rest of this allegory? Remember it was Sarah who caused this problem for Abraham because of her unwillingness to accept her barrenness as God's choice for her life. Could it be that Sarah, representing the Lord's people today, has caused problems for the Lord, causing children to be born into His house using fleshly, carnal methods, because she hasn't been willing to accept God's choice for her? Hagar (the way of the flesh) is the channel she has used, and unfortunately, Hagar and her children live in the same house that Sarah lives in—the Lord's house!

In light of this, it is not at all surprising to find in the last days a revelation of two women. That "other woman" in Abraham's house became a source of great trial and sorrow to Sarah. Likewise, the "other woman" in Revelation will be one of the greatest sources of trials and sorrows for God's people in the end. The Chinese use symbols to convey their concepts instead of using an alphabet to spell words. Their symbol for "war" is a little house with two women inside. Abraham and Sarah, as well as the other men in similar situations, understood through experience what the Chinese have been declaring for thousands of years. Sadly enough, it appears that the heavenly Sarah (spiritual Israel, or the Church) is going to learn this lesson in the end in the same way it was learned in the beginning—through difficult personal experiences.

Who Is the "Son" of the Woman in Revelation 12?

Revelation shows who the "son" is. We reproduce according to our species or "kind." This is a law of God instituted in Genesis 1. Since this woman in Revelation 12 is the Church, she symbolizes a **group of people.** Therefore, the "man child" that she births must also be symbolic of a **group of people.** This interpretation is consistent with the context of the rest of the Book of Revelation, including the rest of chapter 12. Revelation 12:5 and 11 give us two details about her son that are keys to knowing who he is. First, he will "rule all nations with a rod of iron," and second, the statement is made that "*They* [plural] overcame him [Satan] by the blood of the Lamb." Revelation tells us precisely who will rule with a rod of iron: all the overcomers (Rev. 2:26-27). Then, near the end of Revelation, we find, "He that **overcometh** shall **inherit all things**; and I will be his God, and he shall be my **son**" (Rev. 21:7). The inheritance of the Believers is the Kingdom of God (in other words, rulership). So all overcomers are sons, and all overcomers rule with a rod of iron. However, this is the same blessing given to the son in Revelation 12. That "son" is therefore a company of people whose "mother" is the Church and Father is the Lord.

Isaiah shows who the "son" is. In both Revelation 12 and Isaiah 66:7-8 the Church is seen travailing. We can be certain that the woman who travails in Isaiah 66 is the Church for at least two reasons. First, Isaiah declares, "as soon as Zion was in labor she brought forth her sons" (Isa. 66:8 RSV). Zion, the Church, travails and brings forth "sons" (plural). Second, "Zion" is the same woman referred to many times in the last few chapters of Isaiah, beginning with Isaiah 54:1. Not only does Isaiah 54:5 tell us that she is the Lord's wife, and therefore the Church, but also Paul quotes this passage in Galatians 4 and reveals her as the "mother of us all." In Isaiah 66 that same Zion brings forth her sons. Furthermore, in Isaiah 66:6-7 we are shown that God's answer to His enemy, "the old serpent," is the birth of those **sons.** Therefore, Revelation 12 reveals a wonderful and precise fulfillment of God's promise to bring forth His sons. There the enemy, "the old serpent," is overcome in the last days by those sons.

Paul shows who the "son" is. "*I consider that our present sufferings are not worth comparing with the glory that will be revealed in us. The creation waits in eager expectation for the sons of God to be revealed*" (Rom. 8:18-19 NIV).

Consider what Paul is saying here:

1. Many years after the early Church was founded, Paul declared that the creation is still waiting for something. Specifically, it waits for God's sons to be "revealed." From this same Greek word comes the word "Apocalypse," or "Revelation." The creation earnestly awaits the "Apocalypse" or "Revelation" of Christ, and this will occur through the revelation of the sons of God. The Church gives birth to God's sons. This confirms something we have already studied in Chapter 6—He first comes in His people, by a birth.

2. The *"glory that will be revealed in us"* is shown to be Christ's life manifested in and through the Believers in Colossians 1:27 where Paul explains that Christ in the Church is the hope of glory. All the earth will see His glory, as the Scriptures promise, but only when the glory of His life has been formed *in* His people and revealed *through* His people. This "Apocalypse" or "unveiling" of His life is an end-time visitation of God that occurs during the Great Tribulation. (Compare Isa. 60:2 and Hab. 2:14.) We know from many Scriptures that the revelation of the mature sons of God is a future event. Paul confirms this by giving us a definition of "hope" in Romans 8:24-25, saying that we "hope" for things we do not yet possess. This explanation is given in the context of the revelation of the sons of God and the "hope" set before us (Rom. 8:19-20). Romans 8:19 and Colossians 1:27 tell us that Christ being formed in us is the "hope" of the creation, and is therefore something that, as a Church, we have not yet fully experienced. There were glorious differences between the Old Testament Age and the New Testament Age that were brought by the coming of the Son. And there will be even greater differences between this present Age and the Millennial Age, when the Son comes again and manifests Himself through His mature sons. God's people couldn't accept those differences because of tradition (doctrine based on their past experience). Will we make the same mistake?

3. In Chapter 6 we considered the logical question, "But isn't Christ already in us?" This is clarified by Paul when he tells the Galatian *Believers* that he is "travailing in birth" so that Christ would be formed in them. He further explains this in Ephesians 4:13-14 where his desire is that we would grow up into the "measure of the stature of the fulness of Christ: that we henceforth be no more children." The Father's desire is not only to produce babes in Christ, but He is also looking for mature sons who will bring His glory to a needy world. The life of Christ is only formed in us through "travail," and travail involves suffering and sorrow. So this is why Paul mentions that *"our present sufferings are not worth comparing with*

the glory that will be revealed in us" (Rom. 8:18 NIV). That travail will bring forth that glory.

I know that a few readers will immediately link what I am saying here with what is known as "the manifest sons" movement that sprang up in the United States and elsewhere many years ago. I am very much aware of what that movement teaches, and believe that they have taken some wonderful truths from God's Word and twisted them. The major difference that I see between those teachings and what I am sharing here is Christ's role and position in all of this. The essence of that false teaching is that when God manifests His mature sons to the world, they will actually be "little Christs." We know that this is extremely heretical. I believe the issue is that there is only *one* Christ, the only begotten of the Father, and that He has promised to manifest His glory *and* His character through a many-membered Body in these last days. That glory will proceed *from* Him alone and will be *for* Him alone. He alone will be exalted, and all His true servants will choose the lowest of places at His feet. They will be among the humblest and meekest men that have ever walked the earth. As with Christ's ministry, there will be no flashy show, and no "form nor comeliness" that would cause the natural, carnal, sensual man to be drawn to those sons.

Christ Makes the Same Commitment He Asked Joseph to Make

At the beginning of the New Testament, the Lord asked Joseph, the husband of Mary, to make a commitment that was going to deeply affect the rest of Joseph's life. He asked Joseph to bear the reproach of receiving Mary as his wife, even though she was with child before the wedding. By accepting Mary as his wife everyone would assume that he was admitting the child was his. It was a difficult commitment and that would cause him great reproach for the rest of his life. But, oh, what a child! And, oh, what glory came to earth because of that commitment!

The Lord never asks any man to make a commitment that He is not willing to make Himself. And this is exactly the same commitment He makes to His Bride at the end of the New Testament. He, too, is willing for her to be found with child of the Holy Spirit before the wedding. But, oh, what a child! And, oh, what glory will come to those who bear the reproach of having His life formed within them, a reproach that falls on the Lord Himself (Rom. 15:3). Like Joseph and Mary, they too will be mocked, condemned, ridiculed, and despised, but when His glory is suddenly seen upon them, their shame will be turned into great rejoicing. I declare with the Apostle Paul that Christ in us is the only hope of that glory coming.

There Have Always Been Two Streams in the Same House

I have said that the two women of Revelation represent the true Church and a false church. However, I am not implying that the false Church is an organization found in the world. We have seen from the beginning that these two women **live in the same house**. The world does not live in the same house that is occupied by the true Church, God's house. So when I refer to the "false church" I am not referring to the world. I am referring to the two streams that have always been manifested in the same house that the true Church occupies. This happened in the beginning, and it will happen again in the end.

In the beginning, Cain and Abel revealed that there were two streams flowing from the same house and from the same father, Adam. We see this throughout the Bible, where the evil men, who were foreshadows of the Antichrist, always came **out from among** the people of God. For example, there were thirteen tribes, but Jacob calls the father of one, Dan, "a serpent" in Genesis 49:17.[3] Thirteen judges are found in the Book of Judges; one, Abimelech, was wicked. Absalom, a son of David, from the house of David, betrayed his own father and tried to usurp the throne. There were thirteen apostles,[4] but Judas, who walked and ministered with Christ and His disciples, was a "devil" (Jn. 6:70-71).

John confirms the validity of this truth in First John 2:18-19: "Little children...ye have heard that antichrist shall come, even now there are many antichrists...**They went out from us**, but they were not of us; for if they had been of us, they would no doubt have continued with us: but **they went out**, that they might be made manifest that they were not all of us." John experienced this very thing during the Last Supper when Judas went out from them. That event must have had a tremendous impact on John, as well as on the other disciples.

---

3. Jacob had twelve sons, but Jospeh's two sons, Ephraim and Manasseh, were considered to be his own after Genesis 48:5. For that reason we find twelve tribes mentioned in Revelation 7, but Dan, the serpent, is not found among them.
4. This is counting Matthias in Acts 1. He took the place of Judas.

At the beginning of the Church Age, the life and ministry of Judas, the "son of perdition," is one of the most awesome foreshadows of the Antichrist in all of the Bible. Judas lived and walked with the other disciples, and with the Lord Himself. In fact, as one of the twelve, he was given a ministry of power and authority to heal the sick, cleanse the lepers, raise the dead, cast out devils, and preach the gospel of the Kingdom (Mt. 10:6-8). And Judas did so, returning to Jesus along with the eleven, rejoicing in the tremendous power they had manifested.

However, one of the greatest sorrows in the life of Christ was His betrayal by Judas, as seen in Psalm 55:12-14, where He says, "For it was not an enemy that reproached me; then I could have borne it...But it was thou, a man mine equal,[5] my guide, and mine acquaintance. We took sweet counsel together, and walked unto the house of God in company." They all went to church together, but Judas was not flowing in the same stream as Christ and His disciples.

The terrible reality of those two streams flowing together for a time in the same house must have been witnessed by the apostles many times, because John says "many antichrists" went out from the Church. However, during the last days, the spirit of Antichrist will manifest itself as never before. In the near future, the reality of those two streams in the same house will be greater than ever before!

There Were Two "Jerusalems" or Streams in God's House During Christ's First Coming

Within the natural house of Israel, during the days of Christ's First Coming, there was a clear manifestation of those two streams. Part of Israel rejected and persecuted Him, while others accepted Him as their Savior. Nothing has changed today. One of those streams actually crucified Him. Paul likens that stream to Hagar, or earthly Jerusalem and the law (Gal. 4:21,22,25). It is a religious system that walks with the true disciples for a time. Hagar's child, Ishmael, persecuted **a son of promise,** Isaac, in the beginning. Her children also persecuted and crucified *the* **Son of promise**, Christ, when He was born in Israel, which was Abraham's "house" (Gal. 4:25,29). However, the other stream, likened to Sarah, loved His appearing. She became His true Bride, the heavenly Jerusalem or

5. This statement shows to what degree the self-emptying of Philippians 2:7 was a reality in Christ's life. He became a man to such a degree that He called other men His equals. Of course, Hebrews 2:17 confirms this, where we are told that He was made like His brethren "in all things."

Church (Gal. 4:22,26,27,31). Later, the early Church gave birth to many faithful sons of God.

But the Beginning and Ending of the Church Age Are the Same

The characteristics of those two spiritual streams, or "Jerusalems," were clearly manifested at the beginning of the Church Age, and we will see them manifested in the end. The thing that natural Israel manifested in Christ's First Coming was the spiritual condition of two very different types of people. Spiritually speaking, both have lived together in the same house since the days of Cain and Abel.

This is the very same truth that the Spirit is revealing to us through the two women found in Revelation at the end. There will be two types of people among the disciples in the last days also. One type of disciple in Christ's house will be like Judas. Although he had great power and authority given to him by Christ Himself, he did not have Christ's character, nor a love for the will of God. That false stream is composed of natural, earthly, sensual, carnal disciples, who are lovers of the world and not of God. They will be just like the religious leaders of Christ's day, with whom Judas finally became identified and allied in betraying the Lord. They are those who love money, position, the honor of man, ministry, success, and other things, more than they love the presence of the Lord of Glory. In Paul's allegory, these people are called the **"earthly Jerusalem,"** or a false spiritual stream that has been manifested among the people of God since the beginning. It is the spirit of religion that has always plagued mankind, and has always sought to walk with those who are truly spiritual. In fact, the Lord says that they will even be sent by Him, as was Judas, and they will deceive hearts into following them, hearts that are like their own.[6]

The other type of disciple in Christ's house loves Him more than life. Those who do so will follow the Lamb "withersoever He goeth," even though this means a daily dying to self by embracing His cross (Rev. 14:4). These people are not filled with religion, but rather with relationship, a relationship that will cause them to give birth to the divine life. They are

6. Compare Matthew 24:5 and Second Thessalonians 2:11-12. To "come in His name" does not refer to using the formula that many use today of simply saying, "In the name of Jesus." Rather, this scriptural phrase refers to the same thought that is conveyed today if someone delcares, "I come to you in the name of the President." That means that the President sent them through direct communication. As Judas was sent by the Lord, these people will be sent also to gather out the tares. They will be reapers of the impure hearts.

truly spiritually minded, with their heart and eyes fixed on Heaven's values. This is the **heavenly Jerusalem.**

We need not end our lives being part of the earthly Jerusalem as a carnal Christian. Paul, in First Corinthians, gives us great hope of being changed. Near the beginning of that epistle he tells the Corinthians that they are carnal disciples and walk as men. They are filled with envy, strife, and divisions (1 Cor. 3:1-3). Later, near the end of his message to them, he makes it clear that we all have borne the image of the earthly and carnal. We were born that way. However, he says that we will also bear the image of the heavenly (1 Cor. 15:45-49). The context is clear; we must allow the old man in us, the first Adam, to be crucified with Christ by daily denying ourselves and embracing His cross. The Lord is going to transform each sincere Believer into the heavenly image, just as He will also do with the natural city of Jerusalem at the end of this age. He will bring great glory to the efficacy of His grace when Jerusalem, in the Middle East, is transformed into a holy city again and it becomes the capital city of His worldwide Kingdom. It, too, has borne the image of the earthly but will soon bear the image of the heavenly!

Revelation clearly identifies one of the two women, or cities, found in the book as heavenly Jerusalem (Rev. 21:2). However, there is sufficient biblical evidence to show that the other city, called the great harlot of Revelation, is symbolic of a group of people inside the true Church in these last days. In a moment we will see how the details given about Babylon the Great, the mother of harlots, had a **natural fulfillment** in the natural city of Jerusalem in the First Coming. However, I want to emphasize that the end-time fulfillment of these things has nothing whatsoever to do with the natural city of Jerusalem today. In fact, the Lord Himself is going to soon fight to save and rebuild that natural city as the capital of His Kingdom. To understand this we must remember that when Christ came the first time He was changing His natural people of Israel into a spiritual people, and now all of the same events of our "parable" will occur again, being repeated on a spiritual level in Israel, or the Church. Many have observed the tremendous amount of Jewish terminology found in the Book of Revelation, showing that the message is definitely related to the nation of Israel. However, we need to remember that Israel *is* the Church, and God's dealings with her in Revelation are primarily on a spiritual plane and secondarily on a natural plane, although one never excludes the other. For example, in the Old Testament He was dealing with Israel primarily on a natural plane and secondarily on a spiritual plane. In the New Testament this is reversed. With this understanding it is much easier to properly interpret the message of Revelation.

Consider the Proof That the Great Harlot in Revelation is an Earthly, Sensual, Carnal "Jerusalem"

1. Revelation 17:18 calls her the "great city." In the context of Revelation, it is the earthly Jerusalem that is called the "great city" (Rev. 11:8).

2. Revelation 18:24 tells us that "in her [the harlot] was found the blood of prophets and of saints, and of *all* that were slain upon the earth." Jesus said to Jerusalem, "I send unto you prophets, and wise men...and some of them ye shall kill and crucify...and some of them shall ye scourge...and persecute...That upon you may come **all the righteous blood shed upon the earth,** from the blood of righteous Abel unto the blood of Zacharias" (Mt. 23:34-35).[7]

3. The earthly Jerusalem turned into a harlot. "How is the faithful city **become an harlot!** It was full of judgment; righteousness lodged in it; but now murderers" (Isa. 1:21). Isaiah is speaking about Jerusalem here (Isa. 1:8). The "great city" of Revelation 17 is also called the great harlot (Rev. 17:1). Therefore, we find here one more link between the harlot of Revelation and an earthly Jerusalem.

4. Ezekiel 22:2 calls Jerusalem the "bloody city," guilty of abominations. Revelation 17:4-6 describes the harlot there in much the same way, saying that she is full of abominations and drunk with the blood of the saints.

5. Paul says Hagar is earthly Jerusalem (Gal. 4:25). But Hagar was an Egyptian (Gen. 16:1; Gal. 4:25). Revelation 11:8 says that the earthly Jerusalem, where Christ was crucified, is Egypt, spiritually speaking.

6. The merchandise of the great harlot in Revelation links her with Jerusalem, the great harlot of Ezekiel 16. The Lord condemns **Jerusalem** for turning into a harlot with the nations of the earth, and converting the precious things He has given her into merchandise for her harlotry (Ezek. 16:1,9-29). Note the similarity between her merchandise in Revelation 18 and what God gave Jerusalem in Ezekiel 16: gold, silver, precious stones, fine linen, silk, oil, fine flour, etc.

The Woman of Revelation 17 Rides the Beast

When someone rides an animal, or a vehicle, the purpose is generally to reach a goal. Likewise, this woman is using the beast to attain a goal or

7. Compare Appendix C here. Note that this message of Christ was the seventh to the Pharisees in Matthew 23, and it is parallel to the Laodicean Church in Revelation. This will be repeated in the end!

purpose. The beast is shown to be a "king," and also a worldwide empire.[8] Therefore, she is using the kingdoms of this world to reach a goal. In other words, she is riding that beast.

In this aspect also, the end is a repeat of the beginning. During the First Coming, the earthly Jerusalem, or woman, is seen riding the beast. When they crucified the Lord, they "rode" Rome. Meaning, they actually sought and received the help of Rome and the rulers of this world, to attain their evil goal of crucifying the Lord. They did exactly what the earthly, carnal, Jerusalem will do at the end of the New Testament Age. In their blindness, they actually made themselves a part of Rome by their own choice when they said, "We have no king but Caesar" (Jn. 19:15). The harlot of Revelation is called "Babylon," because, through spiritual adultery, she becomes one with the world system, known as "Babylon."

Notice, however, that in Revelation 17:16 the same beast she rides, later turns on her and destroys her. This, too, was fulfilled in the beginning. Just a few years after they had used Rome to kill the Lord, Rome turned on Jerusalem and totally destroyed her in A.D. 70.

Those same religious leaders "rode Rome" again to reach their self-seeking goal to bring an end to Paul's life and ministry. They used the army, governors, and kings of Rome to imprison Paul, and finally sent him to Rome. Their hope was that Rome would send him to his death in the coliseum, or take his life in some other way. Instead, Rome released Paul and destroyed the "woman," earthly Jerusalem.

In these last days the religious leaders among God's people who haven't paid the price to maintain "oil in their lamps"[9] will be filled with jealousy when they see a great company of mature saints manifesting the glory of Christ through their lives. They will ultimately repeat what that wicked "woman" did in the First Coming of Christ. They will turn to the governments of this world to help them fight against those who have put them to shame by revealing the depths of their spiritual poverty. But in the end those same governments will turn on them, and bring upon them God's judgments.

This is not merely doctrine, interpretation, or speculation. Within the last few centuries the true disciples of the Lord have witnessed this very thing happening time and time again. John Bunyan, the author of *The Pilgrim's Progress,* spent many years of his life in a wretched prison. This happened because the religious leaders of his day sought and received the help of the government against him. They refused to allow their own

---

8. Revelation 17:10-11 shows us that the beast is a king, and Revelation 13:1,7 shows us that the beast also speaks of a kingdom.
9. In other words, the blessing of the presence of God on their lives.

spiritual poverty to be revealed on the streets of England by the compelling preaching of that unlearned tinker. Many others experienced the same treatment at the hands of leaders who felt threatened by the preaching of those who had the authority of Heaven resting upon them. This will be nothing new in the last days. It will simply be the last time that carnal, self-seeking disciples will be permitted to use that tactic before **the final victory**. However, those who have the meekness and mind of the Lamb will soon conquer through the strength of the Lion of Judah.

This continues to happen in God's house up to this very day. In one country, a large group of local churches withdrew their affiliation from their denomination, because they were tired of spiritual politics and the continual interest in money that the national leadership manifested. Once it became clear that they were going to leave the denomination, the national leadership went to that nation's government. They told the officials that they had decided to donate a large number of their church buildings to a government-backed institution, wanting them to be used for government purposes. They were, in fact, donating the buildings of all the local churches that had left the denomination.

The government actually ended up turning on them, and said, "We know what you are doing, and we are aware of the internal fighting going on among you who call yourselves 'Christians.' We don't want any part of it, nor do we want the buildings." This is just a small sample of what has been repeated many times, and in many different ways, and it will happen again because of the uncontrollable jealousies of Pharisaism still found in the hearts of men.

This is what "riding the beast" really means. The end of that path will be complete and eternal destruction for that woman—earthly, carnal, sensual "Jerusalem." Those carnal disciples have lived in the same house as the other woman for many centuries. Very soon, however, there will no longer be two Jerusalems, nor two women living in the same house. After "Sarah" has travailed and given birth to her "son," Hagar will be cast out forever, as finally happened in Genesis 21.

Final Conclusions Concerning the Woman of Revelation 12

1. What does this tell us about a pre-tribulation Rapture? The woman found in Revelation 12 is on the earth, protected in a "wilderness" during the last three and a half years (v. 6,14).[10] In other words, she is on earth

10. Personally, I believe that this wilderness is spiritual and not natural because the rest of the characteristics mentioned in this context are spiritual. So why should only this one refer to something natural?

during the Great Tribulation. If we understand that the woman found in Revelation 12 is the Church, we also understand that the Church goes through the Tribulation. This, too, is a repeat of the beginning, because Exodus reveals that God's people were protected from the plagues that Moses brought on Egypt.

2. Why the woman cannot be Mary giving birth to Christ: In Revelation 4:1 the angel tells John that from that point onward he is going to show him things that will happen in the future. John was exiled to the isle of Patmos in about A.D. 96, where he received the Revelation. He, therefore, received this book from the Lord almost one hundred years after Mary had given birth to Jesus. Since he was being shown the future, not history, the woman in chapter 12 cannot be Mary.

3. Why the woman cannot be natural Israel: Some have interpreted the woman in Revelation 12 to be a type of natural Israel in the last days, and that Revelation 4–19 deals with that people. We will see in the next chapter why this is not possible.

Chapter 18

Revelation 4:1

Most pre-tribulation Rapture teachings affirm that the Rapture of the Church takes place in Revelation 4:1 when the angel says to John, "Come up hither." In Appendix B we see that the prophet Ezekiel's experience and his revelation are precisely the same as John's in the Book of Revelation. The Heavens were opened to Ezekiel (Ezek. 1:1). Also in Second Corinthians 12:1-4 Paul was caught up to the third Heaven. There is no reason to conclude that John's experience typifies the Rapture any more than Ezekiel's or Paul's does. In spite of this, several reasons are given in support of a Rapture in Revelation 4:1. The purpose of this book is not to mock or expose others, but rather to discover the truth and to exalt the Lord Jesus Christ for His Body's sake. Let's look at the reasons that are given to "prove" that the Rapture takes place in Revelation 4:1. Let's consider them honestly, and with humility of heart, knowing that regardless of what God has shown to any of us, our knowledge and understanding are extremely limited (1 Cor. 8:2).

1. A change in God's attitude toward humanity. One pre-tribulation teacher says, "There is a marked change in God's attitude toward humanity in general at the beginning of Revelation 4, from that of mercy, found in Rev. 1–3, to that of judgment, found in Rev. 4–19."[1] Let's look at a few thoughts in both of these sections to see if this argument is really convincing. In the first section, Revelation 1–3, we supposedly find an attitude of mercy. However, in that section, God warns Ephesus, a very

1. Dake, Finis, Jennings, *Revelation Expounded*, Dake Bible Sales, Inc., Lawrenceville, Georgia, 1977, p. 53.

diligent church. It is not for gross sin, but merely for a lack of the first love that He warns, "Remember therefore from whence thou art fallen, and repent, and do the first works; or else I will come unto thee quickly, and will remove thy candlestick out of his place, except thou repent" (Rev. 2:5). Further, in Revelation 3:15-17, He warns the Laodicean Church, "I know thy works, that thou art neither cold nor hot: I would thou wert cold or hot. So then because thou art lukewarm, and neither cold nor hot, I will spue thee out of my mouth. Because thou sayest, I am rich, and increased with goods, and have need of nothing; and knowest not that thou art wretched, and miserable, and poor, and blind, and naked..." This definitely does not sound very much like the kind of mercy I would want to receive! And these messages are directed toward the Church, not even toward the world and the ungodly. Even more amazing, He promises that those who do not change their ways will suffer great tribulation. We have seen that each one of us who are alive in that day will be faced with choosing between great visitation and the Great Tribulation.

On the other hand, looking at some references that show God's attitude in chapters 4–19, consider Revelation 7:3, "...Hurt not the earth, neither the sea, nor the trees, till we have sealed the servants of our God in their foreheads." Also we find a very gracious attitude of God in Revelation 14:12-13: "Here is the patience of the saints: here are they that keep the commandments of God, and the faith of Jesus. And I heard a voice from heaven saying unto me, Write, Blessed are the dead which die in the Lord from henceforth: Yea, saith the Spirit, that they may rest from their labours; and their works do follow them."

These passages are from the heart of a merciful God. God has always spoken with great mercy toward the repentant, and with great judgments against any man who will not accept His gift of salvation. John 3:36 declares, "He that believeth on the Son hath everlasting life: and he that believeth not the Son shall not see life; but the wrath of God abideth on him." This is so today, and this will still be the case during the time of the Great Tribulation.

In conclusion then, to say that mercy is seen in the first three chapters of Revelation and that judgment is seen later is not a strong argument. Verses revealing mercy and judgment are found in both sections.

2. The word "church" never appears after Revelation 4:1. It is assumed that since the Greek word "church" never appears in the Bible text between chapters 4 and 19 of Revelation that the Church is not on the earth at that time. This reasoning is followed immediately with the thought that "the enthroned elders are representative of the raptured saints."[2] But in the New Testament there are two principal words used to refer to God's people: "church" and "saints" (1 Cor. 1:2). Both are used more than fifty times. In Revelation 4–19 the word "saints" *does* appear eleven times, and they are clearly on earth and not in Heaven.

For example, speaking of the Antichrist, Revelation 13:7 tells us, "And it was given unto him to make war with the **saints**, and to overcome them." Also, Revelation 15:2-3 says, "And I saw as it were a sea of glass mingled with fire: and them that had gotten the victory over the beast, and over his image, and over his mark, and over the number of his name, stand on the sea of glass, having the harps of God." Therefore, some saints will be overcome by the beast during the last days, whereas other saints will overcome the beast, and all that he represents. This is **the final victory** for which Christ and the Church are waiting! How can we resort to saying that the twenty-four enthroned elders are symbolic of the Church in Heaven when "saints" are clearly still on the earth. We are ignoring the facts for the sake of symbolism, a symbolism that is pure speculation since no other Scripture in the Bible confirms this interpretation. We are never justified in using symbolism that the Bible does not establish. For example, if the Bible likens a "sword" to the Word of God, only then am I justified in doing so.

3. Chapters 4–19 of Revelation have the earmarks of Israel. It is stated by some that throughout chapters 4–19 we see many Old Testament references, as well as thoughts, expressions, and concepts that involve natural Israel and not the Church. For example, the concept of an "altar" in Revelation 8:3 is said to be Old Testament and Jewish. But Revelation 1:4 and 11 clearly state that the message of the entire Book of Revelation is for the Church, which includes both Jews and Gentiles, no longer divided into two different peoples. It is not merely for natural Israel, and saying that Israel and the Church are two different entities is totally unscriptural. This false doctrine has not only birthed many false doctrines regarding the last days, but it is also a huge factor in why the Jewish people have suffered at the hands of "Christians" for centuries. Besides, the Gentile Church will never get to Heaven without being firmly grafted into the root from which Resurrection life flows, because salvation is of the Jews (Jn. 4:22). And the Resurrection that will accompany the Rapture will only be granted when the Jews, as a nation, are part of the Body again (Rom. 11:15).

Actually, every jot and tittle of the Old Testament will be fulfilled in the New Testament (Mt. 5:18). And there is nothing new in Revelation. In fact, if every concept in Revelation cannot be found in the Old Testament, then

2. Dake, Finis, Jennings, *Revelation Expounded*, Dake Bible Sales, Inc., Lawrenceville, Georgia, 1977, p. 53.

Ecclesiastes 1:9-10 is false. There is nothing new under the sun. Revelation is a repeat of the concepts of the Old Testament. It is a repeat of the beginning, and of all that Israel, our "parable," reveals in the Old Testament. The New Testament is full of Jewish concepts and types. If Revelation 4–19 sounds Jewish, try the Book of Hebrews! It was actually written to help Jewish Believers make the transition from the Old to the New Testament Age. As we have seen, the writer of Hebrews shows that all the natural aspects of the Old Testament find a similar spiritual aspect in the New Testament. For that reason he says that we have an altar, a priesthood, a Tabernacle, sacrifices, and a law. The New Testament itself says that His New Testament Temple is the Church.

This lines up with Paul's doctrine in Colossians 2:16-17 that the things found in the Old Testament were shadows of things that were to *come* in the Church Age, *not* things to be done away with. Those things in the Old Testament were natural and earthly, but ours are spiritual and heavenly.

4. The temple found in Revelation is a temple built by the Jews. "Measure the temple of God, and the altar, and them that worship therein," John is commanded in Revelation 11:1. Whether or not this refers to a natural temple and to a natural people is another important point to consider. Those who believe that Revelation 4–19 deals with natural Israel declare that this temple is a natural temple also.

Referring again to Appendix B, where a clear parallel is established between Ezekiel and Revelation, we conclude that when both Ezekiel and John measure the temple with a "reed" or a "rod," we are seeing the same truth. The temple Ezekiel is measuring is not a temple that will be built by apostate, unbelieving Jews and the Antichrist, because in Ezekiel 43 the glory of the Lord fills that temple. His glory will never fill a false temple, but it *will* fill again the true New Testament Temple, His Church. His glory *will* return to the nation of Israel in the end, and all the Gentiles who are grafted into that nation will be visited by that glory also!

What if the Jews were to build another temple? This is something that could very well happen. Would their blood sacrifices be a sweet savor to the Lord? We noted earlier in this study that Paul himself offered blood sacrifices after the cross. So in themselves, there is nothing inherently wrong with sacrifices. However, we also noted that all men of faith offered those sacrifices knowing that only *the* Lamb of God could save them from their sins. They were either looking forward or backward to His coming and the cross. Paul warns the Galatians against keeping the law as a source of either salvation or perfection, saying that if they do so they have "fallen from grace."

The question becomes, "Why would the Jews offer those sacrifices?" They would do so because of their confidence in the spiritual efficacy of those sacrifices. They would feel that they are finally able to receive the cleansing for sins that they believe those sacrifices can bring them. One of the reasons that many Israelites rejected their Messiah in the beginning was that they didn't understand that He had to come the first time to suffer and die, not to reign. They didn't see any need for the death of a sinless *human* sacrifice to take their place, and in general they still don't today. If Israel believed, even today, that a human being had to die in their place to save them, half of their conflict regarding who Jesus was, and is, would be resolved.

It is one thing for Paul, or any of the other thousands of Jews in the early Church, to offer a blood sacrifice as a symbolic way of remembering what their Lamb had done for them, and to thank Him for His sacrifice. It was an entirely different matter for the unbelieving Jews to continue to do so, thinking that they were obtaining the favor of God through those outward works. In fact, if God were to accept blood sacrifices offered with that motivation and attitude, it would be an affront to the shed blood of His own Son, who offered the *only* sacrifice that gives the answer for sins.

Finally, an unregenerate Jew is no different than an unregenerate Gentile. They are both sinners. According to Proverbs 15:8, "The sacrifice of the wicked is an abomination to the Lord: but the prayer of the upright is his delight." So regardless of how a sacrifice is offered to God, or with what sincerity or great desire for blessing, if it is offered by a sinner it is not acceptable and is, in fact, an abomination. Does not the sacrifice of Cain give us this same message, the very first story recorded for us after the fall of man? In conclusion, God would never call a physical temple that was built by unregenerate Jews who were trusting in their own works to save them, "the temple of God." The temple found in Revelation is repeatedly referred to as His temple (Rev. 3:12; 7:15; 11:1,19).

Where is the "temple of God" located? Some say that His temple, mentioned in Revelation 11:1, is a physical temple located in natural Jerusalem. There are at least two serious scriptural problems with this idea. First, at the end of this same chapter of Revelation, and in the context of the very same vision that John is receiving, he refers to this temple again and says that it is in Heaven! (Rev. 11:19) Some would counter that John must be speaking about two different temples in the same vision, because Revelation 11:2 says this temple is in the "holy city." Isn't that the city of Jerusalem? The truth is, if we stay within the context of Revelation itself, the answer to this doubt is actually further confirmation that this temple is not an earthly temple. If, in the context of Revelation 11, the holy city is natural Jerusalem, why is natural Jerusalem called "Sodom" later on in this same chapter? Revelation 11:8 states that the city where the Lord was crucified (Jerusalem) is spiritual Sodom. No one would call Sodom a "holy city," at least not the Holy Spirit! We know that the Lord will restore natural Jerusalem to her former holiness when He comes, but that will not happen beforehand, and certainly not through the efforts of unbelieving Jews. Again, allowing Revelation to give us its own interpretation, we are told exactly what the "holy city" is in Revelation 21:2: "And I John saw **the holy city**, new Jerusalem, coming down from God out of heaven, **prepared as a bride** adorned for her husband." Therefore, the holy city is the Bride of Christ, the heavenly Jerusalem that we considered in Chapter 17.

In addition to the two references to the temple that appear in Revelation 11:1-2, the word "temple" appears in Revelation eleven other times.[3] In every one of those references it is unquestionably the Lord's heavenly temple, His eternal dwelling. In four of those references it is said to be the temple in Heaven. In three references, angels of God are seen coming out of that temple. In three other references it is said to be God's temple. If the temple that John is measuring in Revelation 11:1-2 is not the same temple that is mentioned in the other eleven references, we have a major problem with regard to the principles of scriptural interpretation. Suddenly context would mean nothing!

Why John and Ezekiel Measure the Temple

The Apostle John is commanded, "Measure the temple of God, and the altar, and *them that worship therein*" (Rev. 11:1). If this refers to a physical temple, and physical measurements, we must ask ourselves a question, "Is John going to measure the physical height of those worshipers in Revelation 11? Or is he going to measure their width?" Many of us certainly hope not, because in some cases our width is rapidly approaching our height! Obviously there would be no purpose in those measurements. However, our spiritual stature *will* be measured, to see how we measure up to "the stature of Christ" (Eph. 4:13). Since the measuring and the measurements are seen to be spiritual matters, we can be certain that the "temple" and "altar" found in Revelation 11 are also spiritual. The temple is a spiritual temple, the Church, and the altar is a spiritual, heavenly altar (Heb. 13:10). As living stones, we must be conformed to the required measurements to be a part of His eternal temple.

3. The thirteen references to "temple" in the book are found in Revelation 3:12; 7:15; 11:1,2,19; 14:15,17; 15:5,6,8; 16:1,17; 21:22.

John is measuring the same temple that Ezekiel measured, and he must be doing so for the same purpose—the Lord is giving us a message. God tells us what that purpose is in Ezekiel 43:10. "Thou son of man, **show the house to the house** of Israel, that they may be ashamed of their iniquities: and let them measure the pattern." God wants us to compare **His** house with **our** house, to see if our lives are being conformed to the measurements found in the pattern. We are being shown a spiritual temple, and the measurements obviously have a spiritual meaning. If our lives do not measure up, then we should be ashamed enough to do something about it. We should seek Him for grace to be conformed to His likeness. Otherwise we will not be included in His eternal temple.

So in reference to the doctrinal question of "Israel vs. the Church" in Revelation 4–19, our conclusion is that there is no difference between Israel and the Church. We must understand that Revelation was written *to* the Church and *for* the Church, just as Revelation 1:4 and 11 declare. In Revelation many references to things found in the Old Testament Israel are mentioned, because God continues to deal with Israel during the New Testament Age in accordance with the "parable" of the Old Testament Age.

5. If the Rapture Isn't in Revelation 4:1, Then Where is It? There is one final argument that I would like to lay to rest. Some say that if Revelation 4:1 isn't the Rapture, then the Rapture doesn't appear in Revelation at all. Possibly we are looking in the wrong place. Could it be that we are so conditioned to look for the Rapture at the beginning of the book that we haven't even considered the possibility it might come at the end of the book?

The Rapture is the event that will take us to the Marriage Supper of the Lamb. This is what happens when Christ comes to take His Bride to Himself, to be joined to her. If we believe this, we have no problem finding the Rapture in precisely the place it should appear, at the end of Revelation, after the Church has defeated Babylon in Revelation 18. Then, in Revelation 19:7-9 we find that she is taken to the Marriage Supper. "Let us be glad and rejoice, and give honour to him: for the **marriage of the Lamb is come**, and his wife hath made herself ready. And to her was granted that she should be *arrayed* in fine linen, clean and white...And he saith unto me, Write, Blessed are they which are called unto the marriage supper of the Lamb..." So at this time, after the defeat of all His enemies, and not before, we are told that the "marriage of the Lamb is come." Our heavenly Melchisedek, the everlasting High Priest, comes forth to meet us after the defeat of the kings of this world, and He serves us bread and wine at that Marriage Supper.

In the Rapture we will be "changed" as promised in First Corinthians 15:51-52: "This corruptible must put on incorruption." The Greek word "put on" means "to invest with clothing." At the Rapture we will be "invested with clothing." Let's compare this with Revelation 19:8 where we find a revelation of the Rapture. Speaking of Christ's Bride, we are told, "and to her was granted that she should be **arrayed** in fine linen." "Arrayed" comes from the Greek verb meaning "to be invested with clothing," exactly the same as the phrase "put on," used in reference to "putting on" incorruption.[4] So the Bride is going to be "invested with clothing" here, and Paul affirms that this will take place at the Rapture. This is what being clothed with linen clean and white represents.

A change of clothing also occurs in Zechariah 3:1-5 where the Lord takes away the filthy garments of Joshua and clothes him with a "change of raiment." He is clothed there with the garments of the priest, which were made of fine linen. Can there be any doubt about where the Rapture occurs in the Book of Revelation? It occurs when her filthy garments, which are "spotted by the flesh" (or the "corruption" of the flesh),[5] are taken away, and she is given the fine linen garments of her eternal priesthood, just in time for her wedding day.

4. See *Strong's Greek Dictionary*, #1746 and #4016.
5. Jude 1:23 says that our garments are "spotted by the flesh." Galatians 6:8 says that if we sow to the flesh we shall "reap corruption." So the "corruption" or filth of our garments is caused by the fleshly works, and sowing to the flesh. But this "corruption" is the same Greek word that Paul uses in First Corinthians 15:50-53 (*Strong's Greek Dictionary*, #5356); so Paul is saying that at the Rapture we will take off those spotted, corrupted garments, and put on fine linen.

Chapter 19

Pre-Tribulation Rapture?

It would not be fair to teachers or students of a pre-tribulation Rapture to conclude this subject without examining at least the strongest points that are used by some as evidence of the Rapture taking place before the Tribulation. In this book, all the statements used to support a pre-tribulation Rapture cannot be presented. However, we will try to briefly, yet sincerely, present in this chapter the very strongest reasoning that is used by those who support this doctrine.

First Thessalonians 5:9

God Has Not Appointed Us to Wrath

One of the supposed "proof texts" for a pre-tribulation Rapture is First Thessalonians 5:9, where we find, "For God hath not appointed us to wrath, but to obtain salvation by our Lord Jesus Christ." The argument in favor of a pre-tribulation Rapture is based on the assumption that the "wrath" referred to here is speaking of the Tribulation. We know that God's wrath will be manifested in the last days, according to Revelation 15:1. But we also know that hell is an even greater manifestation of God's wrath against ungodliness. What, then, is this verse saying?

In First Thessalonians 5:9, Paul presents mankind with two options: obtain salvation or face wrath. But if the "wrath" mentioned here is referring to the wrath of the Tribulation, then in light of the two clear options presented here, a question arises. "Is it logical to say that if a person does not obtain salvation, he will face the other option presented in this verse, which is the Tribulation?" If the "wrath" mentioned here is referring to the

Tribulation, then every person in history who did not obtain salvation must return to earth to face the Tribulation, because this verse gives us those two options—salvation or wrath. We know that this idea is not logical, so we must conclude that "wrath" here is something other than the Tribulation. What could "wrath" be referring to here?

The subject of "wrath" appears three times in First Thessalonians (using the same Greek word). In this epistle Paul is writing to Believers who lived almost 2,000 years ago. In chapter 1, verses 9 and 10, he tells them that they had turned from idols to serve the living God and "to wait for his Son from heaven, whom he raised from the dead, even Jesus, which delivered us from the wrath to come." Obviously those Believers were not delivered from the Great Tribulation, but rather from hell itself, God's eternal wrath.

Then in First Thessalonians 2:15-16 Paul again refers to "wrath" in this epistle. He is speaking there about the very same Jews who had crucified Jesus, and who were persecuting Paul also at that time. Concerning them, he said they were "forbidding us to speak to the Gentiles that they might be saved, to fill up their sins alway: for the wrath is come upon them to the uttermost." Obviously the Great Tribulation did not come upon those Jews, and never will, but the fire of hell most certainly did. So once again the context and thought of "wrath" in First Thessalonians is hell, or God's eternal wrath.

Therefore, since the first two references to "wrath" in this epistle are obviously speaking about hell, or God's eternal wrath, then we certainly cannot ignore that context and dogmatically say that the "wrath" in the third and last reference is speaking about the Great Tribulation. We could do that only if there were a clear change of context that would let us know that "wrath" is now referring to the Tribulation. However, far from that being the case, we see that the two options presented by First Thessalonians 5:9 make it clear that Paul continues to speak about the eternal wrath of hell. Man has two options presented to him there, and throughout the Bible. He must either accept the free gift of salvation or face the wrath of God in hell forever.

Titus 2:13

The Blessed Hope and Glorious Appearing

Titus 2:13 tells us that as Believers we are "looking for that blessed hope, and the glorious appearing of the great God and our Saviour Jesus Christ." Some have said that His appearing couldn't possibly be a "blessed hope" if the Church has to pass through the Tribulation first. This mentality is pretty much identical with that of the people of God who lived in Moses' day. They were thrilled with the blessed hope and promise of entering the land that flowed with milk and honey. But when they realized that there was a great and terrible wilderness between where they were and the land of promise, they rebelled against God and Moses and wanted to return to Egypt, which represents the world.

As I have already mentioned, this is exactly what some Believers will do in the last days when they find themselves in the midst of a great and terrible wilderness experience. We have also seen one reason why many believe that only blessing awaits us, and that there is no "wilderness" that must be experienced before arriving at *our* goal. It is because we belong to the Laodicean Church, which does not see its desperate spiritual need. Unfortunately, many in this Church do not see any need for passing through a wilderness first, where the old generation is dealt with (that is, our old man, or old nature).

Deuteronomy 8:16 explains very clearly why God allowed Israel to pass through that difficult time, and why He would allow His Church to pass through a Tribulation in the end. In this reference Moses is speaking to Israel about their God, "Who fed thee in the wilderness with manna, which thy fathers knew not, that he might humble thee, and that he might prove thee, **to do thee good at thy latter end**." Paul informs us that this wilderness journey is an example ("mold" or "type") for God's people living in the last days (1 Cor. 10:11). Therefore, there *will* be a fiery wilderness trial for all the Church and world, as Peter also confirms: "Beloved, think it not strange concerning the fiery trial which is to try you, as though some strange thing happened unto you" (1 Pet. 4:12).

God is willing to allow us to suffer for a time with the goal of giving us everlasting blessing and comfort. In no way is this contrary to His nature, even though it is almost always contrary to ours. This is actually the attitude that exists in the heart of any true father. He is willing to see his child pass through unpleasant circumstances if, in the end, the child will have what is best. But rarely, if ever, does the child agree with the father's assessment of the situation, or the wisdom of his actions.

Luke 21:36

Watch That Ye May Be Accounted Worthy

Many use this as a proof text also of a pre-tribulation Rapture. Jesus says, "Watch ye therefore, and pray always, that ye may be accounted worthy to escape all these things that shall come to pass, and to stand before the Son of man." We fully agree that the context here is undoubtedly dealing with the last days. However, the fact that a person is permitted to "escape all these things" is no proof that the person must be in Heaven to do so. This is where speculation has entered the interpretation. Noah, a clear revelation of the last days according to Christ's teaching, escaped. He was "saved thoroughly"[1] even though he remained on earth throughout the entire time of judgment. In fact, in this very same chapter of Luke (v. 16-19), Christ promises us great trials, but He also promises us that in the very midst of them, "there shall not an hair of your head perish." This is certainly "escaping," without being removed.

One of the ways in which God will glorify Himself in the end is seen by what He did in the beginning. When the plagues fell on Egypt, Israel was kept by the power of God. When the Egyptians saw that they were being judged, and at the same time the people of God were being protected, they knew, without a doubt, who was in complete control of those plagues—Jehovah, the God of the Hebrews. If the same thing doesn't happen in the last days, then the world will never know for sure that the judgments that are falling proceed from God, and that they are completely under the control of the God of the Church.

God Would Never Allow His Wife to Suffer

This is an often heard declaration, although it is frequently stated in a more emotional way, "The Lord is not coming back for a battered wife!" Paul tells us that the woman referred to in Isaiah 54:1 is the heavenly Jerusalem, "the mother of us all" (Gal. 4:26). From Revelation 21:2 we know that the heavenly Jerusalem is the Bride of Christ. As we read a little further in Isaiah 54 we discover a few other details concerning what will happen to that woman in the last days. The context makes it clear that He is speaking there about His wife, the Church, because verse 5 declares, "For thy Maker is thine husband." Then in verse 7 He says to her, "For a small moment have I forsaken thee; but with great mercies will I gather thee."

In case we haven't understood to what time in history this passage refers, He explains in verse 9: "For this is as the waters of Noah unto me: for as I have sworn that the waters of Noah should no more go over the earth; so have I sworn that I would not be wroth with thee, nor rebuke thee." Since Christ taught that the last days will be like the days of Noah, the context is clear. Isaiah is speaking about that difficult journey through the wilderness that awaits the people of God in the end.

---

1. This is the meaning of the Greek word used to refer to Noah's salvation in First Peter 3:20. See *Strong's Greek Dictionary*, #1295.

Once again, the root problem with the concept that the Lord would never forsake His wife is found in the attitude of the Laodicean Church, which fills the hearts of many Believers today. If we could only see that we are dressed in filthy rags instead of wedding garments, we would understand that the Lord will have to do something to awaken and prepare the wife He loves so much. The days that are upon us will indeed accomplish that purpose.

PART III

Another Look At Daniel's Seventy Weeks

Introduction

The prophetic message found in the Seventy Weeks of Daniel is one of the most glorious and precise revelations God ever gave to man. It contains the keys to determining the year of both the First and Second Comings of the Lord. Many interpretations of this prophecy exist today. Most of them reveal a measure of truth and give insights for that passage. For that reason, I am not belittling, or rejecting all the study, searching, and toil invested by those who have gone before us. In fact, much of what they have shared is included here. Nor am I claiming that this fresh insight or look is an exhaustive study, or a complete understanding of the subject. However, some of the details of the traditional interpretations of this passage have no basis in Scripture or history. Therefore, what I *am* claiming here is that the additional insights presented in the following chapters satisfy all the biblical and historical evidence.

Chapter 20

Sir Isaac Newton and Daniel's Seventy Weeks

I am presenting Sir Isaac Newton's interpretation of Daniel's most studied prophecy, the Seventy Weeks, before I present what I believe the Lord has shown me on this subject. I do so because it confirms, in a wonderful way, the revelation God has given me, and also, I believe that it is fitting to honor a man who loved the truth in the way Sir Isaac Newton did.

Just recently I was given a republished volume of Newton's book, *Observations Upon the Prophecies of Daniel,* which is a photocopy of Thomas Jefferson's original, personal copy, still available in the Library of Congress, Washington, D.C.[1] I was first made aware of this book three years after publishing the first edition of *The Final Victory: The Year 2000.* My wife and I were overwhelmed, and at the same time greatly humbled, to discover that this amazing scientist had interpreted the key aspects of Daniel's Seventy Weeks in the same way that we shared in our book. But his revelation came almost three hundred years before most of us were born! It does not seem to be a coincidence that, although his message was first published centuries ago, the republished volume was printed in the same month and year that our book was first published: September of 1991. This made us realize once again that the Lord is faithful to confirm His Word in the mouths of two or three witnesses.

---

1. Reprinted as *Newton's Prophecies of Daniel* by the Oregon Institute of Science and Medicine, 2251 Dick George Road, Cave Junction, Oregon 97523, September, 1991. The quotes we include here are from pages 128 to 137.

Concerning Newton's translation of the Seventy Weeks from the original Hebrew to English, there were few men in history that were more qualified to make such a translation. Not only was Sir Isaac Newton a great scientist with a keen mind, but he was also a whole-hearted Believer who was well-versed in the Hebrew language. His great wisdom in analyzing the world around him is well-known. Because of his scientific laws, the discovery of calculus, and his numerous inventions, he is recognized as the father of both the scientific and industrial revolutions. In fact, it has been said that he was the last scientist in history that knew everything that there was to know in the realm of science. It was through his discoveries that the doors were opened for much greater advancements in science. Most important of all, he knew and loved the Messiah. Just maybe God was using him also to deliver a message to the Body of Christ, and bring glory to His name. I wonder how many have actually listened to what he has shared during the last three hundred years?

Therefore, in honor of a man of his stature, I want to quote a few of the declarations that Sir Isaac Newton made regarding Daniel's prophecy. I am quoting only his declarations that are related to the message of this book, and I highlighted certain key statements that will interest us later. What is probably most awesome to me regarding his understanding of Daniel's Seventy Weeks is that he correctly predicted the restoration of the nation of Israel in the last days, and then, based on that future event, also predicted the year of Christ's Second Coming—three hundred years ago! In his day, to even predict that Israel would some day be a nation again surely inspired ridicule. To then predict the year of Christ's Second Coming, based on Israel's supposed restoration, must have seemed even more ludicrous to many of the Believers of that day. Maybe this is one reason his book has been ignored by the Church for so many years. However, Israel has been restored, and the first part of Newton's interpretation has proven to be correct! I believe that the second part will also be confirmed very soon. Therefore, based on Israel's restoration in this century, we *can* now know the year of Christ's Second Coming. Although we have more precise historical dates with which to work than were available to Newton (because of extensive archaeological work that had not been done yet in his day), that does not affect the most important aspects of the interpretation of this prophecy. In other words, his calculation, as well as ours, of the year of Christ's Second Coming is based on recent events in history that now have precise dates.

Note: Because of the English of Newton's day, you may find that a few of his statements are difficult to understand. There is no need for concern, because we will consider each detail in later chapters.

Newton's Interpretation of Daniel's Seventy Weeks

"**This prophecy of the Messiah...relates to both comings, and assigns the times thereof.** This prophecy, like all the rest of Daniel's, consists of two parts, an introductory Prophecy and an explanation thereof. The whole I thus translate and interpret.

> *Seventy weeks are cut out upon thy people, and upon thy holy city, to finish transgression, and to make an end of sins, to expiate iniquity, and to bring in everlasting righteousness, to consummate the Vision and the Prophet, and to anoint the most Holy.*
>
> *Know also and understand, that from the going forth of the commandment to cause to return and to build Jerusalem, unto the Anointed the Prince, shall be seven weeks.*
>
> *Yet threescore and two weeks shall it return, and the street be built and the wall; but in troublous times: and after the threescore and two weeks, the Anointed shall be cut off, and it shall not be his; but the people of the Prince to come shall destroy the city and the sanctuary: and the end thereof shall be with a flood, and unto the end of the war desolations are determined.*
>
> *Yet shall he confirm the covenant with many for one week: and in half a week he shall cause the sacrifice and oblation to cease: and upon a wing of abominations he shall make it desolate, even until the consummation, and that which is determined be poured upon the desolate.*

Now the dispersed Jews became a **people and city** when they first returned into a polity or body politick...

Know also and understand, that from the going forth of the commandment to cause to return and to build Jerusalem, unto the Anointed the Prince, shall be seven weeks. The former part of the Prophecy related to the first coming of Christ, being dated to his coming as a Prophet; **this being dated to his coming to be Prince or King, seems to relate to his second coming.** There, the Prophet was consummate, and the most holy anointed: here, he that was anointed comes to be Prince and to reign. **For Daniel's Prophecies reach to the end of the world**; and there is scarce a Prophecy in the Old Testament concerning Christ, which doth not in something or other relate to his second coming...

The Israelites in the days of the ancient Prophets, when the ten Tribes were led into captivity, expected a double return; and that at the first the Jews should build a new temple inferior to Solomon's, until the time of that age should be fulfilled; and afterwards they should return from all places of their captivity, and build Jerusalem and the temple gloriously, Tobit 14:4,5,6: and to express the glory and excellence of this city, it is figuratively said to be built of precious stones, Tobit 13:16,17,18; Isa. 54:11,12; Rev. 11, and called the New Jerusalem, the Heavenly Jerusalem, the Holy City, the Lamb's wife, the City of the Great King, the City into which the Kings of the earth do bring their glory and honor. **Now while such a return from captivity was the expectation of Israel, even before the times of Daniel, I know not why Daniel should omit it in his Prophecy.** This part of the Prophecy being therefore not yet fulfilled, I shall not attempt a particular interpretation of it, but content myself with observing, that as **the seventy and the sixty two weeks were Jewish weeks**, ending with sabbatical years; so the seven weeks are the compass of a Jubilee, and begin and end with actions proper for a Jubilee, and of the highest nature for which a Jubilee can be kept: and that **since the commandment to return and to build Jerusalem, precedes the Messiah the Prince 49 years; it may perhaps come forth not from the Jews themselves, but from some other kingdom friendly to them, and precede their return from captivity**, and give occasion to it; and lastly, that this rebuilding of Jerusalem and the waste places of Judah is predicted in Micah 7:11; Amos 9:11,14; Ezek. 36:33,35,36,38; Isa. 54:3,11,12; 55:12; 61:4; 65:18,21,22; and Tobit 14:5, and that the return from captivity and coming of the Messiah and his kingdom are described in Daniel 7; Rev. 19; Acts 1; Mt. 24; Joel 3; Ezek. 36, 37; Isa. 60,62,63,65, and 66, and many other places of Scripture. The manner I know not. **Let time be the Interpreter.**

Yet threescore and two weeks shall it return, and the street be built and the wall; but in troublous times: and after the threescore and two weeks, the Anointed shall be cut off, and it shall not be his; but the people of the Prince to come shall destroy the city and the sanctuary, etc. **Having foretold both comings of Christ, and dated the last from their returning and building Jerusalem;** to prevent the applying that to the building Jerusalem by Nehemiah, **he distinguishes this from that, by saying that from this period to the Anointed shall be, not seven weeks, but threescore and two weeks, and this not in prosperous but in troublesome times; and at the end of these weeks the Messiah shall not be the Prince of the Jews, but be cut off;** and Jerusalem not be his, but the city and sanctuary be destroyed. Now Nehemiah came to Jerusalem in the 20th year of this same Artaxerxes, while Ezra still continued there, Neh. 12:3,6, and found the city lying waste, and the houses and wall unbuilt, Neh. 2:17; 7:4, and finished the wall the 25th day of the month Elul, Neh. 6:15, in the 28th year of the King, that is, in September in the year of the Julian Period 4278. **Count now from this year threescore and two weeks of years, that is 434 years, and the**

reckoning will end in September in the year of the Julian Period 4712 which is the year in which Christ was born...

Thus have we in this short prophecy, a prediction of all the main periods relating to the coming of the Messiah; the time of his birth...and the time of his second coming: and so the interpretation here given is more full and complete and adequate to the design, than if we should restrain it to his first coming only, as Interpreters usually do. **We avoid also the doing violence to the language of Daniel, by taking the seven weeks and sixty two weeks for one number. Had that been Daniel's meaning, he would have said sixty and nine weeks, and not seven weeks and sixty two weeks, a way of numbering used by no nation.** In our way **the years are Jewish Luni-solar years, as they ought to be; and the seventy weeks of years are Jewish weeks ending with sabbatical years, which is very remarkable**...Others either count by Lunar years, or by weeks not Judaic: and, which is worst (sic), they ground their interpretations on erroneous chronology..."

Chapter 21

Any Moment?

"Six million? Did we hear you say six million?" the people of the world asked incredulously. "That's right. We now have confirmed reports that six million Jews were slaughtered by Nazi Germany during the war," responded the leaders of the allied forces who conquered Germany. The entire world was in shock. Undoubtedly, this was one of the worst atrocities committed by human beings in the history of this planet, that is, until abortion became an international institution. It was so despicable that the conscience of humanity could not rest until the Jews had a homeland once again. This was one of the dearest prices ever paid for a homeland—the lives of six million Jews killed by Nazi Germany.

From the very beginning God's plan was to restore the nation of Israel to the Promised Land. God's Word declares that He would gather them from the nations of the earth and restore them as a people. Isaiah 11:11 says, "And it shall come to pass in that day, that the Lord shall set his hand again the second time to recover the remnant of his people, which shall be left, from Assyria, and from Egypt...and from the islands of the sea." We are witnesses of this gathering today, as even hardened Russia has been forced by the Lord to open her doors for the exodus of the Jews. His plan has always been to restore Israel before the Rapture and His return. We know this for two reasons: (1) the Bible reveals it in Isaiah and other places[1] and (2) it has already happened.

---

1. Isaac Newton included many Scriptures that show this. See the last chapter. Furthermore, Acts 3:21 tells us that Christ will remain in Heaven until the "restoration" (NKJV) of everything that the prophets said would be restored. Among the things that will be restored, according to the prophets, is the nation of

Let's take an imaginary trip back in time to A.D. 1945. The world has just learned of the terrible things that happened to the Jews in Europe. However, as Believers living in that day, we know what the Bible says. Like Sir Isaac Newton knew three hundred years ago, we also know that God has promised to restore Israel to the Promised Land, before the Rapture and the Second Coming. However, we are living two years prior to the beginning of that restoration.[2] The question arises, "As Believers living before the beginning of that restoration, can we accept a doctrine that says the Rapture can take place at any moment?" Any attempt to join the truth of Israel's restoration with the concept of a Rapture at any moment would have proven futile to the understanding Believers of that day. Those two ideas were completely incompatible.

There is another question that we should ask ourselves today. Is it possible that there are other things that the Lord has promised to do before the Rapture of the Church? If we are aware of anything that has not yet been fulfilled, we have two options. First of all, we can continue believing that Jesus could come at any moment, and that possibly some of the things He has promised will simply not be fulfilled. Or second, if we see Him as the One who always fulfills every jot and tittle of His Word, we must say that Jesus cannot come today for His Church.[3]

Certainly many would say that to deprive Believers of the doctrine of an imminent return of Christ[4] would not only be heresy, but it would also do much damage to their walk and fervency. According to Christ's evaluation of the lukewarm Laodicean Church of the last days, Believers don't have much real fervency anyway. Furthermore, if this doctrine is *not* true, it will produce a harvest of bad fruit in lives, as is the case with any false doctrine.

An imminent return of Christ was not the apostles' doctrine. They taught that the return of Christ was not near at hand. Consider Peter's

---

Israel (Isa. 1:26; 11:11; 49:6; Hos. 6:1-2). Finally, Jesus said that before He comes, Elijah will come and "restore all things" (Mt. 17:11). Again, the nation of Israel is one of those "things." Zechariah 12–14 tells us that when He comes He will fight for Israel, which will be under attack by the nations of the earth. This could happen only if the nation was restored before His coming. Therefore, a restoration of Israel before the last days is clearly revealed in the Bible.

2. In this example we are living in 1945, and the restoration of Israel began after the United Nations decree, given on November 29, 1947.
3. Of course, we must always be aware of the fact that Christ could come for us personally at any moment; therefore, we must always be ready. This we should preach and teach effectively!
4. The phrase "imminent return of Christ"refers to the doctrine that says Jesus could return, and that we could be raptured, at any moment.

ideas on this subject. He received many wonderful promises from the Lord regarding his ministry to the early Church. However, in John 21:18 the Lord told him that in his youth he did a lot of things on his own.[5] Jesus told him, "But when thou shalt be old, thou shalt stretch forth thy hands, and another shall gird thee..." Thus Jesus declared that Peter would grow old. (Fortunately, growing old requires a few **years**, although not nearly as many as most of us would like.) And then, immediately after this, Jesus revealed to Peter "by what **death** he should glorify God."

So Peter knew that he would spend many years on earth, ministering in the early Church, and that afterwards, when he had grown old, he would die. In Second Peter 1:14, many years later, when he was now old, Peter said, "Knowing that shortly I must put off this my tabernacle, even as our Lord Jesus Christ hath showed me. Moreover I will endeavour that ye may be able after my decease to have these things always in remembrance." So here he was, knowing that he would soon die. During all those years he knew he would die rather than be raptured. Therefore, he did not preach an imminent return of Christ (that Christ could come and rapture the Church at any moment). And anyone who knew Jesus' words to Peter also knew that the Rapture could not take place as long as Peter was alive!

Peter showed that the Lord's coming was not going to happen soon. In Second Peter 3:3-4 he said, "Knowing this first, that there shall come in the last days scoffers, walking after their own lusts, and saying, Where is the promise of his coming? For since the fathers fell asleep, all things continue as they were..." Note that Peter was a Church father, and he had just said he was going to "sleep," or die. Furthermore, he said, "**There shall come...**" He didn't say that he was living in the last days already, nor that these scoffers had already come. So in Peter's writings, we do not see an imminent return of Christ; rather, we see just the opposite.

What did Paul teach regarding this matter? In Second Thessalonians 2:1 he said, "Now we beseech you, brethren, by the coming of our Lord Jesus Christ, and by our gathering together unto him..." The context is the Second Coming and our **gathering together** unto Him, or the Rapture.[6]

Paul then went on to say that the day of the Lord was not at hand (v. 2) and also, "Let no man deceive you by any means: for that day shall not

---

5. This is precisely what Peter was doing in the context of this passage. The chapter begins with Peter saying, "I'm going fishing!" He spent the night fishing, all to no avail.
6. The "gathering together" unto Him occurs at the Rapture, as seen in First Thessalonians 4:16-17 and Ephesians 1:9-10.

come, except there come a falling away first, and **that man of sin be revealed**, the son of perdition; who opposeth and exalteth himself above all that is called God...so that he as God sitteth in the temple of God" (v. 3-4). Neither Christ's coming, nor "our gathering together unto him" can take place until the one who falsely claims to be God, and who sits in the temple of God, has been revealed. At this present moment the Church does not know who the Antichrist is, so the day of "our gathering together unto him...shall not come" yet. The Rapture cannot take place today!

Paul's purpose in Second Thessalonians was, in part, to correct the false doctrine of an imminent return of Christ. Doctrinal errors are not easily corrected, so it persists in the Church to this very day.

Like Peter, Paul knew he was going to die before the Rapture (2 Tim. 4:6). His goal was to participate in the Resurrection (Phil. 3:10-11). No one can participate in the Resurrection unless he has first died. So Paul could not declare that he was going to die, and at the same time teach that the Rapture could take place at any moment.

We know that Peter and Paul's doctrine was consistent, but sometimes our own is not. For example, we preach a great end-time outpouring and harvest, but in the next breath we declare that the Rapture can be at any moment.

A few years ago I was in a meeting where the speaker was a well-known television evangelist. He was sharing with a small group of leaders whom he had invited to a special luncheon. He stirred our hearts for forty-five minutes with Bible passages that declare emphatically that the Church will experience a mighty harvest in the last days. At the end of his very sound scriptural message, he said, "And we know that all of this will take place, if Jesus doesn't come first!" He could plainly see that God's Word promises a mighty visitation, but he did not want to give up his doctrine of an imminent return of Christ.

God is very thorough; He will fulfill every jot and tittle of His Word. Until all is fulfilled, including the end-time harvest, as well as the revelation of the Antichrist, the Rapture will not take place. There will definitely be a great harvest of souls from every part of the earth during the Great Tribulation, as Revelation 7:9-14 clearly reveals.

Chapter 22

Can We Know?

"Newsflash! We break into our regular programming to inform our viewers of a startling development that occurred at 4:25 p.m. today. Millions of people around the world suddenly disappeared into thin air! Some experts on religion claim that this may be what Believers have called 'The Rapture'. Early indications are that indeed only those who claim the Christian faith are missing. Investigators say that people are missing from every city, town, village, and hamlet on the face of the globe. Many relatives are in shock, saying no warnings or explanations were given. We will keep you informed..." Is this how it will happen? Undoubtedly, the Rapture will come as a surprise to the world, but will it come as a surprise to God's people also? Or will we know the time of His coming?

Setting the year for when the Rapture will occur, besides other, more severe reactions, generally evokes the comment, "He will come as a thief in the night." This concept comes from First Thessalonians 5:2. However, if we continue to read that chapter, we will get the whole message and find that Paul declares, "But ye, brethren, are not in darkness, that that day should overtake *you* as a thief. Ye are all the children of light, and the children of the day: we are not of the night, nor of darkness" (1 Thess. 5:4-5). Therefore, when the Lord comes, He will not come upon the Church as a thief in the night, nor by surprise, because the Church does not live in the "night."

In an attempt to prove that we can't know the approximate time of the Rapture, some quote what has become a proof-text, foundational stone for end-time doctrine, and even a doctrinal hobby horse. Most of us know that it is heretical to base an entire doctrine on one verse, yet unfortunately we have probably all been guilty of doing so at one time or another. The proof-text is Matthew 24:36: "But of that day and hour knoweth no man, no, not the angels of heaven, but my Father only." Does this verse indicate we cannot know the time of the Rapture? Consider the possibility that the Lord's reference to our inability to know "the day or the hour" does *not* refer to the Rapture as is commonly believed, but rather to His Second Coming. To see that this is the case, please read Matthew 24:36-37 where He clearly reveals that His coming (that is, the Second Coming) will be similar to Noah's day, and it is the day and hour of that event of which we have no knowledge. This theme of the Second Coming is then reiterated six more times in verses 39, 42, 44, 46, 48, and 50.

It is an amazing thing that many have totally ignored the context of this part of Matthew 24 by applying it to the Rapture and Marriage Supper of the Church! By so doing, it is then commonly taught that the concept of a "surprise Rapture" is confirmed by the words of Christ here, because He says that two will be in the field and one will be suddenly taken and the other left behind (Mt. 24:40). Again, we need to carefully consider the context of this thought as well, and decide whether or not we would want to be "taken" if we were to find ourselves in the field on that day. Notice that He tells us His coming will be a repeat of what happened in the days of Noah when the flood came and "*took* them all away" (Mt. 24:37-39). Remember that His Coming occurs after the Rapture and Marriage Supper. The Lord goes on to say that "then (at the time of His coming), two will be in the field and one will be *taken* and the other left" (Mt. 24:40). Just as the flood came and "*took*" them away, so some will be "*taken*" away. In that context I think I would just as soon be "left" if I were still on earth at that time!

If you still have doubts about whether or not you would rather be taken away or left, don't worry, because the disciples weren't sure themselves about which would be better. Therefore, in Luke 17:26-37, in the same context of His coming, Noah's day, and two being in the field, the disciples asked Him to where they would be "taken." In the Greek His response was, "Where there is a dead body, there the vultures will gather" (NIV). We find many dead bodies, and vultures being gathered to eat them, in Revelation 19:17-18, at the Second Coming of the Lord. This is *after* the Marriage Supper, found in Revelation 19:7-9, and at the time of His *coming* to establish His physical Kingdom on the earth. This whole concept of removing the wicked from His Kingdom at the time of His Coming was explained to us by the Lord in Matthew 13:24-43. When He comes He will first gather out of His Kingdom all those who offend and do iniquity and cast them into the fire, but the righteous will receive blessing.

Some may ask, "Who then would be the ones 'left' to live on earth when He comes, if all the wicked are taken away at the time of His Coming, and all the righteous have already gone in the Rapture that takes place *before* His Coming?" Jesus anticipated that question, and immediately gave the answer in Matthew 25:1-13. He explains that the Kingdom of Heaven is like ten virgins. We must understand that *all* these virgins represent those who are part of the Kingdom, since the Kingdom is likened to all ten. Even though all are part of the Kingdom, yet some are wise and some are foolish. They are all doing exactly the same things, and they are all waiting for the wedding. Unfortunately, the foolish virgins do not have enough oil in their lamps when the call to the wedding goes forth, and they discover that it requires time to get that oil, time they no longer have. The oil speaks of His presence or anointing. They didn't pay the price for that oil soon enough. Therefore, while they are now taking the time to pay the price, the others go to the wedding, and the door is shut. When they seek to be included the Lord makes it clear that it is too late and concludes by saying, "Watch therefore, for ye know neither the day nor the hour wherein the Son of man *cometh*." Note that He is speaking again about His "Coming," and His Coming occurs *after* the Rapture and the call to the Marriage Supper.

In this context of the foolish virgins, the Lord gives an exhortation to "watch" (Mt. 25:13). Some believe that the Lord is directing this exhortation toward all Believers who are waiting for the Rapture rather than the Second Coming. However, this doubt is clarified in Luke 12:35-36 where He gives the same counsel: "Let your loins be girded about, and your lights burning; And ye yourselves like unto men that wait for their lord, **when he will return from the wedding**; that when he **cometh** and knocketh, they may open unto him immediately. Blessed are those servants, whom the lord when he **cometh** shall find watching." The only time that He will "come" after the wedding is during the Second Coming. Here He exhorts these people to be sure that their lights are burning. The problem with the foolish virgins was that their lights were going out, and for that reason they did not participate in the wedding. Therefore, they had no other option than to do what these are doing here—wait for their Lord to **return from the wedding**. They must wait for His return or Coming *after* the Rapture and wedding, and obviously could not have been at the wedding themselves.

Jesus is showing us that the Kingdom has within it some "foolish virgins" who will not be ready for the wedding because of a lack of oil. They *will* have their lights burning, however, when He *returns* from the wedding. They will then be "left" when all the others are "taken away" in the flood of judgment that will come upon the earth at the time of His Coming, just as happened in the days of Noah. We conclude, then, that to base the doctrine of a surprise Rapture on the verse about "two people being in the field and one being taken" is to ignore the context of that verse (Mt. 24:40), and to ignore other Scriptures as well.

Furthermore, we must be careful not to add to the Word of God. Even if we believe that Jesus was referring to the Rapture when He said that no one can know the day or hour, yet He says nothing about not being able to know the week, month, year, decade, century, or millennium. The One who *is* the Truth always speaks precisely the truth! If the Lord had meant to say that no one knows the "hour, day, month, or year," then He would have said precisely that, just as He does in Revelation 9:15 when He revealed that "four angels were loosed, which were prepared for an hour, and a day, and a month, and a year, for to slay the third part of men." In reality, there was no way for the Scriptures to be written to the whole earth and at the same time reveal the day or the hour of His return, because at the moment He returns twenty-four different hours will exist in the different time zones of the earth. Also, at any given moment, two different days are in progress on earth. When it is January 3 on one side of the international date line, it is January 4 on the other side. So Scripture can never reveal the day or the hour of His return, but to make this verse say more than it says is mishandling the Word of God.

A greater issue here is that believing we can't have any idea of the time of His coming actually contradicts other Scriptures. First Thessalonians 5:4-6 is one example. There Paul says that Christ will not come to us as a thief in the night. Also Amos 3:7 declares He does *nothing* without first revealing His secret to His servants. In Matthew 16:1-3 Jesus tells the Pharisees that they can discern the signs in the skies, but not the signs of the times because of their hypocrisy. Hypocrisy was not a unique trait found only in that little group of Sadducees and Pharisees who crucified the Lord. If we really knew the time of His coming, we could not continue to live as though He weren't coming for another thousand years, as many do. For with the knowledge of the times, there would come an urgency to make an unconditional surrender to the Lamb of Calvary, an urgency to live our lives in the light of His soon return. Our consciences wouldn't allow us to continue playing church and pretending to be spiritual when we aren't. Thus, many prefer to hide behind the excuse that we can't possibly know. That way it is a lot easier to sleep at night, though continuing to live like the world! How we need the Spirit and power of Elijah to again prepare the way of His coming—the Spirit of repentance that will cause us to so yearn for His appearing that we will cry with all our hearts, "Even so, Lord Jesus, come!"

Five hundred years before the First Coming of Christ, Daniel received the key to knowing the year of His First Coming, and also the year of His Second Coming. For the people of the Old Testament Age to know the year of His First Coming was as awesome as it would be for us to know the year of His Second Coming. Some *did* know beforehand when their Messiah would come. Joseph, Mary, Simeon, Anna, and other men and women of faith knew the time of His coming.

Again, Amos 3:7 tells us that He will do *nothing* without first revealing His secret to His servants. The Rapture and Marriage are two of the most important events in the Word of God, events the Lord longs for and awaits with patience (Jas. 5:7). As any true lover, He longs for the day of His marriage. How could God, who says He will do nothing without revealing it first, do one of the most important things in history without revealing it to His servants, or to His Bride?

Some may quote Acts 1:7 as proof that we cannot know the approximate timing of the Rapture. Christ's disciples asked Him if He was going to restore the Kingdom to Israel at that time, and His answer in verse 7 was, "It is not for you to know the times or the seasons..." Does this mean we can never know? In the context of the coming of the Lord, Paul tells us in First Thessalonians 5:1-5 that we do know the times and seasons and that He will not come to us as a thief in the night. Is there a contradiction here? The answer is no.

A principle of Bible interpretation is that we must know to whom a thing was said, and under what circumstances. We cannot simply take any verse of the Bible and apply it to ourselves without considering first whether or not it was directed to one specific human being, or to only one group of people, or possibly to only a certain period in history. For example, under the Age of the Law an adulterer had to be stoned with no possibility of obtaining mercy (Heb. 10:28). In the Age of Grace the adulterer can now be forgiven through Christ's atonement. Another example is the promise of "latter rain." According to Acts 2:17 and James 5:7 that promise is for the "last days." It was not given to the early Church. They had the former rain. Furthermore, the Book of Daniel was sealed until the last days, and today we are living in the last days, but the early Church was not. Therefore, the early Church could not receive the blessing of understanding the details concerning the last days as is possible for the Church of today. We conclude, therefore, that just because the early Church could not receive the latter rain, nor understand when it would come, does not say that we cannot. Nor does the Lord's refusal to give them understanding in this area invalidate the promise of Amos that He will do nothing without first revealing His secret. The early Church did not need to know the time when the Kingdom would come, because it wasn't near, but He will show this secret to the last-day Church before it takes place. We should know the times and seasons. Consider this scriptural prayer: "Lord, make me to know my end, And what is the measure of my days" (Psa 39:4 NKJV). The Lord wants us to pray biblical prayers, and He will surely answer them. Many men of faith knew when their end would come, and the Lord wants us to know also. (Examples are Jacob, Elijah, Moses, Paul, Peter, etc.) If we believe that Jesus is coming during our lifetime, then this prayer can only be answered if we know when He is going to return.

Finally, we have already considered the scriptural evidence that the Church will be on earth during the Great Tribulation. Since the Church will be here during the reign of the Antichrist, and since the Bible tells us that his reign will last forty-two months (Rev. 13:5), knowing the year and even the season of the Rapture will be a simple matter. Once the Antichrist is revealed, we will know that the Rapture will take place forty-two months later. If Christ's statement that "no one knows the day and the hour" really means that we can't even know the year and the season, then His declaration will prove to be untrue once the Tribulation begins. I do not believe for a minute that any of Christ's declarations will be untrue. Therefore, His reference to "the day and the hour" must mean exactly what He said—the day and the hour!

We want to consider some very clear revelations of the timing of the Second Coming, beginning with Daniel's Seventy Weeks. Afterward, we will see many other Scriptures that confirm this timing.

Chapter 23

A Meeting With God

One day, twenty-four years ago, a landmark experience in my life forever changed the way my wife and I live and the way we view this world. It has caused us to run the race, at least to some degree, as the Apostle Paul mentions: "I therefore so run, not as uncertainly; so fight I, not as one that beateth the air" (1 Cor. 9:26). While reading some notes I had made on another subject, I was gripped that day by the reality of the hour in which we live. I came upon a quote from Daniel 9, which the Lord used to open my understanding to Daniel's Seventy Weeks. And something took place in my spiritual man that I will never forget; it did an eternal work in my heart.

The experience was similar to being in a completely darkened room, full of furniture, for the first time. Though aware of the surrounding furniture, one is unable to see it, or its arrangement. Then someone turns on the light, and instantly all becomes clear. As I read that simple phrase from Daniel[1] my spiritual eyes were suddenly opened, and instantly I could see each part of those seventy weeks. They were like the pieces of furniture in that darkened room. I could see what those weeks represent, and also how they fit into the plan of God through the ages of history. The Lord has since confirmed that revelation through the Bible, through historical facts, and through other Believers in many, many ways. Obviously, the latest and most impressive confirmation to my own heart was receiving Isaac Newton's book about these weeks!

---

1. In itself the particular phrase I read was not the key to understanding the Seventy Weeks of Daniel. Rather, it was simply the way that God used to draw my attention, at that moment, to Daniel 9 and the thought of those Seventy Weeks.

Chapter 24

God's Countdown: 490

"T minus two minutes and counting... T minus ten seconds... nine... eight...seven...six...five...four...three...two...one...ignition, blastoff!" Most of us have felt the thrill of a NASA countdown and rocket launch sending the astronauts into the heavens. We have also been frustrated, at times, with delays in those launches. But the tragedy of the *Challenger* mishap underscores the importance of patiently enduring those delays. God, too, is preparing for a launch: Spaceship Church. Very soon His people are going to overcome the gravitational attraction and the bonds of this world. They will be lifted into the heavenly realm to be with Him forever. Although man's systems sometimes fail, God's never do. And although man may sometimes rush his countdown, God's countdown continues according to schedule. God does have a countdown, and, even though there are delays, His launch will not be late or fail!

One way to understand when God's countdown will end is through the correct biblical and historical interpretation of Daniel's Seventy Weeks. Furthermore, by correctly interpreting that prophecy, we can actually know the year of the Second Coming of Christ and the time of His "launch." In the ninth chapter of Daniel we find Daniel in Babylon, among the captives of the children of Israel. There, through the writings of Jeremiah, he understood that Israel would experience seventy years of captivity in Babylon. God had promised to restore them to their own land after that period. By now those seventy years were about to expire. So Daniel began to pray that God would fulfill His covenant by restoring Israel, thus putting an end to her desolations (Dan. 9:16-19). However, the angel Gabriel was sent to give understanding about the purposes of God and His schedule for the fulfillment of all He had promised Israel (Dan. 9:20-23).

Gabriel told Daniel that the desolations of the people of Israel would not cease after a period of seventy years, but rather after seventy weeks. In verse 27 Gabriel reveals the problem: Satan, the Desolator. As long as he has not been destroyed, the desolations of God's people will continue.[1]

Seventy Weeks of Years

What does the Lord mean by seventy "weeks"? Leviticus 25:8 shows that a period of seven days is sometimes used in the Bible to mean seven years. There the Lord says to Moses, "Thou shalt number seven sabbaths of years unto thee, seven times seven years; and the space of the seven sabbaths of years shall be unto thee forty and nine years." *Strong's Hebrew Dictionary* actually defines this word "week" as "a week of years" (#7620).

Applying this to Daniel 9:24, Gabriel told Daniel that "seventy weeks," or 490 years (7 x 70 = 490), "are determined upon thy people." In other words, God had set aside, or specified[2] 490 certain, special, years. Gabriel says that during those 490 special years God was going to accomplish in, or through, His people Israel the six things mentioned in the rest of verse 24. Most Bible scholars are in agreement with our interpretation of these seventy weeks up to this point.[3] The differences arise as we seek to determine how these 490 special years fit chronologically into the history of Israel. Differences concerning *when* these weeks are fulfilled in history have brought conflicting interpretations into the Church.[4] However, there is only one correct interpretation, the Lord's. Let's ask Him to give us *His*, without clinging to our own opinion.

In the interpretation of this passage, there are at least two other details with which most of the Church is in full agreement. First, the weeks are divided into three parts in Daniel 9:24-27: a period of 7 weeks, another period of 62 weeks, and also a period of 1 week. This shows that God's clock or "timer" for these years starts and stops at least once or twice during Israel's history. These three time periods do not simply follow one after the other without gaps.

---

1. The NIV translates it as "one who causes desolation." The NAS and AMP Bibles translate it as "one who makes desolate."
2. This is what the Hebrew word translated as "determined" means.
3. Compare Tenney, Merrill C., *The Zondervan Pictorial Bible Dictionary*, Zondervan Publishing House, Grand Rapids, Michigan, 1967, under "Daniel." The following is a quote from there: "Gabriel answered Daniel's prayers and confessions with a revelation of the 'Seventy Weeks' of years (490 yrs., Dan. 9:24-27)."
4. Ibid., under "Daniel, Book of."

Second, the Church almost universally agrees that at least *some* portion of these seventy weeks must yet be fulfilled in the last days. Not all of the 490 special years have passed. We know this for several reasons. Referring to verse 24, some of the six things Gabriel said would be accomplished during that period of 490 years have not yet been accomplished in the fullest sense. We will see this more clearly in a moment.

It is a historical fact that from the year of Daniel's revelation, until this present day, Israel as a people, has existed for over 2,500 years.[5] However, Gabriel specified a period of only 490 years. What, then, is the key to knowing how these 490 years fit into the span of 2,500 years? In other words, when is God's countdown in progress and when is it "on hold"?

How This Countdown Works

How does a countdown work, and why is it necessary? The 490 years "determined" by God for His countdown are very similar to the countdown the United States Space Agency (NASA) uses to launch a rocket. NASA fixes (or "determines") 100 hours, for example, during which a countdown to "zero time," or launch time, is made. Those of us who have heard a countdown in progress have probably been impressed with its formality and especially with the emotion of the last minutes or seconds before launch time. It is very exciting for a space enthusiast to hear a voice come over the radio and say, "two minutes and counting." What is the purpose of all this? Is it just to impress people? Not at all. The purpose is exactly what God had in mind when He said, "My people have 490 years." At the end of that countdown there will be a "rocket launch!"

Why have a countdown? To launch a rocket there are literally hundreds of pre-flight items that must first be accomplished in an orderly sequence. For example, the fuel must be loaded. However, since the fuel is extremely volatile, why load the fuel before all the guidance equipment, communication radios, and flight computers have been installed and thoroughly checked? If one of these systems is faulty there is no need to load the fuel until the faulty item is fixed. For this reason NASA makes a long checklist containing all the items that must be accomplished before a launch, and the order in which they must be accomplished. Then NASA determines the precise number of hours required to accomplish those items, and then places that number of hours on the countdown clock. Once a decision has been made that the astronauts are going to fly, the clock is started, beginning the count backward toward "zero time."

5. Daniel received his revelation of the Seventy Weeks in approximately 538 B.C.

Each person involved in the preparations for the launch is given a list of his or her responsibilities. Next to each responsibility is found the hour, the minute, and sometimes even the second in which that duty must be performed.

Assume that the clock starts its countdown showing one hundred hours. This means NASA has concluded that one hundred hours is sufficient time to accomplish all the necessary preparations. As each hour passes, the clock shows one less hour remaining before engine ignition. Now suppose that the list instructs one of NASA's computer technicians to perform a particular duty at fourteen hours and thirty minutes before launch. He is to verify that all of the computers on board the spacecraft are working properly. Later, with twelve hours and ten minutes remaining, the fuel crew is supposed to load the fuel tanks.

Upon performing the tests of the computers, the technician discovers that there is a malfunction in the computer system. Do preparations continue uninterrupted? Of course not. They will not load the fuel until the computers are working, so they simply stop the countdown clock. This notifies the rest of the people involved that there is a delay in the countdown. No further preparations will be done until the countdown clock begins to run again. Furthermore, the fuel crew knows that the countdown clock will never read twelve hours and ten minutes to launch time until the computer problem is fixed. It is even possible that there will be several days of delay.

Once the computers are fixed, a voice suddenly comes over the public address system, saying, "Fourteen hours, thirty minutes and counting." This notifies the fuel crew to get ready, because the countdown toward twelve hours and ten minutes is proceeding. Their moment for action will soon arrive.

Understanding how a countdown works, we realize that just because our wristwatch and Big Ben in London are running does not necessarily mean that our spiritual countdown clock is running. It only continues its march toward launch as long as the prescribed preparations are being accomplished on time.

This is exactly what we see with God's countdown of 490 years before His "spaceship" is launched. He says that during those years of countdown the six things mentioned in Daniel 9:24 must be accomplished. However, at different moments during history God has stopped the countdown, because, for one reason or another, the next step could not yet be accomplished. The question is, "During which of Israel's 2,500 years of history since the days of Daniel was God's countdown clock actually running?" How do these weeks fit into history?

Chapter 25

Israel as a Political People

The key to fitting Daniel's weeks into history is found in the phrase "Seventy weeks are determined upon thy *people*" (Dan. 9:24). Biblically speaking, what is a "*people*"? Allowing the Bible to interpret itself, let's go to Isaiah 7:8. Here the prophet gives a prophetic message to King Ahaz concerning Ephraim, or the Kingdom of Israel in the north.[1] He tells Ahaz that within a very short time Ephraim would be broken and would cease to be a *people*. This prophecy was fulfilled a few years later when the King of Assyria conquered Israel and carried away the ten northern tribes as captives, scattering them among the other nations under Assyrian rule in that part of the world.

Why would the Word of the Lord say that they would cease to be a *people*? For although they never returned to the Promised Land, for centuries afterward they continued to exist as a distinct nationality, or *people*, with their own customs, religion, and way of life. The citizens of those foreign nations where the conquered Israelites were now living certainly took note of their continued existence and strange ways. In light of these facts, we conclude that God is using the word "*people*" to mean a political people, and not merely a cultural people with their distinct customs and characteristics. In other words, when Ephraim was conquered by Assyria they ceased to be an independent nation, even though they didn't cease to

1. Ephraim, Samaria, and Israel were all names used in the Old Testament to refer to the kingdom of the north that was established after the death of Solomon, when Israel was divided between Judah in the south under Rehoboam, and Israel, or Ephraim, in the north under Jeroboam. Hosea 7:1 is a verse in which all three names are used together for the northern kingdom.

exist as human beings—they ceased to exist as a political people even though they continued to exist as a cultural people. Incidentally, this concept of the biblical definition of "people" was also understood and expressed by Isaac Newton in his book.[2]

Therefore, when God says they would cease to be a "people," He is referring to a political people, governed from within by themselves, and not from without by foreigners. By biblical definition, then, a nationality is no longer considered to be a people by God if their nation has been conquered and subjugated by foreigners who control it from without. Rather than being a "people," they have become slaves. In fact, according to Exodus 12:1-2 God began to count time for Israel, as a people, when they were freed from Egyptian slavery at the Passover and the nation was born. To this day, the Jewish people declare that the Passover was the "birthday of Israel!" As happens with any birth, time for them began to be counted with that event—the birth of their nation. On the other hand, in this life, the counting of time stops at death. When we say that a person lived for seventy years, we understand that to mean that they were born and then died seventy years later. Likewise, when a free nation dies by being conquered, we no longer consider that nation to exist, and the counting of time for it stops. For example, we say that the Roman Empire lasted for over 1,000 years. What put an end to the counting of time for that empire? It wasn't the death of every one of its citizens, or the extinction of all its customs and culture, because these things never happened. Rather, the end came when Rome fell, and the Romans lost their independence and self-rule. Their clock stopped, so to speak.

From Romans 9:24-26 we understand that just because a group of people *exist* on the earth does not necessarily mean they are a "people" in the biblical sense. Paul, writing to Gentile Believers, tells them that in times past they "were not a people, but are now the people of God." The Gentiles existed in times past. Why, then, does Paul say they were not a people at that time? Because they were governed from without, and were slaves to a foreigner—Satan. When Christ enters their life, all that changes. Afterward they are governed from within. Christ sits on the throne of their hearts. Gentiles are "no more strangers and foreigners, but fellow-citizens with the saints, and of the household of God" (Eph. 2:19). So now they are His "people"—citizens of His Kingdom.

Also, when any person, Jew or Gentile, comes to Christ they actually experience self-rule and true independence for the first time in their life. Many unbelievers declare that, unlike the boring life of Believers, they do

2. *Newton's Prophecies of Daniel,* Oregon Institute of Science and Medicine, 2251 Dick George Road, Cave Junction, Oregon 97523, September, 1991, p. 130.

exactly what they want to do in life, and they alone know true independence. The truth is that only those who choose God's way end up having self-determination and control over their own lives and destinies. If the world is experiencing self-rule, then why are there so many suicides, drug addicts who can't conquer their habit, smokers who can't quit, alcoholics who can't sober up, sexual perverts who can't control their appetites without being behind bars, overweight people who can't stop eating, gossips who can't stop gossiping, and liars who can't tell the truth? If this is "doing exactly what they want in life," then I won't mind being "bored" for the rest of my days!

When Gabriel declared to Daniel, "Seventy weeks are specified for your ***people,"*** he was saying that God had determined that Israel would exist as a ***people,*** or an independent nation, for seventy weeks or 490 years. Gabriel further revealed that, during those times of political independence, the six things listed in Daniel 9:24 would be accomplished, like items on a countdown list. This tells us that from Daniel's day until the physical return of Christ in the Second Coming, Israel will be governed from within as a sovereign nation for a total of precisely 490 years.

There is one absolutely amazing historical fact that should be mentioned at this point. If the present-day nation of Israel continues to exist under the independence it currently enjoys until the year A.D. 2000, it will have had at that time precisely 490 years of national independence since the days of Daniel. This is surely no coincidence! I will show, with biblical and historical facts, that this is the case in the following chapters. Understanding "people" to mean a self-governing nation is definitely a major key for correctly interpreting this prophecy, and for determining the arrangement of these weeks in history. We will see how these 490 years of self-rule actually fit between Daniel's day and the year of the Lord's return. It should be understood that when Israel is governed from within, God's 490 year countdown clock is running. When they are governed from without, that clock is stopped.

An Important Scriptural Fact

There is one other biblical definition that we must understand to properly interpret Daniel's Seventy Weeks. We have seen what "people" means, but we must also understand how "Jerusalem" is often used in the Bible. In Isaiah 48:1-2, speaking about those who are "called by the name of Israel," the Lord says that "they call themselves after the holy city" [Jerusalem] (NKJV). In other words, they use "Jerusalem" to refer to themselves as a nation. The Bible itself frequently does this as seen in Revelation 21:2 where Jerusalem, **the holy city,** is said to be the entire Bride of

Christ, or New Testament Israel. The Scripture often uses "Jerusalem" and "Samaria," the capital cities of the southern and northern kingdoms respectively, when speaking of the entire nation of Judah in the south or Israel in the north. Micah 1:1 is an example: "The word of the Lord that came to Micah the Morasthite...which he saw concerning Samaria and Jerusalem." Then in Micah 1:9 he clarifies that his use of "Jerusalem" is in reference to all the people of Judah and not only to the capital city. The prophet laments that an incurable wound has "come unto the gate of my **people**, even to **Jerusalem**." (See the same truth in Isa. 52:9; 65:18,19; Ezek. 16:2-3; 23:1-4, etc.) The context of Daniel 9 also links God's people and Jerusalem, saying that the people *and* the city are called by His name (Dan. 9:19,24). Then Gabriel reveals that, "Seventy weeks are determined upon thy **people** and upon thy **holy city**." When he refers to "people" and "holy city" he is not speaking here about two different things, but rather one and the same. Therefore, in the following chapters when I speak of the restoration of either Israel or Jerusalem I am speaking of the same thought—His people being re-established as a self-governing nation.

Chapter 26

Two Comings in One Verse

Seventy weeks are determined upon thy people and upon thy holy city, to finish the transgression, and to make an end of sins, and to make reconciliation for iniquity, and to bring in everlasting righteousness, and to seal up the vision and prophecy, and to anoint the most Holy (Daniel 9:24).

In this verse Gabriel gives a list of six things that will be accomplished during Israel's 490 years of history as a political people. One or more of these things have not yet taken place. Considering this list carefully, we observe that some things were accomplished by Christ during His First Coming. However, at least one or more will not be accomplished until the Second Coming. In order to prove this important fact, there is no need to examine more than two of these items—one that was fulfilled at the First Coming, and one that will definitely not be fulfilled until the Second Coming.[1]

Accomplished in the First Coming

One of the six works to be accomplished is a "reconciliation for iniquity." According to Hebrews 2:17 this has already happened, because the ministry of Christ, our High Priest, was to "make reconciliation for the sins of the people." In fact, the New Testament is filled with a revelation of

---

1. Some believe that all six things were fulfilled in Christ's First Coming. I believe that it can be proven biblically that there was a partial fulfillment of all these things during His First Coming, but that some of these things will not be completely fulfilled until His physical return.

this wonderful blessing, brought to mankind through Christ's death on the cross. Thus, this part of Daniel 9:24 has already been fulfilled.

Not Accomplished Until the Second Coming

One of these six things that has not yet been accomplished is to "seal up the vision and prophecy." "Seal up" is the same Hebrew word that is used earlier in this verse where it is translated "to make an end of" sins.[2] So this word "seal up" carries the thought of the conclusion or end of a thing. Also, we should note that the word "prophecy" in this passage is really "prophet" in the Hebrew. (This Hebrew word appears 316 times in the Old Testament. Of those, the King James Version translates it as "prophet" 312 times and as "prophecy" only once—in this verse.) This phrase could therefore be translated as, "To make an end of the vision and the prophet." Please refer back to Isaac Newton's translation of this passage, which I gave in Chapter 20, to see that this is correct. We know that this did not happen in the First Coming, because we find prophets operating after the cross in the early Church (Acts 11:27; 13:1). We also understand, through Paul's writings, when prophecy and prophets will cease to exist. In Ephesians 4:11-13 he tells us that Christ gave prophets to the Church until we all come to perfection. This occurs at the Second Coming. Furthermore, in First Corinthians 13:9-12 we are told that prophecy will cease when "that which is perfect is come" and when we see "face to face." Clearly this, too, will be fulfilled at the end. Since this has not yet happened, we know that at least one of the six things mentioned by Gabriel has not yet occurred.

The phrase "seal up the vision and prophecy" can also refer to a fulfillment of the vision or message of the prophets.[3] After His death and Resurrection, Christ returned to Heaven and will remain there until there is a restoration of all the things the prophets said would be restored as Acts 3:21 clearly states. One of the things they said would be restored is the nation of Israel, and we are witnesses that God is indeed restoring that nation today.[4] The prophets mention a number of other things that must be restored, but the point is, Jesus will remain in Heaven until the vision of the prophets regarding restoration is fulfilled. We could, therefore, say

---

2. *Strong's Hebrew Dictionary*, #2856.
3. In the lives of the prophets, the message and the messenger were always one and the same, just as it will be, and must be, in our own lives. They lived what they preached and preached what they lived. They were the message. So "making an end of the prophet" also means "arriving at the fulfillment of their message."
4. Isaiah 1:26; 11:11 are two of the many references to Israel's restoration in the last days.

that when He seals up (or fulfills) the vision and the prophets, this will open the way for Christ to return.

Therefore, our observation concerning Gabriel's list of six things reveals that at least some are related to the First Coming, while others are related to the Second Coming. **So here, in one short verse, the Lord prophetically mixes the events of the First Coming with events of the Second Coming.**

Combining Both Comings in the Same Verse is Common

In the Old Testament prophecies, the Spirit of God frequently combines both comings of Christ in the same verse. This was one of the reasons the Jews had such a difficult time understanding their Messiah when He came the first time. Their concepts of the Messiah were based on verses that mixed facts of His Second Coming with facts about His First Coming. For example, one Scripture declares that Christ came to "proclaim the acceptable year of the Lord, and the day of vengeance of our God" (Isa. 61:1-2). When Jesus read this portion in the synagogue in Nazareth, He stopped right in the middle of the sentence. He then closed the book and sat down, saying, "This day is this scripture fulfilled in your ears" (Lk. 4:17-21). He stopped reading right in the middle of the verse because He was only fulfilling the work of the First Coming—the "acceptable year of the Lord." Not until the Second Coming would the "day of vengeance of our God" be fulfilled.

Prophetic Perspective

The study of the principles of Bible interpretation calls this mixing together "prophetic perspective." It is the same perspective that a person has when looking at two very distant mountain peaks, one behind the other. Both peaks may be clearly visible, and the one that is furthest away may even be much higher. But because the depth perception of the human eye is not precise at such long distances, the person sees both peaks as one single peak. He does not discern a deep valley separating them. Many prophets and men of faith have had this "prophetic perspective" as they beheld things that were "afar off" (Heb. 11:13). Daniel 9:24 contains "prophetic perspective" where two distinct mountain peaks, His First Coming and His Second Coming, appear as though they were one event.

Chapter 27

Two Comings in Another Verse

Not long ago I met four young men who were vacationing in Central America. The Lord opened the door for me to share for a few minutes with them, though I had no idea who they were. I didn't even know their names. As we began to talk, their frustrations with life surfaced. They clearly had no hope for the future of mankind on this planet, and little or no faith in God. They were even unsure of His existence. I felt urged to tell them about the God of Israel, and how He is proving His greatness and power, and also proving that He is real at this very moment to anyone who has eyes to see. I spoke of His great sovereignty and providence manifested in the restoration of the Jews, a tremendous miracle that the whole world is witnessing, though many have never really given it much thought.

Imagine it! Israel, a small nation to begin with, was scattered over all the earth, among many nations. Yet, for almost 2,000 years they maintained their identity, their religion, and in many cases, their physical appearance. But most of all, many continued to maintain a deep longing to return to a homeland they had never even seen. For 2,000 years they faithfully maintained their yearly Passover celebration, and each year they would end it by saying, "Next year in Jerusalem!" Some have said that their religion actually held them together and kept alive their zeal for their homeland. There's one major flaw in that reasoning. To really observe their religion according to its ordinances they needed to offer blood sacrifices in a temple, and in that temple a High Priest had to make atonement for them once every year. But they didn't have a temple in which to offer the sacrifices, nor the High Priest to officiate. They were sort of in the condition that we were sometimes in during our years in the Philippines.

When we were all suffering the lack of some necessity or convenience, the founder of the work would cheer us up by saying, "If I had some ham, I'd have ham and eggs, if I had some eggs!"

What religion could survive 2,000 years without a leader, and without a place to practice it properly, unless something or someone far bigger than the religion itself were keeping it alive? What people would be able to resist being assimilated into the culture where they lived for 2,000 years, especially when they were the target of continual persecution and hatred if they weren't willing to assimilate? Only something far greater than a lifeless, ritualistic, impossible-to-keep religion could have accomplished that! God Himself records in the Scriptures that this would happen, and that when it did, His name would be glorified among the nations of the earth (Ezek. 20:34-44; 36:22-23).

And when Israel finally did return to their homeland, which was nothing but a worthless wilderness, they called their new nation by the same name it had almost 3,500 years before. Within a few years they were being gathered from literally all the nations of the earth, and the desert was blossoming like a rose, just as God had promised them (Isa. 35:1). This is a miraculous proof of the reality of our God. Throughout history other peoples have been scattered among the nations, either by force or by their own choice, and after just a few generations the descendants didn't even know what country their forefathers came from, much less maintain their cultural identity and a longing to return. A notable example of this is the melting pot of the United States. Many Americans today do not know for sure where they came from. A few do know, but I have never met anyone who wants to return. Against these formidable odds, the Jews have lived, and have survived for 2,000 years, never losing the desire for their homeland!

As I shared with the four vacationers about these things, they were visibly moved as their eyes were opened to the greatness of the God of Israel. But I was moved even more when they revealed their identity. One of them said, "We didn't tell you, but we are all Jews." The God of Israel is still reaching out to His people today to reveal His love for them!

> *Know therefore and understand, that from the going forth of the commandment to restore and to build Jerusalem unto the Messiah the Prince shall be seven weeks, and threescore and two weeks: the street shall be built again, and the wall, even in troublous times* (Daniel 9:25).

One of the keys to understanding this verse is to understand that God was planning to restore Israel the second time. "It shall come to pass in that day, that the Lord shall set His hand again **the second time to recover the remnant** of his people which shall be left" (Isa. 11:11).[1]

When Gabriel explained these things to Daniel, God wanted him to understand that from the going forth of the commandment, or decree, to restore and build Jerusalem, until the coming of the Messiah the Prince, a certain number of weeks of years would pass. Most of the Church agrees that between the time the **command** would be given **to restore Israel** and the coming of **the Messiah** a certain number of weeks of years would transpire. Most of the theological discussion on this verse centers around deciding whether or not the proper historical dates are being used to interpret it. But before we get sidetracked by a discussion about which dates should be used, let's note that there is something far more basic that must be determined first if we are to ever understand this prophecy. Gabriel is speaking about Israel's restoration. As Isaac Newton points out, God promised that Israel would be restored two times (Isa. 11:11 and many other Scriptures affirm this). So before we try to determine which dates to use in our interpretation, we should first be certain we know which restoration he is referring to.

Israel went into the Babylonian captivity during the days of Daniel. Seventy years later, God restored the nation through the command of the king who ruled over the land of their captivity. About five hundred years later, after Christ had already come, Israel was destroyed again by Rome in the year A.D. 70. The Jews were scattered once more, but this time all over the world. Now, in our day, God has fulfilled His promise, and done one of the greatest miracles ever witnessed by humanity. He has begun to restore Israel the second time, just as the prophets said He would. According to Acts 3:21 this brings us one giant step closer to His Second Coming, because there we are told that Christ can only return once the promised restoration has taken place.

Since there are two restorations of Israel between Daniel's day and the time of the end, there must also be two commands to restore them. Neither restoration could have taken place without the command being issued by the Sovereign King of the universe. He rules in all the affairs of men (Dan. 4:17). Therefore, there were not only **two restorations**, but also **two commands.**

We should ask ourselves one other question. How many times will the Messiah physically come to this earth? Most people know the answer. There will be **two comings.** This brings us to a problem in verse 25. Since

---

1. The Hebrew text in Isaiah 11:11, referring to Israel's restoration, actually means the "second" time (*Strong's Hebrew Dictionary*, #8145).

there were to be **two restorations, two commands, and two comings** of the Messiah, to which one of these commands, restorations, or comings is Gabriel referring? The precedent is already established for us in this very context. Daniel 9:24 speaks of both comings in the same verse, and we should read verse 25 with both comings in mind also. As Isaac Newton correctly observed, Daniel is prophesying of both comings in the same passage.

Indeed, the fact that verse 25 ends up giving us **two dates** and not just one is a confirmation to this. Note that he speaks of two time periods: "seven weeks" and "threescore and two weeks" (62 weeks).[2] So the Lord is saying to Daniel, "From one of the commands to restore Israel until one of the comings of the Messiah will be 7 weeks. And from the other command, to bring about the other restoration, until the other coming of the Messiah, will be 62 weeks." History bears out that between the first command to restore and the First Coming there were, in fact, 62 weeks. So then, the first part of this interpretation has already been fulfilled. We will see that the second part is now in progress, and will also soon be history.

2. Referring back to Isaac Newton's translation of this passage, these two different time periods aren't even in the same verse.

Chapter 28

Popular Interpretations

We don't need a "spiritual shoehorn" to fit these weeks into Israel's history, nor do we need the "mathematical wonder" of addition. In this chapter we will look at the problems many popular interpretations encounter. Some of those problems are created by joining together the 7 week period and the 62 week period to arrive at 69 weeks. As Isaac Newton said, this "does violence to the language of Daniel" (see Chapter 20), and no nation on earth has ever written a number in this way. Could we be presuming when we do so?

I once asked a well-known Bible prophecy teacher how he could be sure of the date he was using for the command to restore Israel. His date didn't seem to fit biblical or secular history. I was honestly interested in seeing what proof he was using to support that date. With complete assurance he said, "Well, we can be *sure* of that date because Daniel gives it to us right here in the prophecy. He says that there will be 69 weeks between the command to restore and the coming of the Messiah and we know when He came. I believe the Bible. It doesn't matter what *anyone* says."

Among the best-known interpretations of Daniel's Seventy Weeks, almost invariably the first thing done is to add the period of 7 weeks, with the period of 62 weeks, to arrive at 69 weeks, or 483 years.[1] (We are referring to the two periods found in Daniel 9:25.) However, this does not fit very well with verse 26 where we are told that the Messiah will

1. Tenney, *Bible Dictionary*, "Daniel, Book of."

be cut off after 62 weeks, not after 69 weeks. (We will see more about this in Chapter 33.)

In spite of this, these interpretations go on to say that from the command to restore Israel until the coming of the Messiah was a period of 69 weeks, or 483 years (7 x 69 = 483). The Bible prophecy teacher mentioned above didn't seem to notice that Daniel never said anything about "69 weeks." Nor, could he see that one of the foundation stones of his interpretation was a specific, key date, but that the key date itself was founded on his interpretation. This is called "circular reasoning," or proving our argument by using evidence based on our argument. If God did not intend for these two numbers to be added, we have destroyed the whole meaning of this extremely important prophecy. And as Newton eloquently declares, we have done "violence to the language of Daniel."

Problems Encountered by Popular Interpretations

Problem 1: No biblical precedent. Since nowhere else in the Bible do we find a number written in this manner,[2] we have no biblical pattern or precedent for adding these two numbers. All interpretations must be firmly based on other clear passages of Scripture that say the same thing, give an example of the same thing, or that confirm our interpretations and conclusions. And a "firm" basis is not merely one or two other passages, but rather many others. The decision to add these numbers to arrive at 69 weeks, or a period of 483 years, has no scriptural justification whatsoever, so we conclude that to do so is pure speculation and personal interpretation.

Note: If the Lord wanted us to add these two numbers, then this passage is unique in that it is the only passage in all of the Bible where He wrote a number in this way. This would mean that from the moment He gave us this prophecy, the key to its interpretation would have been that someone, somewhere, was supposed to come to that conclusion through personal revelation, since there is no other passage in the Word of God that writes a number this way to justify that addition. To do so, therefore, is "private interpretation," which means that we interpret Scripture without using other Scripture on which to base every detail of our concept. This would be an open violation of God's Word, since Peter clearly says in Second Peter 1:20, "Knowing this first, that **no prophecy of the**

2. In many places in the Bible the units and the tens or hundreds are separated, but in no place are the units themselves separated into two parts. He would write "sixty and nine" but not "seven, and sixty and two," to mean sixty-nine.

scripture is of any private interpretation." If our interpretation of a prophecy is correct we will always be able to find other verses that say exactly what our interpretation says, or does what our interpretation does. There is nothing wrong with personal revelation as long as it leads us to an interpretation that is firmly based on Scripture. Each conclusion that we arrive at in this study of Daniel's Seventy Weeks will be confirmed by other Scriptures that say exactly what our interpretation says. If we were unable to do this, our personal revelation would then be classed as private interpretation.

Problem 2: He supposedly did not come when He came. The second problem encountered in the most popular interpretations is to fit this newly derived 69-week period (483 years) into the historical chronology of those days. The chronology of that period has now been firmly established upon many highly documented dates. Therefore, in an attempt to fit this period of 483 years between the command to restore Israel and the coming of the Messiah, and yet maintain some degree of doctrinal and historical respectability, many differing dates for the "coming" of the Messiah have been proposed. The most popular choice declares that He "came" when He died on the cross. In other words, those who hold to that concept are saying that He actually came when He left. They affirm that He came at the moment He was departing from this world at the cross. It is, therefore, difficult to understand why we should consider this to be the moment of His "coming." Other interpretations affirm that He "came" when He began His ministry at the River Jordan, in spite of the fact that the Bible says He came when He came—at His birth. In addition, there are at least one or two other dates proposed for the time of the Messiah's "coming," all of which are near or after the end of His life, when he departed this world.

However, the angels announced His coming to the shepherds in Bethlehem, with good tidings of great joy (Lk. 2:10-11). They declared that there was born to them *that* day "in the city of David a Saviour, which is **Christ** [Messiah] the Lord." (In Greek "Christ" means the same as the Hebrew word "Messiah." Both words mean "the anointed one.") Surely the Father wanted His people to know that the Messiah, His precious Son, had come on **that day** to save their souls. The Messiah was revealed on *that* day, *not* 30 years later.

The shepherds were convinced. As they knelt at that manger, in the presence of the Anointed One, and saw His glory with their newly opened eyes, something happened in their hearts that became evident to all who heard their story. It would have been virtually impossible for anyone to have convinced those shepherds that the Messiah had not really come on that wonderful night.

Simeon was convinced. "It was revealed unto him [Simeon] by the Holy Ghost, that he should not see death, before he had seen the Lord's Christ" (Lk. 2:26). When Joseph and Mary brought baby Jesus into the temple to dedicate Him, Simeon took Him up into his arms and said, "Lord, now lettest thou thy servant depart in peace, according to thy word: For mine eyes have seen thy salvation, which thou hast prepared before the face of all people" (Lk. 2:29-31). So Simeon saw the *Christ* (Messiah) in the baby who had come to Bethlehem.

Herod the Great was convinced. To this day the blood of all the precious little ones of Bethlehem may still be upon his hands. They died as a result of his jealousies and fears that the Messiah *had* come (Mt. 2:16). Yes, even Herod the wicked one had heard the news of His coming through the wise men from the East. They came seeking the One worthy of worship, the King to whom they longed to yield their lives. Even His star in the East had announced His coming. All Jerusalem had heard the news and was moved by what had been spoken. The Messiah *had* come. The King *had* been born.

The list goes on: Anna knew, Zacharias and Elizabeth knew, and of course Joseph and Mary knew. His arrival was at His birth. The fact that He needed thirty years to grow up in the presence of His Father does not change the fact that He had already come.

Problem 3: Fictitious dates. All this is still only a small problem compared to other difficulties encountered by the interpretations that begin by adding the 7 weeks to the 62 weeks. In order to fit 483 years between the date of the first command to restore Israel and the date of the First Coming of the Messiah there are three other mistakes often made. First, a fictitious and incorrect date for the cross is sometimes used.[3] Second, an incorrect date is chosen for the command given to restore Israel. In very recent years the date of that command has been established with what we could call absolute certainty.[4]

The third mistake is the invention of what scholars have termed a "prophetic year." A "prophetic year" contains only 360 days instead of the 365 days found in a solar year. This imaginary year, based on 12 months of 30 days each, conveniently shaves off 1 year every 73 years.[5] This makes a difference of almost 7 years in a period of 483 years. However, in Genesis 1

3. See Tenney, *Bible Dictionary*, "Daniel, Book of." There the cross is placed at A.D. 33. This is completely impossible, as we will see later!
4. In the month of Nisan of 445 B.C. Refer to Chapter 29.
5. Because if 5 days are lost each year, then 365 days are lost during a period of 73 years (73 x 5 = 365).

God gave the **sun and moon** to determine the years and seasons.[6] The "prophetic year" has no scriptural foundation, and neither Israel nor the Bible ever used such a year at any time in history. As Sir Isaac Newton tells us, these must be Jewish years.[7] How could it be otherwise, when God is giving a prophetic message to His own "people"? Were they supposed to go to the Gentiles to get the interpretation and understanding of what a "year" really is supposed to be, when their own Scriptures and history had already established it for them? Surely that concept is ludicrous!

The fact that Israel adhered to a luni-solar year, as Newton also mentions, is indisputable.[8] In other words, they made adjustments to their calendar on a regular, pre-determined basis, to adhere to a solar year of 365 days.[9] We do the same by using a leap year every **4** years. This is recognized by those who understand the yearly cycle of the **three principal feasts** of Israel, and their **three annual harvests**. Each year Israel celebrated the Feast of Passover at the time of the barley harvest. About two months later the Feast of Pentecost was celebrated during the wheat harvest. Finally, the Feast of Tabernacles was celebrated during the general harvest in the seventh month. If God's people had used any other than a solar year of 365 days to count time, their harvest times would rarely have coincided with the pre-set feast dates, which were established by God.[10] The barley harvest would be in March one year, in February 6 years later, and in December after 6 more years. If we invent a "prophetic year," we are once again pulling out our "spiritual shoehorn" and forcing our interpretation into the biblical and historical panorama, even though it doesn't fit. So let's throw out the "shoehorn," the addition of numbers, the "prophetic year," and proceed to Chapter 29.

6. Appendix D explains the biblical calendar and the biblical year. The year was always adjusted, using leap years to remain synchronized with the solar year of 365 days.
7. *Newton's Prophecies of Daniel*, p. 137.
8. Ibid.
9. See Appendix D of this book. Refer also to: Spier, Arthur, *The Comprehensive Hebrew Calendar*, Feldheim Publishers Ltd., Jerusalem, Israel, 1986.
10. See Leviticus 23 for the dates of each feast.

Chapter 29

Two Critical Dates

To determine if 62 weeks fit, historically, between the first command to restore Israel and the First Coming of the Messiah (His birth), two dates must be established with certainty. We must know the date of the command to restore Israel, and also the date of His First Coming, or birth. Let's consider both dates here.

The Date of the Command to Restore Israel

Daniel was sealed until the "time of the end" (Dan. 12:4). But when does the "time of the end" begin? According to Christ's teaching, the "fig tree" will blossom when the last generation before His coming is alive on the earth (Mt. 24:32-34). Certainly the "last generation" and the "time of the end" refer to the same period of time. The "fig tree" (the nation of Israel) began to blossom with the decree to restore Israel the second time in A.D. 1947, and then it shot out its tender shoots in the decade of the 1950s.

Some have questioned whether we can be sure that Jesus is really using the fig tree as a symbol of Israel in His teaching on the last days. However, if He is not doing so, then we have a context problem in the Gospel of Matthew, because in Matthew 21 He is clearly using the fig tree as a symbol of Israel. There He curses the fig tree because it has no fruit on it, and it withers (Mt. 21:18-21). Later, in the same chapter, using the parable of the vineyard, He makes it clear that it is the nation of Israel that is not bearing the fruit she was ordained to bear and will therefore be judged. His disciples were greatly impressed at how quickly the fig tree withered, but just a few hours later He tells them that the "fig tree" will blossom again (Mt. 24:32). Those must have been comforting words to those Jewish disciples!

Why is it important to understand this? Because the "fig tree" *has* blossomed, and we can, therefore, be certain that Daniel is no longer a sealed book, spiritually speaking, since it was sealed *only* until the time of the end.[1] God wants to unlock for us the secrets of this prophetic book. During the decade of the 1950s, which we could call the beginning of the "time of the end," the Elephantine Papyri were discovered by archaeologists in the Middle East. Through these papyri, along with other discoveries, God has confirmed an essential date for the proper understanding of Daniel's Seventy Weeks. Specifically, the date of the command to restore Israel the first time, was given by King Artaxerxes in Nehemiah 2:1-8 in the year 445 B.C.[2] These papyri merely **confirm** that key date, because Bible chronology also establishes it. A correct interpretation must satisfy both biblical and historical evidence. Isn't it interesting that God waited until the "fig tree" had blossomed to allow these papyri to be found and this key date to be confirmed? We *are* living in the time of the end!

In the Book of Ezra, King Cyrus gave the command to restore the **temple—not** a command to restore Israel as a people or nation (Ezra 1:1-2). He was not giving them back their independence. However, in the Book of Nehemiah, Artaxerxes wrote a letter decreeing that Jerusalem was to be rebuilt under Nehemiah, and as a result the nation was restored or re-established (Neh. 2:5-7). Even the enemies of Israel understood that if the Jews were permitted to have a capital city, they would be a people or independent nation once again. This was precisely the concern of Israel's enemies as seen in their letter to the king of Persia in Ezra 4:11-15. Ezra was never commanded to rebuild Jerusalem, but a clear biblical command to do so is found in Nehemiah 2. In fact, this is the **only place in the Bible** that such a command was actually given. Therefore, to assume that any other passage in the Bible is the fulfillment of Daniel 9:25 would be pure speculation.

1. In Isaiah 29:11-12 a "vision" is likened to a "sealed book" that no one can read. Also, in Revelation 5:1 there is a sealed book that no one can read. Obviously, as a book, Daniel was not sealed physically, because men have been able to read it with their natural eyes. However, men have not had the keys to fully understand it until now, at the "time of the end." God is beginning to open our spiritual eyes to its message.
2. *Collier's Encyclopedia*, Vol. 17, 1988, see "Nehemiah."
   The Illustrated Bible Dictionary, Inter-varsity Press, Tyndale House Publishers, Wheaton, Illinois, 1986, p. 1070, "Nehemiah."

Many Bible publishers have included notes and helps in the Bible margins. A number of them have placed a date of 445 B.C. next to the second chapter of Nehemiah.[3] Of the many historical and biblical dates that have been established, this date is definitely one of the most trustworthy and well-documented.[4] It coincides with biblical as well as historical chronology, and has been confirmed in many irrefutable ways.

Nehemiah even tells us in which month this decree was given (Neh. 2:1). It was the month Nisan (also called Abib), the first month of the biblical calendar. Depending on the given year, it falls somewhere between early March and early May of our present calendar.[5] Therefore, we can accurately establish the year, and the approximate month, of this very important command to restore Israel, found in Nehemiah 2. That command was therefore given sometime between early March and early May of the year 445 B.C.

The Date of Christ's Birth

"Si-lent night. Ho-ly night." What date was showing on the calendar on that night so critical to human history? This is the other date we must establish with certainty to be able to correctly interpret Daniel's Seventy Weeks. That is, we must be able to establish the year and approximate month. What do we know for sure about that date?

1. The Modern Calendar

Our calendar was devised by Pope Gregory XIII and was introduced in the year 1582.[6] It is based on the birth of Christ. The years before His birth are followed by the letters B.C., meaning "before Christ." The years after His birth are preceded by A.D., which stand for the Latin words that mean "in the year of the Lord." The sovereignty of the Creator is seen in this paradox: though much of humanity rejects Christ, they live by a calendar based on His birth, the focal point of history. Though men ignore,

3. For example, The Thompson Chain-Reference Bible, B.B. Kirkbride Bible, Co., Inc., Indianapolis, Indiana.
4. One of many examples: *Collier's Encyclopedia*, 1988, "Nehemiah."
5. Spier, *The Comprehensive Hebrew Calendar*. In 1899 Nisan began on March 2, and in 1967 Nisan ended on May 10. Incidentally, God designated this month as the first month for Israel in Exodus 12 because it was the month in which history, or time, first began for them as an independent nation. This independence came during the Passover and Exodus from Egypt, when they were freed from slavery and indeed, for the first time became a biblical people (a people with political freedom).
6. Morris, William, ed., *The American Heritage Dictionary of the English Language*, Houghton Mifflin Company, Boston, Massachusetts, 1981, "Calendar."

belittle, deny and mock the Son of glory, the Father chooses to honor and exalt Him.

First, we acknowledge that our modern calendar has an error of several years. If our calendar were correct then the date of Christ's birth would be the first day of January, A.D. 1. Because of miscalculations, and facts that weren't available to Pope Gregory, we now understand that Christ was not born at the beginning of A.D. 1. He was born sometime between the year 5 B.C. and March of the year 4 B.C. This is confirmed by many well-documented studies and historical works that deal with the time of Christ's birth.[7] The following evidence establishes the year of His birth.

2. The Year of His Birth

Josephus, a Jewish historian, tells us that a few days before the death of Herod there was a complete lunar eclipse. He also tells us that Herod died just before the Feast of Passover.[8] So we can determine almost the exact date of Herod's death. First, it has been astronomically determined that this eclipse took place on the night of March 13, 4 B.C.[9] Second, the Passover of that year came during the month of April. Therefore, Herod died between March and April of the year 4 B.C.[10] Since Herod was alive at the birth of Jesus, His birth was definitely before March of the year 4 B.C. However, the events associated with His birth require that He was born at least a month and a half before the death of Herod. Those events include His dedication in the temple, the visit of the wise men, and the flight into Egypt.[11] So if Herod died between March and April of 4 B.C., Jesus had to have been born by February or March of that year at the very latest.

In addition to knowing the **latest** year in which Christ could have been born, we must also determine the **earliest** year. In the past few years the biblical chronology from this period has been carefully and accurately coordinated with highly documented dates from secular history. For this reason we are able to give absolute dates at least as far back as the death of Solomon in 931 B.C.[12]

7. Edersheim, Alfred, *The Life and Times of Jesus the Messiah*, Eerdmans' Publishing Co., Grand Rapids, Michigan, 1969, Appendix VII.
8. Josephus, Flavius, *The Antiquities of the Jews*, Kregel Publications, Grand Rapids, Michigan, 1981, XVII. VI. 4, p. 365.
9. Ibid.
10. *Encyclopaedia Brittanica*, Encyclopaedia Brittanica, Inc., William Benton, Publisher, Chicago, Illinois, Vol. 11, 1973, see "Herod."
11. Leviticus 12:2-6 and Luke 2:22 show that there were forty days between His birth and His dedication in the temple. The wise men came after that.
12. Bromiley, Vol. I, p. 674.

We can therefore ascertain the year in which Christ began His ministry. According to Luke 3:1,7,21 John came baptizing in "the fifteenth year of the reign of Tiberius Caesar." The multitudes came out to him at that time and were baptized. Jesus was among those multitudes and was also baptized along with them (v. 21).[13] Therefore, since Jesus began His ministry upon being baptized, we know that He began it when John was baptizing the people in the wilderness, or in the "fifteenth year of Tiberius Caesar." That was A.D. 26. (Documentation of this date is provided in Appendix D.)

One other biblical fact is needed to establish the year of His birth. We must determine the age of Jesus when He began His ministry. Luke gives us that detail also: "And Jesus himself began to be about thirty years of age" (Lk. 3:23). So during the fifteenth year of Tiberius, when Jesus began His ministry, He was 30 years old.[14] Since He was 30 years old in A.D. 26, He was born between the years 5 and 4 B.C.[15] Many knowledgeable texts, history books, encyclopedias, and studies confirm this timing for His birth, as well as the year A.D. 26 for the beginning of His ministry.[16]

3. The Month of His Birth

There is no evidence that He was born in the month of December, much less on December 25. However, there is sufficient biblical evidence to establish the **approximate** month of His birth. In fact, there is so much evidence that it has been placed in an Appendix so that we are not sidetracked from the main theme of this study. Jesus was born around the month of September. For those who are interested in the details, please refer to Appendix D.

---

13. This is brought out more clearly in Mark 1:4-5,9. John preached a message of baptism in the wilderness, as Luke 3:2-3 states, and all the land of Judea went out to him and were baptized (Mk. 1:5). Then we are told that "in those days" Jesus was also baptized by John (Mk. 1:9).
14. Some modern scholars have expressed doubt that Jesus was actually 30 years old when He began His earthly ministry. But surely the One who said that He would fulfill every jot and tittle of the law began His priestly ministry in accordance with that very law, which states that a priest must begin his ministry when he is 30 years old, not 29 or 31 (Num. 4:43). So when Luke declares that He began His ministry when He was "about 30," we shouldn't conclude that He was "about 29" or "about 31." For Luke to make this statement at all points to the fact that He was fulfilling one more part of the Old Testament law, and that although He was not "precisely 30," He was very close to that!
15. This calculation is explained in Appendix D.
16. Packer, J.I., Tenney, Merrill C., White, William Jr., eds., *The Bible Almanac*, Thomas Nelson Publishers, Nashville, Tennessee, p. 64. See also Halley, pp. 459-460.

Chapter 30

62 Weeks

"Will this book be worth what I paid for it?" I asked myself as I was returning from a tour of the Holy Land. Of all the books in that Jerusalem bookstore I just "happened" to pick up *The Comprehensive Hebrew Calendar*. I bought it on the spot, without even a high pressure salesman to blame. (He got his price, though.)

Years later I can thank a wise God for His careful forethought in putting keys into my hands before I even knew I needed them. Little confirmations that He wants me to understand the end still surprise and thrill me. This *Calendar* has definitely outdone its price tag.

Now that we know the date on which the command to restore Israel was given, and the time of Christ's birth, we can determine if there were indeed 62 weeks of years between the command to restore Israel and the coming of the Messiah. For the sake of convenience, let's arbitrarily choose a specific month and day for each of these dates, using our modern calendar months instead of using the names of the biblical months. Let's assume the command to restore Israel in Nehemiah 2 was given on May 8, 445 B.C., and that Christ was born on September 6, 5 B.C.[1] We have no evidence that these are the **precise** dates. However, we know that the year is correct, and that the month is also correct, within a margin of error of

1. For both Nisan and Tishri, the first month and seventh month, respectively, in the biblical calendar, these are possible dates. For example, the last day of Nisan was on May 10 of our calendar in the years A.D. 1929 and A.D. 1967. And Tishri begins as early as the beginning of September. In A.D. 1899 the first day of Tishri was on September 5. For these facts see: Spier, *The Comprehensive Hebrew Calendar*.

two months at most. It will become apparent later why I have chosen these specific dates as possibilities.

The question now becomes, "Are there 62 weeks, or 434 years, between those two dates?" A simple calculation shows there are 440 years and about 4 months between those two dates.[2] Therefore, we have 6 years and 4 months more than an exact period of 434 years, or the 62 weeks we expect. But let's not jump to conclusions just yet. Remember, the countdown clock. These weeks of years cover *only* the time when Israel is to be an independent nation, governed from within.

Could it be that during that period of 440 years and 4 months Israel was not continuously governed from within? The countdown clock runs only while Israel has her independence. Any years in which they are governed from without are not included in the seventy weeks, or 490 years. The answer is found in the Book of Daniel, and in the history books as well.

First, we need to determine approximately how many days there are in 6 years and 4 months. Being able to accurately determine this was one of the many ways that *The Comprehensive Hebrew Calendar* was a real blessing. Using the biblical luni-solar year of 354 days,[3] every third year was a leap year with an extra 30 days. The biblical leap year, then, had a total of 384 days.[4] Knowing these facts, we use simple addition to determine how many days there are in 6 years and 4 months. The calculation is as follows:

354 days .....(year 1)
354 days .....(year 2)
384 days .....(year 3 - a leap year with 30 extra days)
354 days .....(year 4)
354 days .....(year 5)
384 days .....(year 6 - a leap year with 30 extra days)
116 days ......(from May 8 to September 6 using 29.5 days per month)
2300 days .....total days

Now we need to look at one of Daniel's visions, and its God-given interpretation, found in chapter 8. While living in approximately the year 550 B.C., Daniel was permitted to look 200 years into the future, and see

2. From 445 B.C. to 5 B.C. there are 440 years (subtract 5 from 445). And from May 8 to September 6 is about four months. So we have 440 years and 4 months.
3. The biblical lunar year consists of twelve lunar months. A lunar month has 29.5 days. Therefore, the lunar year has 354 days (12 x 29.5 = 354). See Appendix D for an explanation of the biblical calendar.
4. Spier, pp. 14-16.

the conquests of the Grecian Empire under Alexander the Great. As he looked into the future he could see that, after many successful conquests, Alexander's Empire would be divided into four smaller kingdoms. Out of one of those four, specifically the Syrian Kingdom in the north, would arise a "little horn" who would conquer Israel. History gives us the name of that little horn. It was Antiochus Epiphanes, or Antiochus IV.

Antiochus conquered the nation of Israel in 170 B.C. and began to oppress them severely.[5] They lost all religious, and **political** freedom. Daniel said that the sanctuary and the city would be given over to him, and history gives us the details. We know that Antiochus forbade the Jews to exercise any of the rituals of the law of Moses. He was seeking to Hellenize the Jews, that is, to turn them into true Greeks. He actually thought that he could eliminate their spiritual convictions through force. If he could only have looked forward in time to see what the Jews would endure for 2,000 years without being assimilated by the Gentiles, he might have gotten a little discouraged with his plan! On penalty of death, the Jews were forbidden to circumcise their children, or to offer any sacrifice specified in the law of Moses. For how long did this continue? The history books tell us that it was for approximately 7 years.[6] However, concerning this point Daniel is much more specific than the history books. In Daniel 8:13-14 he says it would continue for exactly 2,300 days. Here, in chapter 8, we find an extremely important key for interpreting chapter 9, especially with regard to the 62 weeks. And this interpretation has no need of ignoring, stretching, or shrinking the historical facts, nor those of biblical or secular history.[7]

Remembering that the seventy weeks are in progress only while Israel is governed from within, we see that from the command to restore Israel until the coming of the Messiah there were 2,300 days that cannot be considered as part of the "weeks." During those 2,300 days Syria sovereignly ruled Israel. Thus, Israel was governed directly by a foreigner from without. The "countdown clock" was stopped and did not continue running again until those 2,300 days had passed. So we find that Israel did have

5. Dubnov, Vol. I, pp. 484, 498.
6. Hartom, A.S., *The Book of Daniel Explained,* "Yavneh" Publishing House, Tel Aviv, Israel, 1966, p. 51.
   Dubnov, Vol. I. pp. 484, 498.
7. Please note that we chose arbitrary dates for the command to restore Israel and for the birth of the Messiah. But we know that those dates include the right year and approximately the right month. We chose those dates for two reasons. First, they are feasible, or possible, dates for the first and seventh month, and secondly, they demonstrate that the 62 weeks plus 2,300 days do indeed fit between those dates.

precisely 62 weeks, or 434 years, of independence between the command to restore and the First Coming of the Messiah.[8] This is a historical and biblical fact.

Conclusion

Is this mere coincidence, or was Gabriel actually revealing to Daniel the precise year of the First Coming of Christ? We conclude that this was Gabriel's message, because the biblical and historical facts confirm it. This is what really happened. Regardless of whether our interpretation of Daniel's Seventy Weeks is accepted or rejected, there were, in fact, 62 weeks (434 years) plus the 2,300 days (in which the Jews were oppressed by Syria) between the first command to restore and the First Coming of the Messiah.[9] Daniel 8 actually confirms what history tells us, that there was such a period of 2,300 days. And history, as well as the Bible, clearly pinpoints the dates of the first command and His First Coming. Therefore, it "just happens" that there were in fact 62 weeks of Jewish internal rule and 2,300 days of external rule between those two well-established dates. Coincidence?

---

8. Those who are familiar with the history of the Jews from that period know that there was much outside influence and intrigue exercised over Israel by several foreign powers between Daniel's day and Christ's birth. However, the Jews were not directly or completely controlled by foreigners at any other time during this period. This is confirmed by biblical history. The Jews were defeated and placed under tribute by many conquerors (Nebuchadnezzar, Alexander the Great, etc.), but they never lost their freedom of religion, and they continued to rebel against foreign intervention as soon as the troops withdrew. This pattern began even before their return from Babylon. Nebuchadnezzar defeated Judah in battle several times, and then placed a puppet king on the throne, only to learn after leaving that the Jews continued on, independent of his authority and rule. (Read Second Kings 24–25 to see that this happened repeatedly.) The enemies of the Jews referred to this independent spirit in Ezra 4:11-16 where they told the king of Persia that if the Jews were permitted to have a capital city again they would never be subject to him. This was proven by the fact that they were never subject to anyone before their capital city was destroyed by Nebuchadnezzar. This same independent spirit was manifested during the centuries between Daniel's day and Christ's birth, with the exception of the days of Antiochus, when the Jews couldn't even practice their religion. Antiochus effectively controlled them for almost seven years.
9. We are speaking in round numbers here. But remember that the dates for the command and His birth are accurate within a margin of error of one or two months at most. We know the month in which the command went forth to restore Israel, so that can't be changed, but if Christ was born a month or six weeks later than what we have said, then maybe Israel experienced 434 years of independence plus 2,330 or 2,345 days of Syrian rule between the date of the command and the date of His birth. Either way, this would be almost as amazing, even more so if our interpretation has nothing to do with the fulfillment of this prophecy!

Chapter 31

7 Weeks

November 29, 1947 headlines: "United Nations Resolution Gives the Holy Land Back to Jews." Today, Israel is as much a people as they ever were at any time in history. They are definitely an independent, self-governing nation at this moment. Some military analysts say Israel is the world's third-greatest military power, after the United States and Russia. In fact, one Russian dignitary recently said that the three superpowers, Russia, the United States, and Israel, needed to sit down and talk! What has God done? What a restoration! Israel will never again cease to be a people (Amos 9:9,14-15), even though they pass through fire and water, or through what Jeremiah calls the "time of Jacob's trouble" (Jer. 30:7).

This brings us to the **date of the second command** to restore Israel the **second** time, and the **date of the Second Coming** of the Messiah. For this command it is unnecessary to go to the history books, because many of us were alive when it was given. We know that on November 29, 1947 the United Nations gave the command, or resolution, to restore the nation of Israel. Note again what Gabriel told Daniel:

> *Know also and understand, that from the going forth of the commandment to cause to return and to build Jerusalem, unto the Anointed the Prince, shall be seven weeks*(Daniel 9:25, Sir Isaac Newton's translation).

Therefore, from the second command (November, 1947) until the Second Coming of the Messiah will be 7 weeks, or 49 years. This is the other date that is given in Daniel 9:25. Therefore, the Messiah will come sometime at the end of the year A.D. 1996. Isaac Newton understood this three hundred years ago! The Lord comes as the Prince to reign after

7 weeks (49 years), but comes as the One who is "cut off" after 62 weeks (434 years).

When I first read Isaac Newton's explanation of all this in June of 1994, and realized that he had seen it long before I had, I was not only humbled but also awe-struck by the fact that we have the great privilege of living today on the other side of Israel's restoration. Twenty-four years ago, when I first understood the meaning of Daniel's Seventy Weeks, I had the benefit of knowing two things that Isaac Newton didn't know. First, Israel was, in fact, restored as a nation, and second, we know the exact date when that happened. Their restoration is no longer merely a prophetic message that the prophets gave, but it is a reality, something Newton believed would happen but never saw. We have the great privilege of living during the last 7 weeks (49 years) leading up to the revelation of His glory in Israel and the entire earth.

But remember, in both comings of Christ He comes with a birth. His First Coming was through a natural birth and His Second Coming will be through a spiritual birth. He came the first time through His natural people Israel and will now come through His spiritual people Israel. He will be spiritually birthed in His people during these last days. Before we are too quick to either accept or reject this concept, let's consider a little more about these seventy weeks, as well as many other Scriptures that confirm this date. Please remember that I am *not* excluding a *physical* return of Christ, which will most certainly take place. We will also see in Chapter 43 that the concept of a seven-week period related to the last days was not something new with Daniel. In fact, this concept runs throughout the Bible. God showed, at the beginning of Israel's ancient history, that seven weeks of years will be a part of His last day plan for them.

One question commonly asked is, "If 7 weeks is the time period between the second command and the Second Coming, why does it appear first in Daniel 9:25, before the 62 weeks?" It is a case of stating first **the final victory**, the ultimate purpose. What is the Lord's final goal? For man, the First Coming and the cross are central. However, for the Lord, it is the Marriage with His Bride. Christ endured the cross for the joy set before Him (Heb. 12:2).

Two other biblical examples of stating the final goal first are found in Enoch and in the Tabernacle of Moses. The very first written message of a prophet of God that is found in the Bible speaks about the Second Coming, before there was ever a prophetic revelation of the First Coming. Enoch is the prophet, and his message is in Jude 14 and 15. Also, when God showed Moses the pattern for the tabernacle, He didn't reveal the door first, but rather the ark of the covenant (Ex. 25:10). The door is the first step in our Christian walk, but entering within the veil of the Holy of Holies, where we find the glory of the ark, is the goal (Heb. 6:19-20). Therefore, we see that in other Scriptures also the Holy Spirit employs this pattern of revealing the goal first and then afterward the essential steps to reach that goal.

To conclude, we can say that the First Coming is governed by a time period of 62 weeks, and that the Second Coming is governed by a time period of 7 weeks.

Chapter 32

7 and 62

Why did God choose these two time periods of 7 weeks and 62 weeks? Do they have any special significance in the Bible?

The Number 7 is Called "The Covenant Number"

The number 7 has often been called "the covenant number," because in the Hebrew language the word "seven" actually comes from the verb meaning "to make a covenant" or "to make an oath."[1] We don't have to be Hebrew experts to understand this. It is evident from Genesis 21:28-32 where Abraham set aside 7 ewe lambs from his flock when he was making a covenant with Abimelech. Abimelech asked him what those lambs signified, and Abraham said they signified, or were a witness of, the covenant that they were making with one another. The place was then called Beersheba, which means both "the well (Beer) of the seven (sheba)," and "the well (Beer) of the covenant (sheba)," as is noted in the margins of many Bibles.

The Number 7 and the Second Coming of Christ

The number 7 is related to His Second Coming, because all that He has promised, or covenanted, to His people will be fulfilled at that time. He has promised the Kingdom to His people, and when He comes again He will come to reign with them. This is surely one reason why the number 7 appears so many times in the Book of Revelation. All of His promises will

---

1. See *Strong's Hebrew Dictionary*, #7651 and #7650.

be fulfilled in that glorious day. All He has promised to mankind and His Church will be manifested in the earth. The river of life will be flowing freely, and we will again partake of that wonderful Tree of Life, lost to Adam when he chose a different tree.

The Number 7 and the End

The number 7 is also used by God to measure time. It marks the end of one period and the beginning of another in God's biblical calendar. For example, the year began on the first day of the first month. Then, on the seventh **day** there was a Sabbath, ending the week. On the fourteenth day of the month, Israel celebrated the Passover. Then God's calendar specified 7 **weeks** from the Passover to the Feast of Pentecost. Later, in the seventh **month**, they celebrated the Feasts of Trumpets, Atonement, and Tabernacles. The Bible even refers to this seventh **month** as the "end of the year" (Ex. 23:16). Then in the seventh **year** they observed the Sabbatical year, and finally after seven "sabbaths of years" (that is, 7 weeks of years or 49 years), they observed the Year of Jubilee (Lev. 25:8). So these different time periods ended in 7 days, 7 weeks, 7 months, 7 years, and then 7 "weeks" of years, or 49 years. In each case the number 7 is related to the end of one period and the beginning of another. So, once again, we understand why the number 7 is intimately linked with the Second Coming. It speaks of the end of one time period and the beginning of another.

The Number 62 and Christ's First Coming as a Servant

Does the biblical significance of the number 62 have anything to do with the **First Coming** of Christ? In First Chronicles 26:8 (NAS) Obededom had 62 sons who were "able men with strength for the service." Here the number 62 is found in a context of strength to serve. In His First Coming, Christ came to serve and to be a Servant. His First Coming is related to serving, while His Second Coming is related to reigning. This gives some indication that the number 62 may be related to the First Coming. Incidentally, if we want to return with Him in His Second Coming, after the Marriage Supper, we must also become identified with His First Coming. In other words, we must be willing to be servants in this present life.

The Number 62 in the Book of Daniel

The number 62 appears only four times in the Bible, and three of those times are found in the Book of Daniel. To understand the context in which Daniel uses this number we need to consider another "parable," namely

Nebuchadnezzar, the king of Babylon. As king of Babylon, he is representative of Satan, as seen in Isaiah 14:4 and 12: "...take up this proverb against the king of Babylon, and say...How art thou fallen from heaven, O Lucifer, son of the morning." Just as Satan has done in all ages, Nebuchadnezzar, as a vessel of wrath and judgment, destroyed God's people, and brought them into captivity. He also made a great image, and cast Daniel's three friends into the fiery furnace for not worshipping that image. These are the ways and the works of Satan. In the end Satan will again make an image, and seek to kill those who refuse to worship it (Rev. 13:14-15).

The kingdom of Babylon was destroyed by Cyrus and Darius, kings of the Medes and Persians. Remembering that Babylon represents Satan's kingdom, in reality, who destroyed the works of Satan and took his kingdom from him? Christ, without doubt, took Satan's kingdom and destroyed the works of darkness **in His First Coming** (Col. 2:15). Consider the possibility that the victory of Darius over Nebuchadnezzar is a foreshadow of Christ's victory over the kingdom of darkness.[2]

After His victory at the cross, Christ returned to His place in Heaven. From there He poured out His Spirit on His people, as promised. He established His Church with a divinely ordained spiritual government. But notice from the Book of Acts and Galatians how Christ organized the Church government **after His First Coming.** Of all the people who had witnessed the glory of Christ's three-and-a-half-year ministry, when the Day of Pentecost finally came, only 120 faithful souls were found obeying His command to wait in Jerusalem. They were endued with power from on high, and became the leaders in the first church of Jerusalem.

During the very first official "service" in Acts 2, they spoke the gospel to representatives of the nations that were gathered in Jerusalem. People from "every nation under heaven" were there, each hearing in his own language the wonderful truths of God (Acts 2:5-6). When 3,000 were added to the Church that day, and 5,000 more a few days later, imagine

---

2. In the Bible there are two kings with the name Darius during the period of the restoration of Israel in the time of Ezra and Nehemiah. An in-depth study of what these two kings did reveals that the first Darius is a foreshadow of Christ in His First Coming, while the second Darius is a foreshadow of Christ in His Second Coming. Not only does this become clear as one studies their two lives, but it also opens up our understanding of certain passages of Scripture related to that time. For example, the first Darius defeated Nebuchadnezzar and began the construction of the temple, while the second Darius defeated Smerdis, a usurper of the throne and finished the construction of the temple. The first Darius was a co-regent with Cyrus, and under their rule the decree was given to rebuild the temple (Ezra 1:1; Dan. 5:31). The second Darius is found in Ezra 4:5,24; 6:1,12-13.

how important the 120 leaders became. They were responsible to teach and guide those multitudes.

The three main pillars, James, Cephas (Peter) and John, presided over the Church, with Peter clearly being the principal leader (Gal. 2:9). Peter was presiding in Acts 1, and again in Acts 2 on the Day of Pentecost. In Acts 3 he was involved in the healing of the lame man, and then spoke to the multitude that gathered as a result. In Acts 4 he spoke to the leaders of the council. In Acts 5 he spoke to Ananias and Sapphira when they were judged, and again to the council. He was the first one to carry the gospel to the Gentiles in Acts 10. And finally, in Acts 12, the entire Church sought God for his release from prison. So it seems that Christ's governmental organization after His First Coming consisted of 120 committed ones, with three main pillars over them, and one of those three pillars, Peter, was the final authority.

Returning to Daniel 6:1-3 we discover that Darius (whom I said could be a foreshadow of Christ in His First Coming) established his government in exactly the same way. His government consisted of 120 princes and three governors, but Daniel, who was one of those three, became the chief. Is this mere coincidence, or is it another link between Darius and Christ's First Coming? Consider also Daniel 5:31: "And Darius the Median took the kingdom, being about **threescore and two** years old." Why are we told this otherwise meaningless fact? Because the number 62 is related to the First Coming of Christ.

Darius the Median, then, is a revelation of Christ's First Coming for three reasons:

1. Because he defeated Satan's kingdom (Nebuchadnezzar).
2. Because he organized his government in the same way that Christ organized His after the First Coming.
3. Because the number 62 is related to both the arrival of Darius on the scene and to Christ's First Coming after 62 weeks.

Chapter 33

Messiah Cut Off

After the sixty-two weeks the Messiah will be cut off and have nothing (Daniel 9:26 NAS).

Note again that He is "cut off" after 62 weeks, *not* after 69 weeks. Some translations have added a few words to this verse that do not appear in the original Hebrew. As a result, several versions imply that this verse is speaking about Christ's death on the cross. Some versions even say, "the life of the Messiah will be taken away." Yet the Hebrew only says that the Messiah will be "cut off," as the NAS and KJV translate, as well as Sir Isaac Newton (see Chapter 20). There is no mention of His life being taken away, or of His death. Attempts have been made to fit the 7 weeks, plus the 62 weeks, between the date of the command to restore Israel and the date of His death on the cross because of this mistranslation.

The Hebrew word translated here as "cut off" in the KJV also appears in Exodus 4:25, where "cut off" refers to the rite of circumcision. That rite was certainly a "cutting off" or a "cutting away." There the son of Moses is experiencing a "cutting off." This does not mean that he is dying, nor is his life being taken away, even though his mother, Zipporah, had her doubts. Although being "cut off" in the Bible *can* refer to physical death, of the 280 times this Hebrew word is used in the Old Testament, the majority of times does *not* refer to physical death. The use of this Hebrew word in the context of circumcision in Exodus proves that it is not necessarily referring to physical death. In fact, this Hebrew word also means "to cut a covenant."[1] In English Bibles it is translated as "to make a covenant"

---

1. *Strong's Hebrew Dictionary, #3772.*

many times in all the different versions. For example, in Genesis 15:10-18, where God told Abraham to *cut* several animals in two, we are told that "in the same day the LORD **made a covenant** with Abram." In other words, He "cut" a covenant with Abraham, and this is the same word translated in Daniel 9:26 as "cut off."

This word is further linked to circumcision and the covenant through an amazing play on words in the Hebrew language found in Genesis 17:14: "And the uncircumcised man child whose flesh of his foreskin is not **circumcised**, that soul shall be **cut off** from his people; he hath broken my **covenant**." The English words "cut off" here come from the same Hebrew word that is found in Daniel 9:26. However, in Hebrew "circumcised" also has the meaning of being "cut off" (see Hithpolel's definition). Therefore, the Lord is saying that any man child who is not "cut off" (circumcised) in his flesh will be "cut off" from his people, because being "cut off" (circumcised) is a sign that they are keeping the covenant that He has "cut" with them. It is no wonder, then, that circumcision (being "cut off") was a sign that they were keeping the covenant that God had "cut" with them. Hebrew speaking people understand this connection.

In light of all this, could we substitute "circumcised" for "cut off" in Daniel 9:26? And how would that apply to the Messiah? Circumcision in the physical body is a sign of a spiritual work that God wants to accomplish in us (Rom. 4:11). That work is the cutting away of our "flesh," or natural man and his desires. This is what the cross accomplishes in the life of the Believer.[2] However, was Christ's first encounter with this "cutting away" at Calvary? No, the cross was a way of life for Him. He said to His disciples, "If you want to come after me, if you want to do what I am doing, and be like I am, you must take up your cross daily and follow me, because that is what I am doing. That is the way I am walking every day" (Mt. 16:24 paraphrased). Paul himself said that he died daily (1 Cor. 15:31). Did Christ do anything less?

When did He begin to experience the bitterness of the cross and the way of suffering? He was circumcised when He was eight days old, as were all Jewish male babies. Could this outward sign have been a revelation of the "cutting away" and the suffering and self-denial of the cross He was beginning to experience even at that very tender age?

The answer becomes clear by considering many other Scriptures that use the word "cut off." It is frequently translated in the context of being

2. Colossians 2:11-12 shows that spiritual circumcision is synonymous with the work of the cross, which is the death and burial of the old man so that we may experience the new life found in His Resurrection.

"cut off" from one's people, as in Genesis 17:14 above. However, to show once again that this does not usually mean physical death, consider what Jeremiah told the Jews who had gone down to Egypt to escape from the Babylonians. He said that they had gone down **into the land of Egypt, to cut themselves off from the land of Judah** (Jer. 44:7-8). Therefore, when Jesus was forced into Egypt as a baby to escape from King Herod, was He not also "cut off" from His people, land and inheritance? Comparing again the beginning and ending, the Lord went into Egypt both at the beginning and ending of His life. Revelation 11:8 tells us that at the end of His life He was crucified in the great city "which spiritually is called Egypt."

Probably the clearest proof that the Lord's "cutting off" is not referring to His death on the cross is found right within Gabriel's words to Daniel. He said, "After the sixty-two [weeks], the Anointed One will be cut off and will have nothing" (Dan. 9:26 NIV). His being "cut off" is followed by the statement that He "will have nothing." This is what the Hebrew actually says, as most of the well-known English translations confirm (NAS, NIV, ASV, RSV, NRSV, AMP). It can hardly be said that after His death on the cross He "had nothing." The scriptural facts are that after He died on the cross He inherited *everything*! Philippians 2:8-11 says it well: "...He humbled himself, and became obedient unto death, even the death of the cross. Wherefore God also hath highly exalted him, and given him a name which is above every name."

Perhaps we point to the cross and Christ's physical death as the time when He was *first* "cut off" because we experience so little of the work of the cross in our own daily living. Could it be? If we were to deny ourselves *daily*, experiencing the cross as He did, it would be easier for us to become identified with periods of His life, other than Calvary, where He was "cut off." As we study His life, we would then say, "Oh, *here* is the cross. *Here* He was cut off. *Here* He denied the flesh and died to self so that He could bring life to others. I recognize His sorrow and agony in *that* experience, for I, too, have tasted a measure of that death to self." When Paul said he died daily, he was certainly recognizing the cross in Christ's life as something far deeper than Golgotha.

In conclusion, just exactly as Gabriel told Daniel, Jesus began His life by being "cut off" at His birth, both in a physical sense at His circumcision, and in a spiritual sense as He descended into Egypt. This occurred precisely 62 weeks after the command to restore Israel. He didn't wait until He was 33 years old to experience His first "cutting off."

Chapter 34

The Week That Never Was

"Just military maneuvers. Just military maneuvers," our tour guide shouted to us. We were standing on a bunker on the Golan Heights, and could see fire coming out of the barrels of heavy guns; the sound of machine guns seemed to be everywhere. We would have believed our guide, except he wasn't a very good actor. The look of panic on his face as he glanced over at the bus driver betrayed him. It was time to get out of there, and fast. Later that day we were informed that fighting had, in fact, broken out between Syria and Israel on the Golan Heights. We had witnessed the real thing during our tour of the Holy Land.

Tony, our guide, was not a Believer in any sense of the word. Born and raised in New York City, he had immigrated to Israel as an adult. Far from being an orthodox Jew, he was basically an agnostic, eking out an existence in the Holy Land as a tour guide. During our week-long tour, I often wondered why anyone who didn't believe in the God of Israel would ever choose to live in that country. There is the constant threat of war, and many hardships not faced elsewhere, and Tony was making far less money than he could have been making in the United States. I knew that many Jews lived in the Holy Land because of a deep conviction that very soon the Messiah will come and establish His worldwide Kingdom, with Israel at the center. But Tony? Why would he live there? He didn't seem to believe in anything.

Finally, to avoid the possible embarrassment or offense of a personal question, I asked, "Tony, of all the Jews living in Israel today, what percentage of them would you estimate are expecting a Messiah to come?" He looked at me for a moment with that "What, are you crazy?" look, and then responded, "*Every* Jew is expecting the Messiah to come, causing Israel to rule again. Do you think we would be here suffering if we didn't believe that, and didn't have that hope?"

This may not be the sentiment of every Jew living in Israel today, but Tony certainly speaks for many. They still cling to the promise God made to father Abraham, that he, along with his descendants, would be the heir of the world. Just as those who are born-again believe that they will reign with Christ, so, too, the Jews expect to inherit the world and rule over it as kings with their Messiah (Rom. 4:13,16; Rev. 1:6; 2:26-27). Even after the cross, the apostles understood that the fulfillment of God's covenant with His people involved the coming of the Kingdom (Acts 1:6). Biblically speaking, this is true. In fact, we could say that a one word definition of the "**covenant**" is the "**Kingdom,**" and all it brings with it (authority, power, character, righteousness, peace, and joy in the Holy Spirit, etc.).

> *And he shall* ***confirm a covenant*** *with the many (for) one week. And in the middle of the week he shall cause the sacrifice and the offering to cease, and on wings as a desolator, abominations, even until the end. And that which was decreed shall be poured on the desolator* (Daniel 9:27, Interlinear Hebrew/Greek English Bible[1]—emphasis added).

This brings us to the well-known and well-preached "last week" of Daniel that, in reality, doesn't even exist. What do I mean? We have already seen how the 7 weeks and the 62 weeks fit into history. Daniel 9:27 speaks of one other week, bringing the total to seventy. This week is often erroneously called "Daniel's Last Week." Since Gabriel didn't call it the "last week," maybe we are misleading ourselves to do so, especially since every jot and tittle of the Word are important and will be fulfilled.

Daniel 9:27 makes no reference to the "last" week, but rather says, "and he shall confirm the covenant with many for **one week.**" There is a great difference between the idea conveyed by the phrase "**last** week" and the phrase "**one** week." It has been *assumed* that this other week must come **last**, at the end of the Church Age. It is often referred to as "The Seven-Year Tribulation." However, nothing in Daniel 9 supports this **assumption.**

---

1. Green, Jay, ed., *The Interlinear Hebrew/Greek English Bible,* Associated Publishers and Authors, Inc., Evansville, Indiana, 1978. We resort to the Hebrew text because of the great variety of opinion about this verse between the translators of the various versions. Words have been added in most cases, which sometimes convey the opinion of the translator rather than giving a precise translation of the text. I recognize that this Interlinear Bible is a translation also, but after conferring with several people who read Hebrew, it became apparent that this translation is quite literal with very few additions and subtractions.

Let's consider what we know for sure about this verse, and then what the Bible reveals in other passages about this "other week."

What We Know for Sure

Limiting ourselves to the facts, and excluding speculation, we know the following from the text itself:

1. A period of one "week" or **seven years is revealed here**. That period is divided into two halves of three and a half years each. (The Hebrew word "middle" used here actually means "to divide into halves."[2])

2. A covenant is being **confirmed with many**. "Confirm" in the Hebrew means "to make strong."[3]

3. A covenant is being **confirmed** for a period of "**one week**," or seven years, in this verse.

4. Someone **causes sacrifices and offerings to cease** after the first half of the week, that is, after a three-and-a-half-year period.

5. The latter part of this verse speaks about a "**desolator**," and that there will be "abominations" until the end. Finally, we are told that what has been decreed will be poured upon the desolator.

The Bible Interprets the Bible

Do other portions of Scripture reveal a fulfillment of these details? Our interpretation of one Scripture must always be confirmed by other Scriptures that clearly support what we are saying. Let's consider each of the above points.

1. Do we find anywhere in the Bible two distinct periods of three and a half years? Previous chapters of this book have given us the answer. The New Testament Age begins and ends with a period of three and a half years. Christ's ministry lasted three and a half years at the beginning of the New Testament, and Revelation reveals another period of three and a half years at the end.

2. Do we find in the Bible someone who is confirming a covenant with many? First, Hebrews 9:17 says that a covenant is **made strong**, or confirmed, by the death of the testator.[4] As mentioned above, "to make strong" is what "confirm" means in Daniel 9:27. Second, regarding a

2. *Strong's Hebrew Dictionary*, #2677 and #2673.
3. Ibid., #1396.
4. Ibid., #949 and #2480. It is noteworthy that the Spanish Bible translates Hebrews 9:17 as, "Because a covenant is confirmed by death" (R.V. 1960).

covenant made with many, Jesus said, "This is my blood of the new testament [covenant], which is shed for *many*..." (Mt. 26:28). So here is a covenant being "confirmed" with "many" **through the death of Christ**, death being the only way a covenant can be confirmed according to Hebrews.

3. Are the two periods of three and a half years found in the New Testament related to a covenant that is being confirmed? Paul, Christ, and Isaiah give us the answer. Paul declares, "Now I say that Jesus Christ was a minister of the circumcision for the truth of God, to **confirm** the promises made unto the fathers" (Rom. 15:8). The covenant includes all the promises God has made to His people. Christ's ministry confirmed, or fulfilled, that covenant. However, it wasn't only His ministry that confirmed the covenant, but His very life *was, and is*, the covenant. In Isaiah 42:6 the Father encourages the Son saying, "I the Lord have called thee in righteousness, and will hold thine hand, and will keep thee, and **give thee for a covenant of the people**, for a light of the Gentiles." The Lord Jesus did not make the mistake that we so often make, forgetting that we must *live* the message we preach. He didn't just *preach* the covenant; He was the covenant. There is only one Person in the universe that can confirm the covenant, because the covenant is a Person, the Lord Himself! Christ brought to the Jews the very thing they sought. Like Tony, our tour guide, they longed for the Kingdom, and, as I mentioned, the "covenant" is the Kingdom of God, and everything that comes with it. God has promised to Abraham and his descendants that they will inherit the earth and rule over it. When Christ came, His message and life were a revelation of that Kingdom for three and a half years as He "confirmed," or fulfilled it. He said, "The Kingdom of heaven is at hand," and that Kingdom was within Him (Mt. 4:17).

However, Christ's ministry does not last only three and a half years, but it will last for seven years, because Daniel declares that He will confirm His covenant for one "week." It is quite understandable then that He would promise us another three-and-a-half-year period in which the Kingdom will be manifested. He did precisely that by saying that the gospel of the Kingdom will be preached in all the world for a "witness" to all nations just before the end (Mt. 24:14). That "witness" lasts 1,260 days, or three and a half years, according to Revelation 11. So the covenant will be confirmed, or fulfilled, again at the end of the Church Age, for another period of three and a half years.[5] Therefore, just as Daniel shows, the seven-year period is divided into two distinct periods of three and a half years.

5. We will see more about this in later chapters, and this statement will be proven.

4. Does anyone cause sacrifices and offerings to cease anywhere in the Bible after a period of three and a half years? The Book of Hebrews tells us that Christ put an end to all God-ordained sacrifices and offerings by means of one sacrifice forever—His own. Consider what is said: "But this Man, after He had offered one sacrifice for sins forever, sat down at the right hand of God...For by one offering He has perfected forever those who are being sanctified...Now where there is remission of these, **there is no longer an offering for sin**" (Heb. 10:12-18 NKJV). Although I didn't quote the entire passage, this passage in Hebrews actually links the New Covenant with the fact that Christ's sacrifice did away with all other blood sacrifices. Christ did this on the cross after ministering for precisely three and a half years. He therefore did, in fact, put an end to sacrifices in the middle of the week, or after a period of three and a half years.

We already noted that the Jewish Believers in the early Church continued to offer blood sacrifices. If we compare the declaration of Hebrews that "there is no longer an offering for sin" with what they actually did in those days, we might have cause to wonder whether or not the Lord actually put an end to sacrifice and offering through the cross. But remember that Hebrews was written to help a believing Israelite make the transition from the Old Testament to the New Testament. Hebrews is explaining to them that the issue isn't whether or not they continued to *offer* blood sacrifices. Rather, the issue is that God no longer *required* them. Before the cross, they couldn't be saved without offering blood sacrifices, but after the cross those sacrifices had no redemptive value whatsoever. From His perspective, God Himself had put an end to them, because there simply was no longer an "**offering for sin**" that was recognized by Heaven apart from Christ's. They could continue to offer sacrifices for as long as they wanted, but He no longer considered them to be an "offering for sin." All **offerings for sin** had been ended by Christ.

5. Will the Desolator confirm a covenant? Some have **speculated** that Daniel 9:27 refers to a covenant that the Antichrist will make with Israel for seven years. I call this "the week that never was," because this passage was never referring to this idea. The speculation continues by saying that after three and a half years the Antichrist will violate the covenant. He then will forbid the Jews to continue offering their sacrifices in a temple that, **presumably**, they will build with his permission and help. This interpretation presents several problems:

a. Not even one detail of this interpretation can be found in any other Scripture. This could be rightfully labeled "extreme speculation."

b. Other Scriptures do show that Christ will confirm the covenant seven years, and that He, in fact, did put an end to sacrifices and offerings for sin after a period of three and a half years. We must not ignore these biblical *facts* simply because we prefer a different interpretation.

c. Returning to the translation of the Hebrew text for Daniel 9:27 given above, the first phrase says, "And he shall confirm a covenant with the many (for) one week." It will be noted that the word "for" is in parentheses. This means that it is not found in the original text. The original says only, "And he shall confirm a covenant with many one week." Therefore, regardless of whom this phrase is speaking of, the person who does the confirming will do so "one week" or seven years, not three and a half years. He does not confirm a covenant that is *supposed* to last for seven years, and then break it in the middle. Rather, he "confirms it seven years." He cannot "confirm it seven years" and at the same time break it after three and a half years. This interpretation contradicts itself.

d. There is no basis for concluding that the Desolator found in the last half of this verse is the same person found in the first half, the one who confirms the covenant. However, there is strong scriptural basis for concluding that they are *not* the same person. Throughout history we have seen Satan's nature manifested over and over through wicked leaders of nations who made covenants, or agreements, and never planned to keep them for a moment. First Kings 8:23 reveals the difference between our God and the "god of this world."[6] "There is no God like thee, in heaven above, or on earth beneath, who **keepest covenant** and mercy with thy servants." Satan, the father of lies, is incapable of truly confirming any covenant, by virtue of his own nature. He is a liar and deceiver who is incapable of keeping a covenant for even a second, much less for three and a half years! Jesus said that Satan is a liar and does not "stand in the truth" (Jn. 8:44 NKJV). According to the Strong's Greek lexicon, this means that Satan does not "make firm" or "establish" the truth. A covenant is, by definition, an agreement between two people that contains certain aspects or truths that both parties agree to. Those who believe that Satan is going to keep a covenant with the Jews for three and a half years are attributing to Satan an ability that he simply does not possess! He never has and never will keep any truth or any promise of any kind. The world witnessed this again recently in the peace accord made between Israel and the Palestinians. Most level-headed people knew that

6. Second Corinthians 4:4 calls Satan the "God of this world."

Yasser Arafat was only maneuvering to obtain a place within Israel from which to launch his terrorist campaigns. However, most of us probably thought that he would put on a good show for at least a few months for the sake of obtaining positive international opinion. To the surprise of many, within hours of signing the final accord he declared holy war on Israel, because he wants the city of Jerusalem. *This* is how Satan always has operated and always will!

Seven Year Peace Treaty and 2,300 Days

We need to understand something else about Satan's mode of operation. He fell because he wanted to take God's place of honor and authority in the universe. He deceived a third of the angels into following him, portraying himself as God.[7] Even the Bible gives him the dubious title of "the god of this world" (2 Cor. 4:4). However, he and his fallen angels used to live in the manifest presence and glory of God. They know what God is like. They have seen His glory.

Therefore, Satan has a problem. Although he wants to be God, he cannot conceive of anything that would be an improvement on what he has already seen in the presence of the true and living God. Therefore, anything that Satan could possibly invent or contrive would be inferior to what he and the fallen angels have already seen. Besides that, if he were to invent something new, his cohorts would tell him, "But *that's* not the way God is." So Satan has been reduced to copying and counterfeiting what he has seen in God. And he seeks to do that as precisely as possible. He tries to counterfeit everything he has seen in God. Many Believers run into problems because they are unaware of this. For example, some say that we should have nothing to do with certain subjects or areas of study because Satan promotes similar subjects among the spiritist mediums. If we follow that line of reasoning, we should stop praying because many of Satan's followers pray. However, when Satan emphasizes some subject or area to his followers, far from thinking the subject bad, we should understand that he is counterfeiting the real and the good that he has seen in God. If there is a counterfeit there has to be a real, by definition. Though he can never reproduce the glory and nature of God, he continually attempts to do so. Like anyone who counterfeits money, he seeks to make his "hundred-dollar bills" as exact as possible.

In the first edition of this book I mentioned, at this point, that in these last days Satan might try to counterfeit the concept of a covenant for seven years. In fact, I wrote, referring to Satan, "He may come in the end and

7. Compare Revelation 12:3-4 with 1:20. See also Second Thessalonians 2:4.

manifest his way for a period of seven years." Now, in this second edition, I can write that this has already happened. On September 13, 1993, seven years before the year A.D. 2000 Israel's enemies, the Palestinians (which means "Philistines") signed a peace accord with Israel. Furthermore, it "just happened" to be exactly 2,300 days from the first day of the new millennium, January 1, 2000.

Unfortunately, many Believers paid little attention to the "signs of the times." The Church has declared for decades that in the last days the enemy of Israel would sign a peace agreement with the Jewish people for a seven-year period. However, in spite of the fact that the ceremony for that peace treaty involved the greatest gathering of international dignitaries on the White House lawn in the history of the United States, it has been discounted and ignored by the Church as though it were totally unrelated to the hour in which we live. Furthermore, the extreme importance of that event is ignored in spite of the fact that even the President recognized the significance of the hour when he said, "This is the first time in history that Ishmael and Isaac have made peace." It was actually hailed as one of the most important events in human history by the news media. Of course, one reason that all this is discounted is due to a love for the pre-tribulation Rapture doctrine. If any of these events indicate that we are already in the last seven years, then the idea of a Rapture before those seven years begin is obviously false. One of the gravest dangers that exist in the pre-tribulation Rapture doctrine is the spiritual blindness that it causes in the hearts of Believers around the world at this very moment. Even though we are already living in the last seven years before the return of Christ, many Believers are discounting everything that is happening simply because they assume that these things can't be significant. Their reasoning is that we would already have been Raptured if we were really living in the last seven years. Only the truth will take away this veil.

For whatever reason, much of the Church continues to ignore what is happening. I'm not exactly sure what those Believers expect to happen in the last days, but I have an idea that we have forgotten the seven exhortations given to us at the beginning of Revelation. Seven times the Lord exhorts, "He that hath ears to hear let him hear" (Rev. 2–3). Apparently some Believers have the concept that Gabriel is going to visibly fly through the heavens blowing a trumpet that is audible to all. God has *never* worked that way at any time in history. If things were going to be so obvious to the natural man, I don't believe that He would have exhorted us concerning having an ear to hear. Furthermore, in the last days people are going to continue on with "business as usual" according to Matthew 24:37-39. They will be eating and drinking, marrying and giving in marriage, just like they did at the time of the flood of Noah until the first drop of water in history fell on them, but then it was too late to get into the ark! I doubt that it would be "business as usual" in the end if everyone knew that something was amiss on earth because an Antichrist with horns and a tail were governing the world. May the Lord grant us what we need to awake from spiritual sleep and recognize the lateness of this hour.

One other thought should be mentioned concerning the peace treaty and the 2,300 days. In that treaty Israel gave her enemies permission to form a separate nation inside the Holy Land, and thus tread under foot that Holy Land, as well as facilitate terrorist attacks against her armies. Daniel 8:13 tells us that the enemies of Israel will tread down the Holy Land and the armies of Israel for 2,300 days. This is what the Hebrew text in that verse actually means.[8] Is it significant that this treaty was signed precisely 2,300 days before January 1, 2000? I believe that God is calling our attention to the things that are happening in our world at this very moment. After having lived, personally, in the light of the message of this book for 24 years, it is thrilling to see it come to pass right on schedule!

8. See The Revised English Bible and *Strong's Hebrew Dictionary*.

Chapter 35

The Week That Was

Israel Was Governed From Without After Christ's Birth

"Stop the clock! Interference by Rome—countdown on hold." Again our key to fitting these weeks into history is to determine when Israel was governed from **within**. Many historians recognize Herod the Great as the last king of Israel,[1] the last to rule over **all** of the Holy Land. At the birth of Jesus, around September of 5 B.C., Herod the Great tried to take His life. This was basically the last cruel work of this vessel of wrath, because just months later Herod died. Herod had been able to negotiate with Rome, and maintain himself on the throne of Israel for many years. However, with his death, Rome stepped into the land and divided it into four parts. Those four sectors were governed by different leaders placed there by Rome. Some years later we find Pilate governing in Judea; Herod Antipas, the son of Herod the Great, was over Galilee in the north; and Philip and Lysanias were tetrarchs of the other two portions of the Holy Land.[2] In other words, Israel lost its independence and was governed by foreigners from the time of Christ's birth onward. Therefore, God's countdown clock, counting the 490 years, stopped running from Christ's birth onward.

This situation was one of the greatest thorns ever in Israel's side. They hated the Romans with a passion, and longed for their Messiah to come and deliver them. Their Messiah offered to do that very thing for them,

---

1. Tenney, *Bible Dictionary*, see "Herod."
2. Luke 3:1 gives us these details, as does secular history.

but they refused His offer. For three and a half years, during His ministry, He actually did deliver them from Rome; they just didn't recognize it. Some may question this last statement, so we will look at the gospel narrative with this in mind.

Israel Was Again Governed From Within for Half a Week, During His Ministry, at the Beginning of the New Testament

"Repent: for the kingdom of heaven is at hand," was Jesus' first message (Mt. 4:17). The Kingdom had finally come, and He was the King. The Bible tells us He preached and revealed the Kingdom of God in Israel. We find here an interesting situation. The **Son of man**, to whom was given all power in Heaven and earth, was living in the Promised Land, and manifesting the authority, power and character of the Kingdom.[3]

At the same time, Tiberius Caesar was telling the world that he was in control, and that he was the only king who ruled. As Jesus revealed His authority and manifested the reality of **God in the flesh**, who was really in control of Israel? Or of the earth? Was the Son of man ruling, or was Rome ruling? Some may answer that Christ has always ruled. However, I am not speaking about Christ, the Son of God, here. Rather, I am speaking about the human being that Christ truly became. He emptied Himself, and became a man in every sense of the word (Phil. 2:7-8; Heb. 2:17). In fact, He was a Jew, living in Israel, manifesting real Kingdom authority. He was a descendant of David, and was as much a Jew as anyone else. Was that Jew from Galilee really ruling or not? Jesus Himself gives us the answer in John 17:2 where He tells the Father in His prayer, "Thou hast given him [the Son] power over all flesh."

However, let's allow Pilate, a Roman governor, to answer that question. When they crucified Him, Pilate placed on the cross this writing for all to see: "JESUS OF NAZARETH THE KING OF THE JEWS" (Jn. 19:19). This "respect" Pilate paid Christ may not appear significant, since Pilate was, at the same time, granting permission to crucify Him. However, in those days Caesar proclaimed himself to be god over all the earth and the only king, demanding this level of reverence from all his subjects. When, during the trial of Christ, the Jews said, "We have no king but Caesar," they revealed the tremendous hypocrisy in their hearts. They hated Rome, and wouldn't submit to Caesar's authority. But in order to crucify the

3. In John 16:33 (NRSV), before the cross, Jesus said, "I have conquered the world."

Lord Jesus, they were willing, for a moment, to recognize Caesar as their only king.

When Pilate wrote, "JESUS OF NAZARETH THE KING OF THE JEWS," those were not the words of a hypocritical Pharisee trying to obtain his evil goal and perverted purposes. He was a Roman governor who wanted to give the impression that he submitted wholeheartedly to Caesar's evil "tenets of faith." He was a man who confessed that Caesar was the only king. By writing that statement for all of Judea to see, Pilate risked losing his seat in Caesar's government over Canaan, and possibly his very life. So why did he write it? Not to please the Jews over whom he governed. They were irate, as he knew they would be. So why then did he write it? Because even Pilate believed what the King of kings had told him: "Thou couldest have no power at all against me, except it were given thee from above" (Jn. 19:11). Even Pilate's wife had told him the truth. Yes, Pilate recognized who was really ruling in Israel, though he didn't have the necessary fiber in his character to resist the Jews and set the King free. But neither could he resist the impulse to write the truth concerning Him.

But what about King Herod Antipas? What does his life teach us concerning who was ruling in Israel? In Luke 23:8 we are told that, during the ministry of Christ, King Herod wanted to see Jesus. Imagine it. Herod, the king of Galilee, the king who was supposedly reigning over Jesus, wanted to see Him.

If the President of the United States requested to see us in the White House, we would probably be on the next flight out to Washington, D.C. Afterward, we would probably accept the most "fruitful-looking" invitation to some Christian conference to tell what had happened. Maybe we would tell the people how we prayed with the President, and that he accepted the Lord while we were with him. Jesus knew that King Herod wanted to see Him. But He also knew who was reigning in Israel. And totally contrary to how a subject of a kingdom would respond, throughout His ministry King Jesus said, in so many words, "Audience denied."

At long last, it looked as if Herod's desire would be fulfilled. He finally obtained that long awaited audience with the Carpenter from Nazareth. In fact, Jesus was on trial, and His very future depended on finding Herod's favor. Herod thought so, anyway. And maybe, to one degree or another, some of us have evaluated that scene in the same way. So Herod began to ask Him questions. Once again, in so many words, the One Who rules the universe responded, "Audience denied. Take him away." Herod thought that *he* was taking *Jesus* away. But in fact, it was Jesus who was taking Herod away. Can there be any doubt of that today? Herod is gone, and Christ reigns forever!

So, during the ministry of Christ as He manifested the King and the Kingdom in the Promised Land, Israel was once again being ruled from within. Several times Jesus revealed to what extent He was ruling in the natural realm also. He showed that He could even give orders to the sea, and it obeyed (Mk. 4:39). Wasn't He also controlling all the natural elements in Israel, even the lives of those who thought they were ruling? The problem was that they recognized neither the King nor His Kingdom. Or did they? In John 6:14-15 they tried to take Him by force and openly make Him King over the nation. He refused at that time, because it wasn't the Father's will. But later, in His triumphal entry He allowed them to do that very thing. They proclaimed, "Hosanna: Blessed is the King of Israel that cometh in the name of the Lord" (Jn. 12:13-16). He was **literally** proclaimed "King" by the Jews themselves.

Two doubts are often raised here: "Yes, but wasn't His Kingdom *spiritual* and not natural? And didn't Jesus Himself say that His Kingdom was not of this world, so that He wasn't really ruling on the earth?" (Jn. 18:36) It is true that His Kingdom was a heavenly Kingdom. However, even wicked Nebuchadnezzar recognized that the Heavens rule in the affairs of men (Dan. 4:17, 26). The natural governments of this world are simply a reflection of the powers that rule in the heavenly realms. When Jesus said that His Kingdom was from Heaven and not from earth, He was not speaking of having less authority in the earthly realm, but rather more. For that reason He could inform Pilate that he didn't have one bit more authority than the Heavens had allowed him to have, and that He, Jesus, was the King of the Jews, and King of Heaven.[4]

The religious leaders who wanted to hold onto their own kingdoms were the ones who crucified Him. They rejected His rule, at that time, over the natural realm. Although He could have called twelve legions of angels and destroyed the world, He chose to lay down His life (Mt. 26:53). Therefore, after His death, the Romans continued their cruel reign over Israel until the nation was destroyed by them in A.D. 70. For the sake of man's redemption, and by His own choice, He laid down His life for His sheep. Neither the Romans nor the Jews had the power to take it from Him (Jn. 10:18).

---

4. He didn't actually tell Pilate that He was the King of Heaven. However, He is (Mt. 28:18).

Christ Wasn't Reigning, or Manifesting the Kingdom During the Years Between His Birth and the Jordan

Some may ask, "Wasn't Christ ruling in Israel during His 30 years of preparation also?" That is a logical question, but consider the answer given by Scripture. When Jesus came to earth in Bethlehem's manger, He emptied Himself of His glory, authority, power, and position in Heaven (Phil. 2:7). He made Himself to be like any other man. In fact, Hebrews 2:17 says, "In **all things**...it behoved him to be made like unto his brethren." If He became like us in all things, then His "self-emptying" or "*kenosis*" (the Greek word for this event) was complete and total. He literally became a man, and limited Himself to natural man's position and authority. From the manger to the Jordan we are told that He submitted to Joseph and Mary and that He "increased in wisdom and stature, and in favour with God and man" (Lk. 2:51-52). His self-emptying had been so complete that He allowed Himself to be ruled over by these earthly parents whom He had actually created. When He was born, He had no more wisdom than a normal newborn. Furthermore, the statement that He "increased in wisdom" described Him after He appeared in the temple at the age of 12. Had He been all-wise, He couldn't have grown in wisdom. He even grew in favor with God.

At the Jordan River something happened. The Heavens were opened to Him, and a mantle from Heaven descended and rested upon Him again. From that day, until His death on the cross, He moved under Heaven's power and authority. The One who had emptied Himself when He became a baby now reigned again as King over everyone and everything as He preached and manifested the Kingdom. In John 2:4 He even made it clear to Mary, His mother, that He was no longer in submission to her. Israel was ruled from within once again.

Israel Will Again Be Governed From Within for Half a Week, During His Ministry, at the End of the New Testament

For three and a half years, or half a "week," Christ exercised direct rule over Israel at the beginning, and He will do so again at the end. He will not only rule over Israel, but also over all the world. The Jewish people are ruled by fellow Jews at this very moment, but soon the King of the Jews is going to take direct control of the nation. As He approached the end of His earthly ministry He told His disciples in Matthew 24:14, "...This gospel of the kingdom [the gospel He preached] shall be preached in all the world for a witness unto all nations; and then shall the end come." Therefore, just before the end, there will be a revelation of Kingdom power, authority, and glory on a scale such as this world has never seen. In the world today, it seems that the enemy is bending humanity to the will of Satan through secular humanism, atheism, spiritism, violence, the New Age movement, and so on. The world even seems to be aiding Satan in his plan. But very soon, mankind will see that the glory of Christ's Kingdom is well able to cause every knee to bow before the King of kings.

The gospel of the Kingdom is the gospel that He revealed through His **life** and **walk**, not just through His **words and miracles**. In the last days, He will do even "greater things" through those who are His true disciples, those who are prepared vessels that will reveal His glory (Jn. 14:12; Dan. 11:32). "Practice what you preach" is not outdated advice. The world wants to see how our theology works out in our own daily living, and only then will they listen to our preaching. God will not judge the world for rejecting a gospel they have never really seen in practice. There are literally millions of honest, sincere hearts in the earth today that have heard the loud and sometimes flamboyant preaching of the Church. Sadly enough, they have come to the sincere conclusion that the Christ they see in the Believers is really not the answer to their needs, nor to the deep longing of their hearts. Often the *lives* of the Believers who preach the gospel shout such an un-Christ-like message that no one can hear what they are preaching with their *mouths*.

Oh, that we could hear the cry of the Gentiles today, "Sir, we would see Jesus." He certainly hears that cry and will soon respond to it as never before. They want to *see* Him, not just hear *about* Him. They want to see His truth being *lived* in us, to know that the gospel really does work, and that our religion affects our walk and not just our talk. The Lord has promised to respond to that cry, and all flesh shall see His glory (Isa. 40:5). All the nations of the earth will see the glory of His gospel lived out before them for a true witness, and then the end will come. This will be the other half of that "week," coming at the end of the Church Age. I call this week "the week that was," because it is the week that Daniel 9:27 has referred to from the beginning. (See the diagram at the end of this chapter.)

The Two Witnesses

The witness which Christ's ministry gave lasted for three and a half years at the *beginning* of the New Testament. Going now to the *end* of the New Testament, we find two witnesses in Revelation 11 who minister for a period of 1,260 days. (This is three and a half years or forty-two months on the biblical calendar.) Could these two have something to do with the preaching of the gospel of the Kingdom that will give a true witness to all nations? We must remember that the Bible is one Book, from one Author, with one message, and that it uses terms throughout the Book that carry the same significance in both the natural and spiritual realms. Jesus says that just before the end there will be a "witness" (Mt. 24:14). Here, just before the end, we find two "witnesses" who minister for three and a half years just as He did.

There has been much doctrinal discussion concerning these two men and exactly who they are and what they will do. Without going into speculation, we just want to take note of the principal details that Revelation gives us about them. That should be enough information to get a clear picture of what will happen during the last three and a half years.

1. They will "prophesy" for 1,260 days (Rev. 11:3). The word "prophesy" means to speak under divine inspiration. Therefore, we know that they will speak forth the living Word of God for three and a half years.
2. They will be the olive trees and lampstands that stand before the God of all the earth (Rev. 11:4). These two olive trees are described in Zechariah 4:11-14, and are also called the two anointed ones that stand before the God of all the earth. They will move under the anointing of the Spirit. In other words, they will carry the Lord's presence, and they will be lampstands that give light to those around them. These things are obviously spiritual attributes.
3. They will bring judgment on the wicked who seek to hurt them (Rev. 11:5).
4. They will bring plagues on the earth as often as they desire (Rev. 11:6).
5. The beast will kill them, but only after they have finished their testimony to the world (Rev. 11:7).
6. All the earth will see their dead bodies for three and a half days (Rev. 11:9).
7. All the earth will make merry and rejoice at their death because they were tormented by their ministries (Rev. 11:10).
8. After three and a half days they will be resurrected and taken up to Heaven (Rev. 11:11-12).
9. Immediately after their resurrection the seventh trumpet will sound, which will bring the Rapture of the Church, as we have seen in Revelation 11:15.

From the details of this list we can be certain about several things. It is clear that they will speak forth words of life and light under a mighty anointing of the Holy Spirit, as no one has ever done before. Some of the things they will do are the "greater things" that Jesus said His disciples would do. Their ministries will bring the message of God to all the earth for three and a half years just before the end and the Rapture. They will move under Kingdom authority, because the very lives of the inhabitants of the earth will be in their hands, as is the case with any true king on earth. At will, they will be able to devour their enemies with the fire that comes from their mouths. There won't even be a need for lengthy, expensive trials in the perverse courts of this world! This fire of the Spirit that will come forth from their mouths in a Word of judgment, was manifested through Peter against Ananias and Sapphira in Acts 5. Their ministries will be world-wide in scope, because they will bring plagues on the entire earth, and as a result the entire earth will rejoice at their death. They will be overcome by the beast and killed. But as in the case of Christ, this will not be permitted to happen until they have finished their work. They will actually lay down their lives by their own choice. They will have the power to continue devouring all their enemies with the fire of God if they choose to do so. The enemy will have no power that Heaven does not permit him to have, as Christ reminded Pilate.

One thing is clear. With this tremendous ministry manifested throughout all the earth for three and a half years, all the nations of the earth will definitely receive a witness of God's Kingdom power and authority. Without going into the scriptural reasons for saying so, it is quite clear that these will be the sons of God that the creation so longs for (Rom. 8:19). We have seen that the man child who is born in Revelation 12 is representative of a company of people. I believe that these two men are also representative of companies of anointed servants that will touch the entire earth for three and a half years before the Rapture and the end. This period of three and a half years of mighty Kingdom glory is none other than the second half of Daniel's "other week." It will come at the end of the Church Age, at a time in which the gospel of the Kingdom will be preached as a witness just before the end. What a glorious day God has called us to live in and be a part of! (See the following diagram.)

Notes Regarding Chart That Follows

1. I arbitrarily chose precise dates for the first command and the birth of Christ. Although we are not sure of the exact day, we are sure of the year and month, with a margin of error of two months at the very most. I arbitrarily chose these exact dates only to demonstrate that 434 years plus precisely 2,300 days fit between the command and the coming of Christ.

2. After the Rapture and the Marriage Supper the Lord returns to earth with His Bride and physically establishes His Kingdom on earth. This is known as the "Second Coming," and Jesus says no one knows the day or hour of that event (Mt. 24:36-42). However, we are given to understand from other passages that it will take place shortly after the Rapture.

3. The dotted line on the chart indicates that the countdown clock is not running, because Israel does not have political independence during those times.

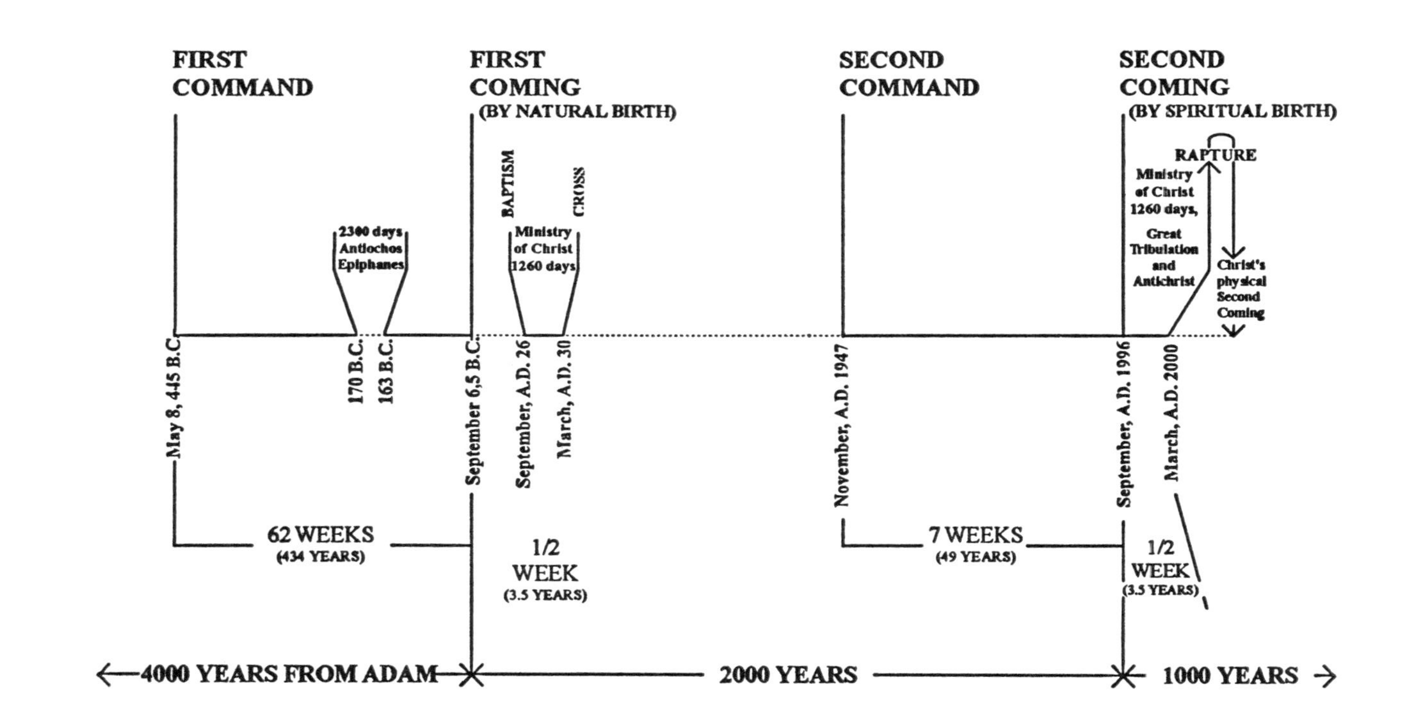
TIME LINE FOR DANIEL'S SEVENTY WEEKS
FIRST COMMAND
FIRST COMING (BY NATURAL BIRTH)
SECOND COMMAND
SECOND COMING (BY SPIRITUAL BIRTH)
2300 days Antiochos Epiphanes
BAPTISM
Ministry of Christ 1260 days
CROSS
RAPTURE
Ministry of Christ 1260 days, Great Tribulation and Antichrist
Christ's physical Second Coming
May 8, 445 B.C.
170 B.C.
163 B.C.
September 6,5 B.C.
September, A.D. 26
March, A.D. 30
November, A.D. 1947
September, A.D. 1996
March, A.D. 2000
62 WEEKS (434 YEARS)
1/2 WEEK (3.5 YEARS)
7 WEEKS (49 YEARS)
1/2 WEEK (3.5 YEARS)
4000 YEARS FROM ADAM
2000 YEARS
1000 YEARS

Chapter 36

What Then?

The following are established and proven facts, and logical conclusions based upon those facts.

Facts Regarding the First Coming

1. The command to restore Israel the first time was given between March and early May of the year 445 B.C.

2. Christ's birth was around September of the year 5 B.C.

3. According to Daniel 8 and related historical facts, between the command and His birth there were 2,300 days when Israel was governed from without.

4. He came the first time by means of a birth. The ministry of His First Coming lasted for three and a half years. Through that ministry He confirmed the promises made to the fathers (Rom. 15:8).

5. After Christ had confirmed the promises made to the fathers for three and a half years, or one half of a week of seven years, He offered Himself as a living sacrifice, and thus caused all **God-ordained** animal sacrifices to cease. In other words, they were no longer recognized in Heaven as the answer for sin after Heaven had received Christ's sacrifice for sin.

6. Christ is our example, and in all things He was made like the ones whom He would not be ashamed to call His brethren (Heb. 2:11,17). After He had ministered for three and a half years, and had offered Himself as a sacrifice, Christ was physically "raptured" or caught up to Heaven in the

clouds. Also, many Old Testament saints were resurrected at that time (Mt. 27:52-53).

Conclusions Based on the Facts

1. Israel had precisely 434 years, or 62 weeks, of independence between the command to restore and His First Coming.

2. Since He was made like His "brethren" in all things, since we are going to be "conformed" to His image, and since the end is like the beginning, we should expect a ministry similar to His if we are His sons. In reality, it will be Christ ministering through His people. He will be finishing His own ministry of seven years, or one "week." Christ Himself will minister through prepared vessels in the end for three and a half years, after which time they will be physically raptured and taken up into the clouds, just as their Pattern experienced with His Father. The New Testament saints will be resurrected at that time, just as happened in the case of Christ and the Old Testament saints.

Facts Regarding the Second Coming

1. The command to restore Israel the second time was given in November of the year A.D. 1947.

2. Israel is as much an independent nation today as they ever were in their entire history. Seventy weeks were determined upon His *"people"* to accomplish six things. Those things have not all been accomplished, but Israel is a *"people"* today.

3. If He comes in His Temple at the end of 1996, then modern Israel (the Israel of today) will have had precisely 49 years, or 7 weeks, of independence by that time.

4. He has promised that the gospel of the Kingdom will be preached throughout the world as a witness just before His physical return to earth (Mt. 24:14).

5. The "witnesses" found in Revelation minister with Heaven's authority for 1,260 days, or three and a half years, just before His physical return (Rev. 11).

6. If the Rapture and His return take place in the year 2000, after three and a half years of testimony by the witnesses, Israel will have been governed from within for exactly 490 years, or 70 weeks, during the last 2,500 years since Daniel's day.

7. The New Testament reveals two periods of three and a half years during its history, one at the beginning and the other at the end of the New Testament Age.

8. Isaiah 66:8, Micah 4:9-10, John 16:21-22, and Galatians 4:27, along with many other Scriptures, tell us that in the last days the travail of Zion, the Church, is going to cause the birth of the sons of Zion. In Revelation 12 we find a woman who travails and gives birth. According to Revelation 12, after that birth there will be a period of three and a half years.

Conclusions Based on the Facts

1. The facts seem clear enough that they need little or no interpretation.

2. The beginning and ending are the same. Therefore, since He came the first time with a birth, and ministered for a period of three and a half years, we should expect Him to come the second time with a birth (in a spiritual sense, through His people), and minister for a three-and-a-half-year period. We find an indication of this in Revelation 12. We also see Paul travailing in birth until **Christ** is formed in the Church in Galatians 4:19.

3. If the life of Christ is brought forth by the woman of Revelation 12 at the end of 1996, and He manifests the Kingdom for three and a half years as a witness to all the world, then the Rapture and His physical return will occur in the year 2000. The covenant will have been confirmed or fulfilled for a total of seven years, or one week, counting the three and a half years found at the beginning of the New Testament.

The Last Days Will Be a Revelation of Christ in His People

The Book of Revelation is a "revelation of Jesus Christ." This word "revelation" in the Greek is "apocalypse," which means an "unveiling," or a "manifestation," or a "discovering." This same word is found in First Peter 1:5. Peter declares that we are "kept by the power of God through faith unto salvation ready to be revealed in the last time." ("Revealed" here comes from the same word as "apocalypse.") The Greek words that make up the phrase "the last time" here can also be translated as "the very last opportunity," "the uttermost opportunity," or "the ends of opportunity."[1] He says this "unveiling," or "apocalypse," will take place in the "last time," during man's very last opportunity.

1. The Greek word "time" here is translated as "opportunity" in Galatians 6:10 and Hebrews 11:15. The Greek word "last" here is translated as "ends of" in Acts 13:47, and as "uttermost" in Acts 1:8 and Matthew 5:26. It means the extreme limit of time or place.

Peter goes on to say in First Peter 1:13, "Wherefore gird up the loins of your mind, be sober, and hope *to the end for the grace that is to be brought unto you at the revelation of Jesus Christ.*" This is not only the same word, but also the same phrase that appears in Revelation 1:1 ("the revelation of Jesus Christ"). So then, great grace will come upon the Church in the end, just as it happened to the early Church in the beginning (Acts 4:33). This is the glory that the world will see—His grace on the Church in the last days. Consider that the "last days" come *before* the end, not *after* the end. So this will happen *before* the end, as Jesus has promised.

So what should we expect to find in the last days? An unveiling of Christ in a manifestation of power, glory, and Kingdom authority and character. Since Revelation is an unveiling of Christ, He should come forth somewhere in that book. We see that He does come in chapter 12, with a birth, just as He came the first time! The Gentiles who cry out, "Sir, we would see Jesus," will indeed see Him in His Temple, the Church. What a privilege to be alive in this hour when He will come *in* His people, *for* His people, and then *with* His people.

PART IV

Other Scriptures and a Visitation That Confirm the Year of His Coming

Introduction

Any true interpretation of prophecy must be firmly established and confirmed by many other Scriptures. From the beginning, the year of the Second Coming of the Lord has been revealed throughout the Bible. Part IV presents other Scriptures that confirm the year A.D. 1996 as the time of Christ's coming, and the year A.D. 2000 as the year of the Rapture of the Church.

The truths of God's Word can also be revealed to man by the Lord Himself. Although we cannot base doctrine on personal experiences, those experiences *can* confirm to our hearts what God's written Word declares. The One who has appeared to His people since the beginning, and has given them understanding in the light of His presence, has never changed. One such encounter with His glory is shared in Part IV.

Chapter 37

Solomon's Temple

> *What think ye of Christ? whose son is he? They say unto him, The son of David. He saith unto them, How then doth David in spirit call him Lord, saying, The Lord said unto my Lord, Sit thou on my right hand, till I make thine enemies thy footstool? If David then called him Lord, how is he his son? And no man was able to answer...* (Matthew 22:42-46).

As seen in this passage, the people of God living in Christ's day did not understand who the "son of David" was. Today we think we understand, but I wonder if we do. We say, "Why, of course we know who the son of David was. He was Christ." But the riddle for us, God's people of this present day, becomes, "But who then was Solomon, the son of David?" Do we understand how Solomon, the son of David, fits into this mystery that Christ presented to the Jews? They knew who Solomon was, but they didn't know who Christ was. We understand today who Christ was, but do we really know who Solomon was in God's plans?

In Luke 1:32 Gabriel told Mary that Jesus would inherit the throne of His father David. This was a fulfillment of the Davidic covenant: "And when thy days be fulfilled, and thou shalt sleep with thy fathers, I will set up thy seed after thee, which shall proceed out of thy bowels...**He shall build an house for my name**, and I will establish the throne of his kingdom for ever" (2 Sam. 7:12-13). Christ came forth from David, and said, "I will build my church" (Mt. 16:18). He is the son of David who builds God's house, His eternal dwelling place.

However, when Solomon ascended to the throne of David, he thought that he was a fulfillment of God's promises made to David, his father. He said, "...Thou hast showed unto thy servant David my father great mercy...and thou hast kept for him this great kindness, that thou hast given him a son to sit on his throne, as it is this day" (1 Kings 3:6). Solomon also said, "...I purpose to build an house unto the name of the Lord my God, as the Lord spake unto David my father, saying, Thy son, whom I will set upon thy throne in thy room, **he shall build an house unto my name**" (1 Kings 5:5).

Was Solomon mistaken in believing that when he inherited the throne of his father David, God was fulfilling the promise He had made to David? It is obvious that he *was* the son of David, and he *was* inheriting the throne of David, his father. He was also ordained by God to build the house of the Lord.

This "son of David" may very well continue to be a great mystery. Jesus draws our attention to this riddle when He asks who the "son of David" really is. Then He gives a hint in Matthew 12:42, "A greater than Solomon is here." Christ was a greater Moses, a greater Adam, a greater David, and a greater Solomon.[1] But every one of these men was a clear scriptural foreshadow of Christ Himself. Once again we see that Old Testament Israel, as a people, was a parable or foreshadow of the New Testament Age. Therefore, the leader or king of the Old Testament people was often a foreshadow of Christ, the Head of the Church.

But each of the Old Testament characters reveals only certain specific aspects of Christ and His work. None of those shadows give a complete picture of the Christ, in whom dwelt the "fullness of the Godhead bodily" (Col 2:9). For example, Moses was the mediator of the Old Covenant; Christ is the Mediator of the New Covenant. Adam was the "son of God" (Lk. 3:38) and the father of the human race; Christ is the eternal Son of God and the father of the family of God. David was a man of war who won the victory over the enemies of our God; Christ is also the Man of war who won the victory over Satan. However, the fallen human nature that was revealed in all these men was *not* a foreshadow of Christ. Christ did not make the mistake that Moses made in the wilderness, nor commit adultery and murder as David did, nor partake of Adam's disobedience.

Solomon Is a Shadow of Christ's Millennial Reign

Solomon was the man of peace. His name actually means "peaceful." His was a reign of peace, whereas David's was a reign of wars and tremendous conflicts necessary to establish the kingdom. We want to observe here that in the Bible many details confirm that Solomon and his reign were a foreshadow of Christ's thousand-year reign of peace after the conflicts and wars are past. Revelation 20:4-5 tells us there will be a reign of

1. In other words, all these Old Testament figures were foreshadows of Christ. He is even called the last Adam in First Corinthians 15:45.

one thousand years on this present earth. David's life, work, and kingdom could be compared to Christ's ministry during the Church Age, a time of great conflict and spiritual warfare. However, Solomon's ministry and kingdom have much to do with Christ's millennial reign, which comes after the Church Age. In one sense we have already experienced Christ's Kingdom throughout the Church Age. However, we will experience it in a deeper and more physical way during the "Kingdom Age," or Millennium. That is, we have experienced "David's reign," but soon we will also experience "Solomon's reign."

Some may wonder how Solomon, with all his wives and sinful living could be a foreshadow of Christ in the millennial reign. One of the problems that we encounter in our understanding of the Scriptures is that we often see only the good or the bad side of the men and women found in the Bible. However, what we need to understand about many Bible characters is that very often they manifest both the old man as well as the new man, or, in other words, the way of the flesh *and* the way of the Spirit. This started with Adam. It is true that he disobeyed and sinned, manifesting a negative side to the story. But it is also true that he did what Christ would do for His Bride. He became identified with her in her sin, thus manifesting a positive side to those events. The result of these two sides are then seen in the fruit of his own life. He gave birth to a Cain, a symbol of man's ways and a sinful person, and then he gave birth to Abel, a clear symbol of Christ Himself. In Romans 7 Paul explains this phenomenon. He says that after Christ has come to dwell in our hearts we all have two natures dwelling in us—the old man (our flesh) and the new man (Christ). Unfortunately, we *all* manifest two sides in this life, not just Solomon!

When Solomon took the throne to begin his reign, the earth "rent" (1 Kings 1:40). This same Hebrew word is used in Zechariah 14:4, where we are told that the Mount of Olives will "cleave" when Christ's feet touch it as He comes to begin His millennial reign on the earth.[2] We also see that all the nations of the earth came to Solomon to hear his wisdom (1 Kings 4:34). During the millennial reign all the nations of the earth will come to Jerusalem unto Christ (Zech. 14:16). Christ is the personification of wisdom in Proverbs 8, and He will rule by wisdom. Solomon was the wisest man to ever live.

Another similarity between Solomon and Christ in His millennial reign is found in the construction of the Temple of Solomon. We call it "Solomon's Temple," but in reality we know that David received its design from the Lord, and provided most of the gold, silver, stones, wood, and other necessities, to build that temple (1 Chron. 28:11-13; 29:2-5). In

2. *Strong's Hebrew Dictionary*, #1234.

fact, the stones were actually cut to size beforehand, and when the temple was assembled on Mount Moriah, the sound of a tool was not heard; everything had been prepared before being brought to the mountain (1 Kings 6:7). As Believers, we are the stones of His house (1 Pet. 2:5). In this present life we are being conformed to the proper measurements so that we will fit into an eternal position and ministry in His Temple. At the Rapture the One Who is "greater than Solomon," the "son of David," will simply assemble the living stones on His Holy Mount, and the sound of a tool will not be heard on that Mount either. In that day we will experience no more chipping, cutting, or polishing. (Let's submit to that process now, so we'll be ready!) To the amazement of the saints and angels, each life will fit precisely into the place God has ordained for it.

What does all this have to do with the year of His coming? On the same day the Lord gave me understanding of Daniel's Seventy Weeks, He led me to two other Scriptures that confirm the year of the Second Coming of Christ. (We will consider one here, and the other in the next chapter.) I was not looking for other Scriptures to confirm the year He had shown me through Daniel, but He sovereignly caused me to open to the right places in the Bible. My natural eyes were providentially directed to take note of these Scriptures, and my spiritual eyes were opened to understand them.

One of those references is First Kings 6:1, where Solomon begins to build the temple. We will consider this verse in light of two previously established principles: (1) Solomon is a shadow of Christ's millennial Kingdom and (2) Every jot and tittle found in the Old Testament Israel will be fulfilled in a spiritual way in the New Testament Israel. Writing about events in Israel's history, Paul says, "Now **all these things** happened unto them for ensamples: and they are written for our admonition, **upon whom the ends of the world are come**" (1 Cor. 10:11). Should we therefore expect First Kings 6:1 to have a spiritual fulfillment during the time of the "ends of the world"?

> *It came to pass in the four hundred and eightieth year after the children of Israel were come out of the land of Egypt, in the fourth year of Solomon's reign over Israel, in the month Zif, which is the second month, that he began to build the house of the Lord* (1 Kings 6:1).

In review, we saw that the Kingdom begins at the end of 1996 as Christ is birthed through His Church. He manifests the power and authority of that Kingdom for three and a half years, and at the end of that period the Rapture takes place. At the Rapture, *our* "Solomon" will assemble (gather together) the living stones on His Mount to "build the Temple" as Solomon was doing here. The above Scripture tells us that this will take place in the "fourth year" of His reign. The "fourth year" means He will have reigned for more than three full years, but less than four years.

So if Christ's reign begins near the end of 1996, then the fourth year of His reign will come in the year 2000. However, if First Kings 6:1 is to be fulfilled, then the fourth year of *our* "Solomon's" reign must also be 480 years after spiritual Israel, the Church, has come out of a spiritual "Egypt." If we go back in history 480 years from the year A.D. 2000 we come to the year A.D. 1520. The question is, "What happened in the year 1520, and did the Church come out of a spiritual Egypt in that year?" In July of 1520 Martin Luther was excommunicated from the Catholic Church and the Reformation officially began. Yes, we did indeed come out of a spiritual Egypt in that year.[3] So then, 480 years later brings us to the year 2000, in which the living stones of the Temple will be assembled in the Rapture. And this will be the "fourth year" of "Solomon's reign," and therefore, the reign of the "greater Solomon" (Christ) must begin in the year 1996.

Some may ask, "Since Solomon's reign was a reign of peace, how can Christ's millennial reign begin in 1996, at the same time that the Great Tribulation begins?" This is a good question, which actually becomes another confirmation of these things. During the same day that Jesus referred to Himself as the "greater than Solomon," He linked His Kingdom and its beginning to the way in which Solomon's began (Mt. 12:42; 13:1). Referring to the time of the end and of harvest, Jesus said, "...so shall it be in the end of the world. The Son of man shall send forth his angels, and they shall gather out of his kingdom all things that **offend**, and them which **do iniquity**" (Mt. 13:39-41). Solomon began his reign with great judgments and a thorough cleansing of the Kingdom. He destroyed those who **offended**, and those who had **done iniquity**. Examples are Adonijah and Joab, respectively (1 Kings 2:17-24,27-34). Adonijah had **offended** the king concerning Abishag, King David's concubine. And Joab had **done iniquity** by slaying several righteous men. Other judgments fell also at the beginning of the kingdom. Solomon did exactly what Christ will do during the first three and a half years of His Kingdom; He will remove the wicked, **before** assembling the stones of the Temple.

Jesus declares that He will send His angels to "gather out of his kingdom all things that offend, and them which do iniquity" (Mt. 13:41). He can only gather *out* of His Kingdom this type of people if they are actually *in* that Kingdom. So the Kingdom must begin while many wicked people are still alive on the earth. Once the Kingdom of the "greater Solomon" (Christ) begins there

3. In Part III, Chapter 33, we saw that Christ had more than one "Egypt experience." So, too, the Church in the last days will have more than one. For example, as a Church, we left Egypt in A.D. 1520 in a spiritual sense, and at the very end we will leave Egypt, the world, in a physical sense during the Rapture.

will be a time of severe judgments and a deep cleansing that will take place on the earth. The Great Tribulation will indeed be that time. It will also be a time of tremendous blessing and harvest when "this gospel of the kingdom shall be preached in all the world for a witness...and then shall the end come" (Mt. 24:14). But the "**end**" of what? This word "end" in the Greek means the "goal" or the "conclusion of an act or state."[4] When Christ physically comes again it will not be the end of the earth; rather the earth will continue on for another one thousand years. Nor will it be the end of the righteous, because they will live and reign with Him during that entire period. But it will be the **end** of both the **wicked** on the earth, and of the present **state** of the earth, which is filled with violence and corruption.

Another clear indication that the millennium begins with a time of judgment is found in the Scriptures of Peter and Paul. They both tell us that "the day of the Lord will come as a thief in the night" (1 Thess. 5:2; 2 Pet. 3:10). When Peter refers to that "day of the Lord," he is referring to the thousand-year reign of Christ. We know this for two reasons. First, that statement appears in the context of a "day" meaning a thousand-year period (2 Pet. 3:8). Second, he confirms this by saying, "But the day of the Lord will come as a thief in the night; in the which the heavens shall pass away with a great noise, and the elements shall melt with fervent heat, the earth also and the works that are therein shall be burned up." We know that the heavens and the earth do not pass away at the time of the Second Coming. Yet Peter reveals that this occurs during the "day of the Lord," which must, therefore, be the Lord's millennial reign. The earth *does* pass away at the end of that thousand-year "day" (Rev. 20:7–21:1). Therefore, the "day of the Lord" to which both Peter and Paul refer must be Christ's millenial reign, and it begins with travail and destruction according to Paul (1 Thess. 5:2-3).

Conclusion

Because the events and dates considered up to this point dovetail together in such an amazing way, we conclude that only the Almighty could have accomplished such a thing. It would be worthwhile to consider a few of the threads that will come together in the years A.D. 1996 and A.D. 2000. First, if the "living stones" of the Temple are gathered at the Rapture in the year 2000, that will be exactly 480 years after the Reformation began, when the Church came out of spiritual Egypt. The year 2000 will also be the fourth year after 1996, the year of the "birth" of the Messiah through His people, and the beginning of the reign of "Solomon." But, the year 1996 just happens to be precisely 49 years, or 7 weeks, after the decree to restore Israel as a nation in 1947. He is definitely ruling in the affairs of men!

4. *Strong's Greek Dictionary*, #5056.

Chapter 38

One Day Is as a Thousand Years

But, beloved, be not ignorant of this one thing, that one day is with the Lord as a thousand years, and a thousand years as one day (2 Peter 3:8).

This is the other scriptural confirmation for the year of the Lord's coming that I received along with Daniel's Seventy Weeks. This declaration appears in Peter's discourse concerning the return of Christ. He says that scoffers would come in the last days, saying, "Where is the promise of his coming? For since the fathers fell asleep, all things continue as they were from the beginning of the creation" (2 Pet. 3:3-4). Peter then gives us a very important key regarding the timing of Christ's coming, in verse 8, quoted above. Why is this "one thing" so important for understanding the last days?

One of Peter's favorite Old Testament prophets, Hosea, has the answer. We know he was a favorite of Peter because he is quoted in First Peter 2:10. Peter certainly understood the Book of Hosea. Like Daniel and other prophets, Hosea reveals details of both the First and Second Comings within the same passage. For example, in Hosea 5:14-15 the "lion to the house of Judah," the Lord Jesus Christ, is speaking concerning His First Coming and His rejection by His people when He came to them. He says, "For I will be unto Ephraim as a lion, and as a young lion to the house of Judah: I, even I, will tear and go away; I will take away, and none shall rescue him. **I will go and return to my place, till they acknowledge their offence,** and seek my face: in their affliction they will seek me early" (Hos. 5:14-15).

He came to His people as the Lion, or King, when He came preaching and revealing the King and His Kingdom. He did so with the mind and nature of the Lamb. However, they rejected Him, so He returned to His place. Peter makes reference to this in his preaching when he says, "Repent ye therefore, and be converted, that your sins may be blotted out...and he shall send Jesus Christ, which before was preached unto you: Whom the heaven must receive until the times of restitution..." (Acts 3:19-21). So Christ returned to Heaven, and shortly afterward brought judgment on His people in a literal way, when Titus destroyed the nation in A.D. 70. To this day the nation of Israel, in general, still refuses to "acknowledge their offense" or to seek the face of their Messiah, but their time of affliction has not yet come to its fullness.

Yes, Israel already has experienced a degree of affliction: the sorrow of the utter destruction of their nation in A.D. 70, followed by centuries of persecution in the nations of the world where they were scattered. There was the Holocaust of World War II, and the wars in Israel immediately after their restoration as a nation in 1948. Add to that the Six-Day War of 1967 and the War of 1973. And even as I write these very lines the world has just received notice of the Mideast War between the Allied forces and Iraq, whose leader believes it is his call to destroy the nation of Israel. Unfortunately, the end of the suffering has not yet come, because Israel's God loves them so much that He will never stop bringing discipline until His people turn back. I trust that God will do the same for me every time I leave the path! Hosea, Jeremiah, and other prophets tell us that more pressure is coming to Israel to turn the nation back to their God and to the Lion of the tribe of Judah, whom they rejected.

Jeremiah refers to the period of difficulties that is just ahead in Israel's history as the "time of Jacob's trouble." "Ask ye now, and see whether a man doth travail with child? wherefore do I see every man with his hands on his loins, as a woman in travail, and all faces are turned into paleness? Alas! For that day is great, so that *none is like it: it is even the time of Jacob's trouble*; but he shall be saved out of it" (Jer. 30:6-7). Many prophets speak of a time of travail in the last days for God's people. Concerning this latest war in the Middle East (in 1991), we were told that there has never been such a powerful air assault in the history of mankind. This sounds like the **beginning** of the day of which Jeremiah says, "None is like it." The threat of being attacked during this latest outbreak caused great concern in Israel. That concern is surely part of the reason that Israel is *talking* peace and *making* peace with her enemies all around. We know that the time of "travail" is at the door for God's people, because in the context of the last days, Paul is saying that when they say, "Peace and safety," then sudden destruction will come upon them, *as travail upon a woman with child...* (1 Thess. 5:3).

Since the first edition of this book was published, Israel has signed a peace agreement with two of her enemies, the PLO and Jordan. Is this merely a coincidence? Or is the calendar I am presenting in this book based on Scripture and being confirmed by world events? The continual topic of conversation in the world-wide news media is peace in the Middle East. Not only Paul tells us that the time of travail is at hand, but the prophets speak over and over of a "destruction" that is coming. Thankfully, they also reveal in very clear terms the end of the matter. Israel will be saved out of it and will survive all the conflicts; she will turn to her God in the midst of the affliction.

In light of the "travail" seen by Jeremiah, an amazing bit of news came out of Israel on the first night of Operation Desert Storm. I personally heard reports on a major news network that one of the hospitals in Israel experienced an interesting phenomenon. During the very first hours of the conflict there were more babies born there than during any other single day in the history of the hospital. Could it be that once again the natural is a revelation of the spiritual? Is it possible that not only the Israeli women are entering a time of travail, but the entire nation is doing likewise as the time of "Jacob's trouble" intensifies and draws to a conclusion? The fruit and new life of that travail will be wonderful. As the events of the coming years unfold, we will see that her travail will bring Israel back to her God.

Returning to our passage in Hosea, we find the outcome and the fruit of this "affliction" in Hosea 6:1-3. God's people cry, "Come, and let us return unto the Lord: for he hath torn, and he will heal us; he hath smitten, and he will bind us up." At long last they come to recognize that all their troubles have been caused by the Lion of the Tribe of Judah, and not simply by prejudiced, bigoted men. Notice the reference to "days" in Hosea 6:2, keeping in mind Peter's key thought that "one day is as a thousand years," and also that he understood the message of this prophet. Hosea says, "After two days will he revive us: in the third day he will raise us up, and we shall live in his sight." Israel is being revived today, and that restoration will be complete 2,000 years after Christ's First Coming.

This restoration of Israel will be followed by a thousand-year reign of Christ on the earth, after the Second Coming.[1] This is the "third day," which is mentioned here in Hosea, the day in which His people will "live in his sight." The next verse clarifies this. "Then shall we know, if we follow on

1. This is based on a very clear declaration found in Revelation 20:4-6.

to know the Lord: **his going forth is prepared as the** ***morning; and he shall come*** **unto us** as the rain, as the latter and former rain unto the earth" (Hos. 6:3). **Hosea compares His coming to the morning, a new day, and to the latter and former rain.** James 5:7, speaking of the Second Coming, says, "Be patient therefore, brethren, unto the coming of the Lord. Behold, the husbandman waiteth for the precious fruit of the earth, and hath long patience for it, until he receive **the early and latter rain.**" Therefore, can there be any question that the context of Hosea's message here is the Second Coming of Christ after 2,000 years, on the morning of the third day?

Therefore, the "third day," when we will "live in his sight," is the millennial reign of Christ on the earth. His reign will last one day, or a thousand years. As we said, Peter was familiar with Hosea's book. So it is understandable why he wanted us to know "one thing." When he declared, "One day with the Lord is as a thousand years," he was giving us the key to this passage, and to other similar Scriptures that speak of these "days."

We need to understand that Christ will not return to earth and give man the blessing of "living in his sight" on that "third day" until He has finished the restoration of Israel "after two days," or 2,000 years. Acts 3:21 tells us that He will remain in Heaven until the "restoration" of all the things spoken of by the prophets is completed. Israel is one of the "things" that must be restored (Isa. 11:11). So when He has finished restoring Israel after "two days," then He will return to this earth.

Will it be **approximately** two days, or **exactly** two days? And will the third day be only **approximately** 1,000 years? Revelation 20:4-6 implies that it will be **exactly** 1,000 years. We will see in later chapters that the Lord is the Master Mathematician of the universe; He does everything with mathematical precision and exactitude. If He says the Church Age will be two days, or 2,000 years, then He is going to fulfill this precisely and not approximately.

By comparing the message of Peter with Hosea, we find another confirmation for the time of September, 1996. This is because September, 1996 will be precisely the end of the 2,000th year, or two days, since Christ's birth in September of 5 B.C. At that time the Kingdom Age, or "third day," will begin. At first glance, there appears to be a five-year error in our calendar, but there is no year "zero." Therefore, since our modern calendar goes from the year 1 B.C. directly to the year A.D. 1, there is an error of approximately three and a half years.[2] (If you don't like numbers and dates, skip this footnote and just take our word for it!)

I recently received a pamphlet from Jerusalem, that included an announcement from its mayor. He declared that in A.D. 1996 Israel will celebrate the 3,000th anniversary of King David's proclamation that made Jerusalem the capital city of the Kingdom. How amazing and coincidental! Incidentally, it can be proven both biblically and historically that A.D. 1996 is, in fact, the proper year for the anniversary. This 3,000th anniversary of Jerusalem's establishment as the center of the kingdom "just happens" to be exactly 2,000 years after the birth of Christ, the Son of David. So, in the very year that the nation of Israel will be celebrating the anniversary of this important date, their *heavenly* King David, the Lord Jesus Christ, will proclaim that Jerusalem is the center of *His* Kingdom also. Oh what glory is coming to the nation of Israel and to all true Believers very soon!

Finally, let's note one other detail from Hosea. "In the third day he will raise us up" (Hos. 6:2). This word "raise" is translated as "resurrect" in the Authorized Version in Spanish.[3] It appears in the Hebrew text in Second Kings 13:21 in the context of the resurrection of a dead man. This resurrection will take place "in the third day," during the very dawning, or beginning "minutes," of the third day. As we have seen, the Resurrection, as well as the Rapture,[4] take place in the year A.D. 2000, during the opening "minutes" of the Kingdom Age, so to speak.

The Resurrection and Rapture take place at the *beginning* of the Kingdom Age and *not* at the end of the Church Age, as has often been

---

2. Bromiley, *Chronology of the New Testament*. Vol. I, p. 686. To understand how this works consider the following. From September of 5 B.C. to January of 4 B.C. is only about four months. Therefore, for the sake of easy calculations, let's assume that Christ was born in January of 4 B.C. Now, we will calculate how many years transpired between January of 4 B.C. to January of A.D. 1. Afterward, we will add those four months to our final calculation. So then, from 4 B.C. to 3 B.C. is one year. Then, from 3 B.C. to 2 B.C. is the second year. From 2 B.C. to 1 B.C. is the third year. Finally, from 1 B.C. to A. D. 1 is the fourth year. (There is no year "zero.") Therefore, when our calendar shows January of A.D. 1 it is really Christ's fourth birthday, assuming that He was born January of 4 B.C. So then, we must add a correction factor of three years to the year of our calendar to determine His actual age at any time. For example, A.D. 1 plus three years gives us His correct age of four years, and on January of A.D. 1997 His age will be 1997 + 3 = 2000 years since birth. But don't forget that He was born four months before January (in September), so His 2000th birthday will be in September, 1996.
3. Reina Valera (in both the 1602 and 1960 versions).
4. According to Paul, the Resurrection occurs at the time of the Rapture (1 Thess. 4:15-18).

taught. The Rapture takes place when all the enemies are under His feet, and the saints of the most High have taken the Kingdom (Dan. 7:18). When Christ comes, the Church will arise as one man and crown Him King of all. This is what our "parable" (Israel) did in the Old Testament, when they crowned David as king over all the nation. However, the Kingdom must first be ours before we can proclaim Him as King. The work the Lord has given to His people is to defeat all His enemies through the power He has invested in us.

For this reason Paul tells us in First Corinthians 15:26 that the last enemy that will be destroyed is death. However, Paul goes on to say in that chapter that death is destroyed at the Rapture (1 Cor. 15:51-54). Therefore, the Rapture cannot occur until every **other** enemy has first been conquered. And certainly the Antichrist and his cohorts are "other" enemies. Jesus gave us power over all the power of the enemy, and is now seated at the right hand of His Father, waiting until we use that power. He is waiting until all enemies are put under His feet as First Corinthians 15:25 and Hebrews 10:13 tell us.

In the next chapter I want to share what was, for me, one of the most precious experiences of my entire Christian life. It is the continuation and conclusion of what began on that day when the Lord opened my heart to understand the Seventy Weeks of Daniel, Solomon's Temple, and Hosea's "three days."

Chapter 39

A Heavenly Visit

During the night following that very important day in my life, the day when the Lord revealed the year of His coming, I experienced a "vision of the night" (Job 33:15). In a vision of the night one is neither fully awake nor fully asleep, so it is neither wholly a "vision" nor wholly a dream, but somewhere in between.

In this vision of the night I was at a banquet, seated across the table from a person for whom I had great respect. For many years, I had witnessed his deep personal relationship with the Lord Jesus. He knew and understood the Bible in a way that few people do. As I often did in real life, I began to ask him many doctrinal questions. (A love of the truth causes us to search for the hidden treasures of knowledge and wisdom.[1])

I asked this friend one question after another, but to my deep sorrow he didn't respond. Even worse, it was as though he didn't even hear me or see me. After quite some time he stood up, and for the first time he directed his attention to me, saying, "I am sorry, but I must leave now. I have a very important appointment." With that, he turned and began to move very quickly toward the door.

At that moment I remembered the Scriptures about the year of Christ's coming, which the Lord had shown to me the day before. I instinctively leaped to my feet and ran after him. I said, "Just one more thing...what about...?" He was moving very quickly toward the door. Time was running out, and I had been wasting this opportunity by asking so many other less important questions. Why hadn't I thought of this revolutionary

1. Compare Second Thessalonians 2:9-11 and Proverbs 2:1-6.

revelation sooner? All of my other doctrinal concerns at the time suddenly seemed to be of very little importance compared to this most precious truth. I asked him if what I had received the previous day about the specific year of the Lord's coming was correct or not. It was instantly obvious that he had been waiting for me to ask that precise question that he had been sent for that very purpose. I will never forget that moment. He stopped immediately and turned around, but it was no longer my friend standing there; rather, it was the Lord Jesus Christ Himself. Nor, will I ever forget the overwhelming flood of anointing that poured down upon me as He spoke to me, and said, "That's right, within one year." And there the vision ended.

The fact that He said my understanding of the year of Christ's return was "right within one year" was one of the most perplexing things I have ever experienced. You see, just the day before I had received this wonderful revelation of a *specific* year, and now He told me that it didn't line up, at least not exactly. It wasn't until several years later that this great perplexity became one of the greatest confirmations of all that I had truly heard from the Lord. For several years after receiving this revelation I did not share it publicly, so I had not studied any more about it, nor prepared formal notes. I had placed my few simple notes, made on the day I received these truths, in the flyleaf of my Bible, and had not looked at them again for several years. Some years later, when I finally took them out, I was awestruck by the exactness of the Lord. Why? Because I realized that there had been several misconceptions in my knowledge of history. As a result, I had asked the Lord about the wrong year. The first error was that I had used 1948 for the date of the *command* to restore Israel. That is, in fact, the year the nation was re-established. However, the *command* was given in 1947 and Daniel tells us there will be 7 weeks from the command to the coming of the Messiah, not from the birth of the nation. The second mistake was made regarding the exact year of His birth, nor had I understood that there is no such thing as a year "zero" in the modern-day calendar.

When I posed the question to my friend in that vision, I was sure that 1997 was the correct year. For the Lord to say, "That is right within one year," was definitely disconcerting, but it turned out to be one of the greatest confirmations that the "vision" was not a product of my own mind. If this hadn't happened, then today, twenty-four years later, the enemy could come to me with doubts and say that the vision was a product of my own mind and heart. However, I went to bed that night absolutely certain of one thing—that I knew the precise year of Christ's return. If my own mind had fabricated this vision, then my own mind would also have told me that I was exactly right, but that is not what I heard.

The overwhelming anointing that flooded my heart when He spoke to me in that vision of the night left no doubt whatsoever in my own heart that it was the Lamb of Calvary Who was speaking to me. He wants us to know the time of His coming. He does not want that day to come upon us unawares, nor does He want to come to His bride as a "thief in the night" (1 Thess. 5:4-6). Do we have an ear to hear what the Spirit is saying today? May we cry out, "Lord, open my ear to hear Your voice, and 'make me to know mine end, and the measure of my days, what it is' " (Ps. 39:4).

Chapter 40

Ezekiel

Over the years the Lord has given many other Scriptures that confirm the year of His coming. We can also see through Ezekiel that A.D. 1996 is the year His life will be birthed by the Church, the year in which His glory will fill His Temple. As Appendix B shows, Ezekiel is an Old Testament parallel to the Book of Revelation. It begins with the same experience that John the Beloved had in Revelation 4 and 5, and continues with the same basic truths that are seen in the Book of Revelation. Ezekiel most certainly reveals a message for the end.

Ezekiel Represents the Nation of Israel

God chose Ezekiel to be a personification of the nation of Israel. He told Ezekiel that what happened to him personally was a revelation of what would happen to the nation of Israel as a whole. "Speak unto the house of Israel, Thus saith the Lord God...Ezekiel is unto you a sign: according to all that he hath done shall ye do: and when this cometh, ye shall know that I am the Lord God" (Ezek. 24:21-24). God tells Ezekiel this same thing in Ezekiel 4:3: "Moreover take thou unto thee an iron pan, and set it for a wall of iron between thee and the city...This shall be a sign to the house of Israel."[1]

Ezekiel Represents Israel in the Last Days

Ezekiel personifies the nation of Israel, and reveals what will happen to them, but specifically, **in the last days**. We know this because of the

---

1. Compare also Ezekiel 12:6,11,18-19 for the same thought.

indisputable apocalyptic nature of Ezekiel's message, and its parallel to Revelation. We also know this from Ezekiel 24:24, where we are told that when the things that happened to Ezekiel have happened to Israel, *then* they shall know that He is the Lord God. Israel has not yet come to that awareness. The nation, as a whole, continues to reject their Messiah, and, as Jesus said, if they reject Him they also reject the One Who sent Him (Jn. 5:23). We understand today that Israel will know who their God really is only at the very end of this Age. So the things that happened to Ezekiel for a sign are things that will happen in the very end, because only then will Israel come to know their God.

Ezekiel Visits Tel Aviv

Consider what Jesus says about the last days and the "fig tree" in Matthew 24:32. When her shoot or branch is tender (from new growth) this is a sign that summer is near. He is using "summer" here as a symbol of His coming or of the fulfillment of all that He has spoken concerning the last days in Matthew 24. Summer is a new time or a new day, a time of harvest and blessing after the winter, and after the labor of spring sowing has passed. We have already seen that the fig tree represents the nation of Israel. When Israel became a nation again in 1948, they chose the city of "Tel Aviv" as their capital. God used that name to give a message to all the earth, because "Tel Aviv" in Hebrew means "the mound of the tender growth" (or shoot).[2]

Ezekiel had an experience that links him and his message to Israel of the last days, specifically to "Tel Aviv." In fact, Ezekiel experienced much the same thing that John experienced in Revelation 1:10. John says, "I was in the Spirit on the Lord's day, and heard behind me a great voice, as of a trumpet." The "Lord's day" throughout the Bible refers to the time of Christ's coming (and not Sunday as some commentators have said). In other words, John was carried forward in time by the Spirit, and personally saw what would happen in the future, on the day of the Lord. It is no wonder that he heard a trumpet, because there will be a trumpet associated with the day of the Lord.

Ezekiel's experience was similar to John's: "So the spirit lifted me up, and took me away...but the hand of the Lord was strong upon me. Then I came to them of the captivity at Telabib..." (Ezek. 3:14-15). When Ezekiel says, "the hand of the Lord was upon me," he means that he was "in the Spirit" (Ezek. 37:1). And by the Spirit he came to those of Telabib. In the

2. Compare *Strong's Hebrew Dictionary*, #8512 and #24.

Hebrew this is exactly the same as Tel Aviv.[3] This Telabib is not the modern Tel Aviv, but the name is the same. The question is, "Why would God carry Ezekiel by the Spirit to Telaviv, the 'hill of the tender shoot'?" Was He trying to reveal a truth to His people? This is a further indication that there is a link between Ezekiel and the end-time nation he personifies.

The Telabib that Ezekiel visited was near the River Chebar, which means "a long time."[4] Also note that he sat where they sat, and "remained astonished among them seven days." We have seen that the number seven is intimately linked with the last days.[5] These two details further show that Ezekiel is related to the last days, days that will come "a long time" after Ezekiel's day. This, coupled with the fact that Ezekiel and Revelation are parallel messages, further confirms that Ezekiel has a message for Israel in the end.

Ezekiel Gives Us His Age As Well As Many Other Dates

Ezekiel was in his "thirtieth year" when he began his ministry (Ezek. 1:1).[6] Because the biblical system of counting a person's age was different than the system of the Western World today, it is necessary to explain what the biblical terminology is telling us here. Ezekiel had passed his twenty-ninth birthday and was living in his thirtieth year. In the second verse of chapter one he says the nation was in their fifth year of Babylonian captivity when he began his ministry. Therefore, they were in their fifth year of captivity when Ezekiel was 29 years and some months of age.

Throughout his writings, Ezekiel gives a multitude of precise dates for many of the prophecies, revelations, or events found in the book. God's Word has nothing included in it by chance, or simply for historical records. Jesus says that every jot and tittle will be fulfilled. Therefore, these dates surely have meaning and importance. Since the man Ezekiel represents the nation of Israel in the end, and since that which happened to Ezekiel will happen to Israel (Ezek. 24:24), then the age of Ezekiel is given to show how old the newly resurrected nation of Israel will be when certain specific events take place in the last days.

---

3. Tenney, *Bible Dictionary;* refer to "Telabib" to see that it is the same as the Hebrew "Telaviv." Refer to *Strong's Hebrew Dictionary* under #3529 for the meaning of "Telabib" or "Telaviv."
4. *Strong's Hebrew Dictionary,* #3529.
5. Refer to Part III, Chapter 32.
6. Unger, Merrill F., *Unger's Bible Dictionary,* Moody Press, Chicago, Illinois, 1978; "Ezekiel."

Ezekiel Confirms the Year of A.D. 1996

The Book of Ezekiel ends with a revelation of a temple that has not yet existed, again pointing us to the last days. Ezekiel 43:1-7 explains which temple he is referring to. It is the place where God will dwell forever, the house of Israel (v. 7). Therefore, we know it is a spiritual temple, because He will not live forever in a house made with hands (Acts 7:48). His people are the only eternal dwelling He has chosen. But how old will the nation of Israel be when this takes place? Ezekiel's experience gives us the answer.

Ezekiel entered a tremendous experience with the Lord where the "glory of the Lord filled the house"(Ezek. 43:5). Remembering that what he experienced will be experienced by Israel, we can be sure that Israel will see the glory of the Lord returning to the house of the Lord in the last days. He is going to visit His people in a wonderful and tremendous way. But how old was Ezekiel when he had this experience? Ezekiel 40:1 says this meeting with God came to Ezekiel during the twenty-fifth year of Israel's captivity. His ministry began in the fifth year of captivity, when he was 29 years old (Ezek. 1:1-2). This was now 20 years later, so he was 49 years old. Since he is a personification of Israel in the last days, this experience of Ezekiel shows us that Israel will be 49 years old when the glory of the Lord returns to the nation. In other words, the blessing and glory of God will flow in Israel beginning with her fiftieth year as a nation. This shouldn't surprise us, because this will be her very first **Year of Jubilee** after her restoration as a nation, and in the jubilee everyone is set free and the land is liberated!

If Ezekiel's age were only casually mentioned in the book, or the use of dates by Ezekiel were only sporadic, then we might be justified in doubting just how much real significance they have in his message to Israel for the last days. However, the very first verse in the book gives Ezekiel's age, and the second verse gives the date of Israel's captivity. From then on, one of the outstanding characteristics of his prophetic message is the constant use of exact dates, from which we always know his exact chronological age. If this is of no importance, then there is a tremendous amount of information given in Ezekiel that is simply superfluous.

The decree to restore natural Israel was given in A.D. 1947. So Israel, as a nation, will be 49 years old in A.D. 1996, which is coincidentally 7 weeks of years after their restoration, confirming Daniel's prophecy that links 7 weeks with the last days. Therefore, in that year we should expect the glory of God to fill His "house," and that He will come to His eternal dwelling in a way He has never done before. We have seen that His coming is with a birth. His people will give birth to the Son of promise; He will "suddenly come to his temple" (Mal. 3:1).

Chapter 41

Two Days

The Church Age will last for a period of 2,000 years. This truth is brought out in several ways in the Bible. The number 2,000 actually appears in some passages. In other cases the revelation of this period is based on Second Peter 3:8, where Peter, speaking specifically about the Second Coming of the Lord, says, "One day is with the Lord as a thousand years."

In Chapter 38 we considered the passage where Hosea declared that Christ will return to His people after two days, or 2,000 years, and that in the third day His people will live in His presence for a thousand years, during the millennial reign of Christ. There are many other places where we find that He returns after two days, or 2,000 years. But before we go on, there is one important characteristic of God that we should observe.

God Is a God of Mathematical Precision

God always does things with mathematical precision. He is a God of exactness. He didn't merely "invent," or even create mathematics, but rather it is a part of His very nature. Those who have studied higher mathematics understand that mathematic principles were only discovered by mathematicians, not invented by them.

This divine characteristic of precision is seen in the events associated with the flood of Noah. Noah is a foreshadow of Christ's Second Coming and the events of the last days (Mt. 24:37-39). Noah entered the ark on a precise day, month, and year, and then, on the very day of his 600th birthday, he removed the cover of the ark (Gen. 8:13).[1]

Another example of God's mathematical precision is found in His dealings with Israel in Exodus 12:40-41 (NKJV), "Now the sojourn of the children of Israel...was four hundred and thirty years. And it came to pass at the end of the four hundred and thirty years—on that very same day—it came to pass that all the armies of the Lord went out from the land of Egypt." They began their sojourn in a strange land on a certain day of the year, and on that very same day of the year, 430 years later, they left Egypt. This type of exactness obviously glorifies the Lord, because in spite of all the hardness and rebellion of Pharaoh, when the day came for them to leave, the Sovereign One saw to it that they were permitted to leave.

To foretell an event, and pinpoint its timing, brings great glory to God. But even greater glory comes when He precisely fulfills what He has spoken right on time, in spite of all the obstacles man or Satan can devise. This reveals His greatness, His providence, and His sovereignty in a wonderful way.

If the God of precision tells us the Church Age will last for a period of 2,000 years, then we can expect the Church Age to be exactly 2,000 years. We saw in our study of Daniel that Jesus was born around September of 5 B.C., when the Church Age began.[2] So 2,000 years will end sometime around September of the year 1996.[3] Therefore, if there are other Scriptures that show that the Church Age will last for 2,000 years, they will be further confirmations of this year.

Jesus Casts Out Devils for Two Days

Continuing with the thought of a day being a thousand years, Jesus makes a very interesting statement in Luke 13:32. Certain Pharisees were trying to strike fear into His heart by saying that Herod was going to kill Him. His response manifested anything but fear. However, His response *was* a manifestation of truth, as were all of His responses. Referring to

---

1. Note that Genesis 8:13 says: "In the six hundredth and first year..." But it says that this was the first day of the first month of the six hundredth and first year, so that he is just completing 600 years, and on that very day he is beginning the 601st year of his life. Note Genesis 7:11 to see that the Bible is referring to Noah's age here.
2. Some say the Church Age began on the Day of Pentecost, but isn't it a little presumptuous to say that the Church Age began with us, the Body, and not with the coming of the Head of the Church, the Lord Jesus Christ?
3. Remember, as we saw before, there is no year zero ("0") in our modern calendar. Therefore, we add a correction of only four years to 1996 instead of five years. (See Chapter 38, footnote 2.)

Herod, Jesus said, "Go ye, and tell that fox, Behold, I cast out devils, and I do cures today and tomorrow, and the third day I shall be perfected."

When He made reference to casting out devils for two days, He was not referring to two days of 24 hours. This is clear because Jesus cast out devils throughout His three-and-a-half-year ministry. Here the Lord was referring to two days in which He would work. If He was referring to a "day of the Lord," which is a thousand years, then this is a period of 2,000 years.

Why did Christ say that He would cast out demons for two days, or 2,000 years? Because He will not cast demons out of people during the millennial reign, since there won't be demons on the earth then. Satan and his servants will either be bound, or else cast into the lake of fire, for that period of 1,000 years (Rev. 19 and 20). In Mark 16:17 we see that He will cast out demons using His Church. However, that ministry will last for only "two days," or 2,000 years.

Mark 5:13 gives us another insight into this same truth. There Jesus casts many devils out of a man and permits them to enter a herd of swine. The entire herd runs headlong down a steep hill into a lake and drowns. Spiritually speaking, Second Peter 2:22 likens swine to human beings who are unclean. The Bible shows that demons actually do seek to enter the lives of men. However, we learn from this event in the ministry of Christ that they can do so only with His permission. When permission is granted, what happened to the herd of swine in Mark 5 happens in a spiritual sense to the men they possess. The inhabited "swine" always run headlong toward destruction and the pit.

How many swine were there in Mark 5:13? We are told that there were about 2,000. Remembering that God's Word never gives unimportant details, what is the significance of this number? It is this: "swine" (unclean people) will be inhabited by other spirits for 2,000 years, or two days, as we learned from Jesus' message to Herod.

Another question: "Why will He heal people for only two days?" Won't there be healing in the Millennium? Psalm 105:37 says that when Israel left Egypt at the Passover, there was not one sick person among them. And when the Church leaves this world to enter the millennial Kingdom, there won't be one sick person among us either. We won't need the ministry of healing in that day.

Finally, He declares, "The third day I shall be perfected," referring to the perfection or completion of His Body, the Church. He will finish or perfect His work in His people during the third day, His millennial reign. There is a tendency in the Church today to preach that the end of God's purposes with this earth is at hand. But we must remember that this present earth will continue to exist for another thousand years. We are not coming to the end of the world, but rather to the end of this present order or system, and to the beginning of the Kingdom Age. The Millennium will definitely not be a waste of time. He has a divine purpose in giving the earth one more "day" of existence, and He will perfect and complete His work with His people and with this earth during that time.

The Marriage At Cana

"And the third day there was a marriage in Cana of Galilee; and the mother of Jesus was there: And both Jesus was called, and his disciples, to the marriage" (Jn. 2:1-2). In this marriage Jesus serves the best wine at the very end of the feast. Again, let's keep in mind that everything Jesus did and said revealed truth; we are even told in this passage that this miracle was a "sign."[4]

At what moment in time will Jesus and His disciples be together at a wedding where He will serve the very best wine of all? Every Christian knows the answer; it is one of our great hopes. This will happen at the Marriage Supper of the Lamb mentioned in Revelation 19:9. This "sign" at Cana revealed the glory of the Lord. He will serve the very best wine at the end. This is a revelation of His nature or glory. The marriage in John 2:1 took place on the third day. This again confirms that after two days have passed, and at the beginning of the third day, the Lord will come, and that eternal Marriage will take place.

The Ark of the Covenant Crosses the Jordan River

The ark of the covenant in the Old Testament was a wooden box covered with gold within and without. That ark carried the manifest presence of God in the midst of Israel during Old Testament times (Ex. 25:10-22). As such, it was a symbol of the Lord Jesus Christ in the New Testament, the One who would carry God's presence and glory in the midst of His people during this present age. Consider the details of how the ark led God's people across the Jordan River under Joshua.

> *And they commanded the people, saying, When ye see the ark of the covenant of the Lord your God, and the priests the Levites bearing it, then ye shall remove from your place, and go after it. Yet there shall be a space*

4. See John 2:11 in the NKJV and also "miracles" in the *Strong's Greek Dictionary.*

> *between you and it, about two thousand cubits by measure: come not near unto it, that ye may know the way by which ye must go...* (Joshua 3:3-4).

In the four Gospels of the New Testament, we find a spiritual fulfillment to one part of this passage. We find that Christ, *the* Ark, was baptized in the Jordan River. There His glory was openly manifested, and from the moment the Ark, the Lord Jesus Christ, was baptized in the Jordan by John, Israel saw the Ark because He began to openly reveal Himself to them. At that moment, many in Israel began to follow the Ark, just as Joshua had commanded them to do many years before when they saw the physical ark crossing the Jordan. Christ's **first** disciples began to follow Him in the context of the River Jordan in John 1. His **last** disciples still need to follow the Ark, because without Him we do not know the way. The Ark actually *is* the way, and He has opened up the way for us through a spiritual Jordan, as happened when the ark of Joshua's day entered the Jordan and the waters were divided.

Our Journey From Egypt to Canaan Ends at the Jordan

We have already noted that the New Testament explains to us that God's last-day people are also on a journey from Egypt to Canaan (1 Cor. 10:11). Canaan is referred to in many Scriptures as the inheritance that the Lord has promised to His people, and we know that it is the Kingdom of God that we are called to inherit. The Jordan River is the border or gateway between the wilderness and Canaan. The longest part of our journey is through the wilderness, where there are trials and times of spiritual drought. Canaan symbolizes the promised inheritance, or the land of the Kingdom. In light of this, it is very interesting that once Christ had been baptized in the River Jordan He began to preach and reveal the Kingdom of God to Israel. For the Lord, His experience in the Jordan was indeed the gateway into the manifestation of the Kingdom. Could it be that the gospel of the Kingdom that will be preached in all the world for a witness during the last three and a half years will only be revealed through prepared vessels that have finished their spiritual journey and crossed a spiritual Jordan into a spiritual Canaan?

If every jot and tittle of the Old Testament must be fulfilled in the New Testament, then it is important to note that after the ark entered into the Jordan, then all the armies of Israel crossed over into Canaan. We are expecting to enter the authority and character of Kingdom living very soon, but note furthermore, in the Scripture we quoted above, that Israel crossed over "about 2,000 cubits" after the ark entered the Jordan. It is already a historical fact that Jesus Christ, crossed the Jordan and entered the Kingdom life of Canaan about two thousand years ago. I believe that this Scripture is telling us that the Church will follow the Ark at a distance of "about two thousand cubits," or two thousand years. Very soon the Church will cross its spiritual Jordan and begin to manifest the glory of the Kingdom to a needy world.

Why does Joshua 3 say, "**About** two thousand cubits"? Since God is a God of mathematical precision, if He says "about," then it won't be exactly 2,000. We have already noted that there will be exactly 2,000 years from His birth at the First Coming, until His "birth" at the Second Coming in 1996, when He will come in His people. However, Jesus was baptized in the Jordan when He was thirty years old, not at His birth. Therefore, He crossed the Jordan "**about,**" not exactly, 2,000 years ahead of us. How precise the Word of God is, and how carefully the Holy Spirit has worded each passage.

Chapter 42

Six Days

Six Days to Rest

"Six days shalt thou labour, and do all thy work: But the seventh is the sabbath of the Lord thy God: in it thou shalt not do any work..." (Ex. 20:9-10). Remembering that one day is a thousand years, and a thousand years is one day, He tells us from the very beginning that man will do all his works for six days, or 6,000 years. As is often the case when God speaks, this is prophetic. It reveals far more truth than is found on the surface. Speaking again of a day of rest, Hebrews 4:3-4 gives a scriptural basis for declaring that there is a deeper significance to the day of rest than simply a literal day each week for man to rest from his physical works.

What are the works of man in a spiritual sense? Paul calls them the "works of the flesh" (Gal. 5:19). At this very moment, we are seeing the end result of the works and ways of man throughout the world. We are facing worldwide total chaos. Referring to the last days, Jesus calls it a time when there will be "distress of nations" with men's hearts failing them for fear (Lk. 21:25). And things are going from bad to worse almost daily. This is the way of man, and this is the fruit of his works. However, he will do those works for only 6,000 years, and then he will rest for one day, or a thousand years, in the "millennial reign of Christ" (Rev. 20:4-6).

According to the Bible chronology determined by Ussher, Adam was created in the year 4004 B.C.[1] If we use this date, man will end his six days,

---

1. Tenney, *The Zondervan Pictorial Encyclopedia of the Bible;* see "Chronology of the Old Testament." I am aware of the fact that, although for many years Ussher's Bible chronology was highly esteemed, today many scholars do not accept his

or 6,000 years around A.D. 1996. He will then begin a day of rest, a day that will last a thousand years. One man that probably had access to information that was a little more precise, regarding Old Testament chronology and the history of God's people, was the Apostle Barnabas, Paul's companion, living 2,000 years ago. He also wrote an epistle, called the epistle of Barnabas. In that epistle he mentions the idea that from Adam to Abraham was 2,000 years, and from Abraham to Christ was 2,000 years, and from Christ's First Coming until His Second Coming will be 2,000 years. We don't have long to wait to see if Barnabas was right.[2]

Six Days Before Entering His Glory

Mark 9:2 tells us that "after six days Jesus taketh with him Peter, and James, and John, and leadeth them up into an high mountain apart by themselves: and he was transfigured before them." We know that in the last days the people of God will indeed be taken up into a very high mountain. It is called the "mountain of the Lord" (Isa. 2:3). We will be raptured, and at that time we will see His glory. Is the fact that He took His disciples up into a mountain "after six days" a revelation of truth, or merely an unimportant detail? We declare that man will see His glory after six days, that is, after 6,000 years, again confirming the date of 1996.

---

dating as accurate. However, in the light of the study found in this book, it seems that this date is, in fact, highly probable, in spite of what some consider to be "problems" in the biblical chronology.

2. Halley, H., *Halley's Bible Handbook*, Zondervan Publishing House, Grand Rapids, Michigan, 1965, p. 33.

Chapter 43

The Feast of Pentecost

The last scriptural confirmation we will consider is possibly one of the clearest. It is related to the Feast of Pentecost spoken of by Peter in Acts 2:16-21. To understand this glorious truth, we must first understand a few basic truths about the feasts of Jehovah found in Leviticus 23.

There Are Three Principal Feasts

People of all cultures enjoy holidays, usually associated with feasting, festivity, and rest from the usual labor. Israel also had national holidays, called "feasts." According to Exodus 23:16-17 the three principal feasts celebrated every year were the Feast of **Passover**, the Feast of **Pentecost**, and the Feast of **Tabernacles.** In any culture a national holiday usually commemorates specific historical events in the nation's past. Likewise, the seven feasts in Leviticus 23 were commemorations of the seven principal stages in the journey of Israel from Egypt to Canaan.[1] Israel actually became an independent nation on earth as a result of that journey. During the years that followed, Israel celebrated those feasts yearly to remember those major events. Every man in Israel had to journey to Jerusalem three times each year, and "appear before the Lord" who dwelled in the temple (Ex. 23:17). There are many wonderful truths to be found in these feasts. One truth is that mankind will experience three direct divine interventions in the affairs of this world. There will be three times in the course of

1. The seven feasts are as follows: Passover, Unleavened Bread, Firstfruits, Pentecost, Memorial of Blowing of Trumpets, the Day of Atonement, and Tabernacles.

history that the Lord will appear to man on earth, and man will "appear before the Lord." Let's briefly consider these three events.

The Truths Revealed by These Three Feasts

1. The Passover. The first time that God visibly appeared to man was during the Passover of Moses in the Old Testament. The Lord physically and visibly descended among His people, and they saw a literal cloud by day and a pillar of fire by night. Days later, on Mount Sinai, they presented themselves before Him as He visibly descended on that mountain. That Passover, accompanied by a physical, visible, intervention of God in the affairs of men, actually became the basis of our Old Testament. If He hadn't visited His people at that time, then Moses would not have written the first five books of the Bible, nor would we have the rest of the Old Testament, which is basically a history of the nation of Israel that was founded at that Passover and God's Word to them.[2] As a result of that intervention, the course of history was changed. Egypt, the most powerful nation on earth, was crushed, and Israel became the principal nation on earth for many years.

2. Pentecost. But 1,500 years later the Lord physically and visibly intervened once again in the affairs of men, at Christ's coming. As a result of that appearance, the people of God were brought into the blessing and fulfillment of Pentecost in Acts 2. If there had not been a Pentecost in the early Church, we would not have received the New Testament Scriptures. Just as the basis of the Old Testament was the Passover, the basis of the New Testament is the Feast of Pentecost. In fact, all of the New Testament was actually written *after* the fulfillment of Pentecost in Acts 2. But wait a minute. If Christ had not **first** become our Passover Lamb, there would not have been a Pentecost. Therefore, just as the Feast of Passover under Moses was the basis of the Old Testament, likewise the Feasts of Passover *and* Pentecost are the basis of the New Testament, under the second Moses, Christ. Consider also that the course of history was again changed as a result of this second intervention of God in the affairs of men when Christ came physically. Rome, which had been the world's greatest power, sought to destroy Christianity. However, it was Rome that was changed, at least in name, when it was conquered by Constantine and Christianity became the official religion in A.D. 313.

---

2. Exodus 12:2 makes it clear that, for them as a nation, time actually began at the Passover.

3. Tabernacles. There is one more principal feast, and therefore one more great intervention of God in the affairs of men, where all His people will appear before Him. It is the Feast of Tabernacles, which is the feast of ingathering, or general harvest, at the "end of the year" (Ex. 23:16). The people of God are waiting expectantly for this feast, and again the course of history will be changed. History's most powerful empire ever, the Antichrist spirit and his system, will be ruling the earth. As in the days when Israel was in Egypt, the Church will be oppressed, but God will change all that as He again visits His people. That powerful empire will be conquered by the anointed Church, which will subdue the kingdoms of this world under the feet of Christ.

If the foundation of the Old Testament Age was the Passover, and the foundation of the New Testament Age is both the Passover and Pentecost, then it follows that the foundation of the Kingdom Age will be the Passover, Pentecost, and Tabernacles. God is a wise Master Builder who plans ahead, and nothing ever upsets or destroys His plans. Therefore, He never needs to cast away a foundation He has laid. He always builds upon what has gone before. He has done this with the covenants in the Bible, and this is what He is doing with the feasts as well. He is going to fulfill all three of these principal feasts—Passover, Pentecost, and Tabernacles. They will form the foundation of the blessing and glory of the Kingdom Age. Let's consider what the Bible says about this.

The Passover Will Have a Fulfillment in the Last Days

The Passover shall be observed forever, according to Exodus 12:14. The Lord Jesus changed the Passover of Moses, which was celebrated during the Age of the law, to the Lord's Supper, which has been celebrated during the Age of the Church. It will be changed once again, but then celebrated forever. Jesus said to His disciples, "With desire I have desired to eat this passover with you before I suffer: For I say unto you, I will not any more eat thereof, **until it be fulfilled in the kingdom of God**" (Lk. 22:15-18). So there is a fulfillment of the Passover in the Kingdom Age also; it is the "Marriage Supper of the Lamb" (Rev. 19:9). This supper will be celebrated throughout the ages of eternity, a feast forever with the Lord.

Note, too, that the complete fulfillment of the Passover of Moses has not yet been given to the Church. There were two principal aspects related to the Passover of Moses' day: the blood of the Lamb, and leaving Egypt (Ex. 12). The Church today has the cleansing and protection of the blood of the Lamb, but we have not yet left "Egypt," the world. That blessing will come when we leave this world behind at the Rapture, and are taken to the final Passover Supper, the Marriage Supper of the Lamb. So the complete fulfillment of the Passover will come at the end of the Church Age, as we enter the Kingdom, just as Jesus said.

Pentecost Will Also Have a Fulfillment in the Last Days

Quoting Peter's principal declarations concerning the Day of Pentecost, we read:

> *But this is that which was spoken by the prophet Joel; And it shall come to pass **in the last days**, saith God, I will pour out of my Spirit upon all flesh...And I will show wonders in heaven above, and signs in the earth beneath; blood, and fire, and vapour of smoke: The sun shall be turned into darkness, and the moon into blood, before that great and notable day of the Lord come: And it shall come to pass, that whosoever shall call on the name of the Lord shall be saved* (Acts 2:16-21).

It is important to observe several things here. First, Peter said that what they were experiencing on that Feast of Pentecost was similar to what Joel had promised would happen in the *last days*. However, it is clear from the context that not everything Peter mentioned here was fulfilled during the days of the early Church, such as the sun being turned into blood and the moon into darkness. Nor to this day has there been a complete fulfillment of those things. Second, he stated that these things will take place before "that great and notable day of the Lord come." So Pentecost, just like Passover, will find its complete fulfillment in the last days. This is very understandable, because the passage in Joel, from which Peter quoted, begins by saying, "Be glad then, ye children of Zion [the Church]...for he hath given you the former rain moderately, and he will cause to come down for you the rain, the former rain, and the latter rain in the first month" (Joel 2:23). So the rain of the early Church (Pentecost), as well as the rain of the last-day Church (Tabernacles), will be given at the same time.

These Three Feasts Form the Foundation for the Three Ages

The three ages (the Age of the Law, the Age of Grace, and the Kingdom Age) are founded upon these three principal feasts (Passover, Pentecost, and Tabernacles). However, each time a new age begins, it builds on the Feast and blessing of the age that has gone before. The Lord does not take away one blessing to give us another, but rather He always retains the previous blessing and adds another. So the Old Testament Age was founded on the Passover. The New Testament Age is founded on the Passover and Pentecost. And finally, the Kingdom Age will be founded on the Passover, Pentecost, and Tabernacles. Furthermore, in each succeeding age God gives a greater and more complete fulfillment to these feasts. The following diagram clarifies this.

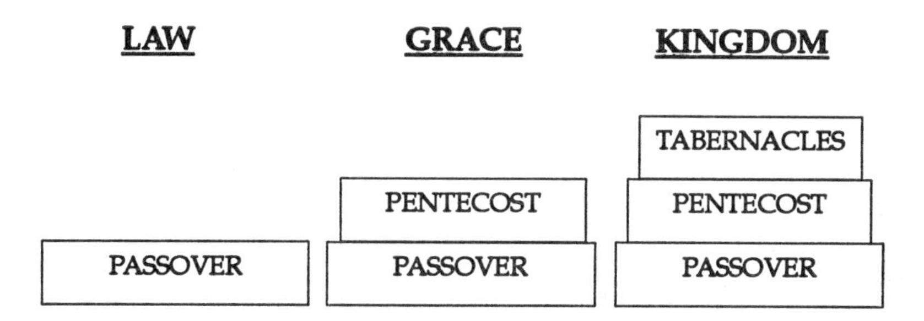

How Then Will Pentecost Be Fulfilled in the End?

How does all this show us the time of His coming? Peter says the Feast of Pentecost is going to be fulfilled in the last days (Acts 2:17, 19-20). However, God will only fulfill it according to the details outlined in His own Word. In the Old Testament "parable" we find several of those details given about how the Feast of Pentecost must be observed. They clearly reveal the time of His coming in the end.

The Experience at Mount Sinai Was on the Day of Pentecost

According to Jewish history, God descended on Mount Sinai on the very Day of Pentecost. In fact, to the Jewish mind the Feast of Pentecost is a commemoration of Mount Sinai and the giving of the law. Indeed, we find in the Bible that Moses went up the mountain at the season of the Feast of Pentecost. Pentecost was always celebrated 50 days after the offering of the firstfruits of the barley harvest, which were offered during the Passover and the Feast of Unleavened Bread.[3] Israel left Egypt on the

3. See Leviticus 23 for this order of events, and Exodus 9:31-32, where we are shown that the Feast of Passover and the Exodus from Egypt took place at the time of the barley harvest.

night of the fourteenth day of the first month, that is, on the night of the Passover (Ex. 12:2,6,42). So counting 50 days, we come to approximately the fifth day of the third month.[4] Note that in Exodus 19:1 they came to Mount Sinai on the first day of the third month. This was 45 days after Passover. Then, reading the context of chapter 19, we find that God descended on Mount Sinai 4 or 5 days after they arrived. This brings us to the very time of Pentecost, 50 days after the Passover and the Firstfruits.

Pentecost Is a Revelation of the Second Coming

The fulfillment of Pentecost is related to the last days, but the first Pentecost, which took place in Exodus 19, gives us the details, or the "jots and tittles," that must be fulfilled in the end. We find there an amazing revelation of the physical return of Christ in the last days. Let's consider the details of the first Pentecost, and compare them with other Scriptures that are also related to the last days and the coming of Christ.

In Exodus 19:4 God tells His people that He bore them on "eagles' wings." This statement refers to His help and protection as He brought them out of Egypt and into the wilderness to begin their journey. This is definitely similar to something that will happen in the last days. Speaking of the woman of Revelation 12, whom we saw to be the Church in the last days, we are told, "And to the woman were given two wings of a great eagle, that she might fly into the wilderness" (v. 14a).

Returning to Exodus 19, we find, "And the Lord said unto Moses, Go unto the people, and sanctify them today and tomorrow, and let them wash their clothes, And be ready against the third day: for the third day the Lord will come down in the sight of all the people upon Mount Sinai" (Ex. 19:10-11). This is an amazing passage, in the light of a day representing a thousand years. First, we know that those in the Church are washing their garments in the blood of the Lamb (Rev. 7:14). We also know that they will do this for "two days" or 2,000 years, and that on the very morning of the third day the Lord will descend from Heaven in the **sight of the people**, just as Revelation 1:7 says, "And every eye shall see him." However, Hosea 6:2 makes it even clearer. "After two days will he revive us: in the third day he will raise us up, and we shall **live in his sight.**" This is a revelation of the physical return of the Lord.

---

4. Between the fourteenth day and the thirtieth day of the first month there are 16 days. Then 29 days for the second month give a total of 45 days from Passover to the first day of the third month. So then the fifth day of the third month would have been 50 days after the Passover they celebrated in Egypt.

Again, we need to keep in mind that all these events in Exodus 19, which symbolize the Second Coming of Christ, occurred in the context of the Feast of Pentecost. No wonder Peter, in Acts 2, links the fulfillment of Pentecost with the "great and notable day of the Lord," the day of His coming. That is precisely what Exodus 19 does. Surely Peter understood these things, but we want to consider more Scriptures as a confirmation.

Continuing in Exodus 19:12-13 we find that, "Whosoever toucheth the mount shall be surely put to death." Mount Sinai and this very experience are referred to in Hebrews 12:18-21. The children of Israel are found saying that they did not want to hear God's audible voice anymore, because the message "If so much as a beast touch the mountain, it shall be stoned, or thrust through with a dart" was too fearful for them to bear. Hebrews then makes a clear comparison between the shaking that occurred at Mount Sinai and the shaking of Heaven and earth in the last days (Heb. 12:25-29).

The principal message of Hebrews 12:18-29 is a comparison of Mount Sinai with Mount Zion. We are told that in the last days we will not draw near to an earthly mountain (Sinai), but rather to a heavenly mountain, Mount Zion (v. 18-24). We know that we will ascend Zion in the Rapture, because Mount Zion appears in Revelation 14 as the dwelling place of the Lamb, and the redeemed are with Him there in heavenly places. So once again, a clear connection is made between the events of Pentecost, where they ascended Mount Sinai in Exodus 19, and the return of the Lord, when we will ascend the heavenly mountain, Zion. We have, then, a strong scriptural foundation for concluding that Mount Sinai is definitely related to Christ's coming and Mount Zion.

Finally, in Acts 2:19 we come to an interesting thought that Peter relates to the fulfillment of Pentecost. He says there will be "**signs** in the earth beneath; **blood**, and **fire**, and **vapour** of smoke." And when God descended on Mount Sinai there were literally signs in the earth, seen on that mountain. There was blood, because any "beast" that was on the mountain died, and there was also fire and smoke, according to Exodus 19:18. Can there be any doubt that both the Pentecost found in Exodus 19 and the Pentecost referred to in Acts 2 by Peter are referring to the last days and the return of Christ, just as Peter declared? But let's continue this comparison a little further.

The Last Trumpet and the Rapture in Exodus 19

The coming of the Lord is associated with a trumpet.[5] Knowing the connection that exists between Exodus 19 and His return, it should not

5. Compare First Corinthians 15:51-52 and First Thessalonians 4:16 for the trumpet of His coming, when He comes to His people.

surprise us that the sound of a trumpet is also involved in Exodus 19:13. Not only is a trumpet involved, but note what happens when this trumpet sounds. "When the trumpet soundeth long, they shall come up to the mount." Hebrews and Revelation tell us that we will ascend Mount Zion in the end, and we know that this will happen at the sound of a trumpet.

Exodus 19:16 and 19:18 are comparable to Revelation 11:15 and 11:19. In both passages, the trumpet sounds, and there are voices, thunderings, lightning, and an earthquake. Once again, we see the importance of comparing Scripture with Scripture, and the absolute importance of understanding the beginning in order to understand the end. At this point there can be little doubt that Exodus 19 is a type of the last trumpet and of the Rapture of the Church.

We, therefore, have a very clear connection between what is occurring in Exodus 19 and the seventh or final trumpet in Revelation 11:15-19. This is further evidence that the Church is raptured at the seventh trumpet of Revelation, again showing that she passes through the Great Tribulation.

So then, in the end there will be a total fulfillment of Pentecost, but it will be in accordance with the pattern given in Exodus 19 at the first Pentecost. In the same way, there will be a total fulfillment of the first Passover, seen in Exodus 12. In the next chapter, we will consider the end-time fulfillment of Tabernacles also. We understand from Peter that the end-time fulfillment of Pentecost will begin with a mighty outpouring of the Holy Spirit throughout the world. This outpouring will begin in A.D. 1996. Pentecost will reach its culmination at the physical return of Christ, which involves "blood, and fire, and vapour of smoke" on the third day as He descends on Mount Zion and calls His people up into that Mount. This will occur in the year A.D. 2000.

The Celebration of Pentecost Starts "Seven Weeks" After Israel Enters Their Land

Knowing that the Lord is going to fulfill Pentecost in the last days, we know that He must do so in accordance with His own written instructions regarding the keeping of that Feast. They are found in the Old Testament Scriptures, and every detail must be fulfilled. Leviticus 23:9-16 gives a few additional aspects related to Pentecost that must also be fulfilled in the last days. The Lord tells Israel that when they enter their land, they were to offer a firstfruits offering to Him from the land (v. 10). The date of this offering was then used to determine when Pentecost actually began, because they counted 7 weeks, or 49 days, from this offering, and began the Feast of Pentecost on the fiftieth day (v. 15,16).

When did Israel enter their land? They entered their land, Canaan, on more than one occasion. The first time was under the leadership of Joshua. They entered again in these last days as a result of the 1947 United Nations' Decree. Therefore, as before, the date on which they entered the land this last time, and offered the firstfruits, will be used to determine when the Feast of Pentecost will begin in the last days. So, the fact that Israel has literally entered their land again makes it possible for even this little detail to be fulfilled in these days.

The Hebrew word "Pentecost" actually refers to the fiftieth day, that is, the day following the 7 weeks or 49 days. How is God going to fulfill this detail in these last days? I believe that we have already received the answer to that question from our study of Daniel's Seventy Weeks. Remember that the Hebrew word "week" can actually be translated as a "week of seven years." God is going to begin the celebration of Pentecost, and that wonderful outpouring of the Holy Spirit, "seven weeks of years," or 49 years, after Israel has entered their land again. At this point, some may wonder if we are justified in applying the "seven weeks" between Firstfruits and Pentecost mentioned in Leviticus 23 to the 7 weeks of years of Daniel, or 49 years. The Word of God gives us the answer just two chapters later, in Leviticus 25:8. In the same discourse to Moses, the Lord continues to give Israel various ordinances for their life as a nation. He tells Moses, "And thou shalt number seven sabbaths of years unto thee, **seven times seven years**; and the space of the **seven sabbaths of years** shall be unto thee **forty and nine years**." Isn't it interesting that in these same instructions the Lord reminds us of the way in which He uses the biblical concept of "seven weeks of years"?

So Daniel's revelation of "Seven Weeks to Messiah" was not totally new. In fact, it is a theme that runs throughout the Word of God, starting from the very beginning of Israel's history under Moses. As every detail regarding the celebration of Pentecost must be fulfilled, there must be a period of seven weeks of years between the time they enter their land and the beginning of Pentecost. This is understandable, because 7 weeks of years, or 49 years, will be the time between their restoration and their first year of jubilee, when they will be delivered from their enemies! As we have seen through an abundance of Scriptures, this is exactly what will happen. Israel received their land back in 1947, and 49 years later, in the year 1996, we can expect that the Feast of Pentecost and the outpouring of the Spirit described in Joel will begin. That Feast will finally end with the coming of the Lord.

The Beginning of Pentecost Will Be the Beginning of Rest

In Numbers 28:26 God commands us, "Also, in the day of the firstfruits, when ye bring a new meat offering unto the Lord, *after your weeks be out,* ye shall have an holy convocation; ye shall do **no servile work.**" Therefore, when the Feast of Pentecost is celebrated we will cease from our own works ("servile work"), and enter His day of rest. There will be no works of the flesh manifested in the revival and visitation that are coming. In fact, this Scripture indicates that 1996 will be the beginning of the rest of God, the Kingdom Age, or the Millennium, because the Day of Pentecost is associated with a day of rest.

The Former and Latter Rain Are Associated With These Weeks

"Let us now fear the Lord our God, that giveth rain, both the former and the latter, in his season: he reserveth unto us the appointed **weeks of the harvest**" (Jer. 5:24). Here is a connection between the former and latter rain and the seven weeks of the Feast of Pentecost, which is also called the "feast of harvest" in Exodus 23:16. This passage shows that the outpouring of the latter rain is connected with the 7 weeks, or 49 years, of the Feast of Pentecost. So the latter rain of Joel should begin in A.D. 1996 and culminate in **the final victory** over death, at the Rapture.

PART V

Putting It All Together

Introduction

The year A.D. 1996 is a pivotal year in the plan of God for this earth. We have seen a good number of Scriptures that reveal this, and there are still others. Part V of this book will show that God will bring together many historical and prophetic threads in that year. A.D. 1996 has also been confirmed as the year of His coming through other members of the Body of Christ. Some of those confirmations will be presented here. Finally, the fulfillment of the Feast of Tabernacles, which will also begin in A.D. 1996, will be considered, along with how 1,260 days relate to that Feast and other last-day events.

Chapter 44

Considering "Coincidences"

A servant of the Lord was once testifying of the many miraculous experiences God had granted him along life's way. Later, an unbeliever told him, "Those things you shared aren't miracles. They are just the coincidences of life." His response was, "Whether or not they are coincidences, I would rather not discuss. All I know is that when I stop praying the coincidences stop happening." He knew that a sovereign God was causing and controlling those "coincidences."

There are simply too many "coincidences" related to the year A.D. 1996 to ignore the handiwork of an Almighty and Sovereign God. In the light of Scripture, that year is a pivotal year in the history of mankind and the fulfillment of Bible prophecy. God ties together the threads of many biblical and historical events in that year in a way that only He could possibly do. Let's consider some of the "coincidences" related to A.D. 1996:

1. A.D. 1996 will be precisely the 2,000th year since the birth of Christ, around September of 5 B.C.

2. A.D. 1996 will be precisely the 3,000th year since David declared Jerusalem to be the capital city of the kingdom.[1]

3. A.D. 1996 will be the 6,000th year since Adam was created.[2]

4. A.D. 1996 will be precisely 7 "weeks," or 49 years since the command to restore Israel was given by the United Nations in November, 1947. God had to coordinate world events to cause the United Nations to give that decree precisely 49 years before His 2,000th birthday, or 49

1. We refer to this in Chapter 38, "One Day Is as a Thousand Years."
2. This is according to Ussher's biblical chronology. See Chapter 42, footnote 1.

years before the 3,000th anniversary since David declared Jerusalem the capital of the Kingdom, or 49 years before the 6,000th anniversary of the creation of man.

5. A.D. 1996 will be the beginning of the "seventh day," the day of rest for man, after he has done all his own works for "six days," or 6,000 years. Since the Kingdom Age begins in A.D. 1996, the year A.D. 2000 will be the **fourth year** of Christ's millennial reign. The year A.D. 2000 will be when the Rapture will occur, and the living stones of the Temple will be assembled. It will also be precisely 480 years since Martin Luther was excommunicated from the Catholic Church and the Reformation began, in A.D. 1520. Therefore, A.D. 1996, along with A.D. 2000 and A.D. 1520, are key dates for fulfilling First Kings 6:1, as we saw in Chapter 37 ("Solomon's Temple").

Again, note that God had to coordinate the events of history to cause a Martin Luther to be born, prepared, and excommunicated by the year 1520, so that it would be 480 years before the year 2000, the fourth year of His reign.

6. Finally, God, through His sovereignty and providence, has permitted our calendar (the Gregorian calendar) to have an error of about three and a half years. Proverbs 25:2 tells us that the glory of God is to conceal the truth, and the honor of those who are kings is to search it out. Why did God permit the error of approximately three and a half years in our calendar? He has hidden the fact that, in reality, the year A.D. 1996 will actually be the change of a millennium.

Changes in Decades, Centuries, and Millennia

Many people take note every time we pass from one decade to the next. Some expect significant worldwide events to come with that change in the calendar. There is even a tendency in the news media to characterize each decade as a time of specific progress, problems, or changes in the world.

However, when there is a change of century, people's interest is even greater. Not everyone who has lived on earth has experienced the change of a century during their lifetime. So it's a significant event for those who do. For example, most of the world today speaks of how the twenty-first century will be and what it will bring.

But the change of calendar that gets the greatest attention is the change of a millennium, which is just ahead. One can already hear people talking of what they expect for that year. In the late 1990s all attention will be focused toward the milestone—the year 2000.

So why did God allow the error in our calendar? Because it is God's way to hide the truth, so that those who love the truth will search for it as for hidden treasure. This is a characteristic of those who will become kings (Pro. 25:2). Few will consider the year A.D. 1996 to be an important year, but it will be the actual year in which the millennium will change, not the year A.D. 2000. Furthermore, the events of A.D. 1996 will be of far more eternal significance than the events of A.D. 2000. Yes, the Rapture will occur in A.D. 2000, but only those who recognize that He already came, manifesting Himself in and through His Body, in A.D. 1996 will participate in that Rapture. Some will reject Him, because they are not able to recognize the Lord who dwells in His Body, just as many rejected Him when He came in the body of Jesus, the Carpenter of Galilee. They could not recognize the glory and authority of the Lion of Judah because He came with the mind, nature and meekness of the Lamb.

In a measure, He has always manifested Himself in His Body ever since the cross. In fact, He tells us that what we do to one of the least of His brethren we are really doing to Him (Mt. 25:40). However, the manifestation of Christ in the Church will be greater than ever before at the end of the Church Age. The glory of the latter house will be greater than the glory of the former house (Hag. 2:9), and the latter rain will be greater than the former rain, beginning in A.D. 1996. Let us be ready for *that* coming and for *that* year, so we may have a part in **the final victory** in **the year 2000.**

Chapter 45

Confirmations From the Body

According to the Scriptures, the Lord establishes every word in the mouth of at least two or three witnesses (2 Cor. 13:1). Usually His Word is established in the mouth of *many* witnesses in the Body of Christ. Although I have personally talked to many others who have, in one way or another, received an understanding that A.D. 1996 will be the year of His Coming, I would like to mention here just two such witnesses. The first confirmation came through a child and the second through a minister.

God's Love for Little Children

"Lord, I know that what I am hearing is from Your heart. A deep conviction has gripped me that You will indeed come to Your people in 1996. But what about my little girl? She is only nine years old, and doesn't seem to understand spiritual things. She would never accept this message if I were to share it with her, and yet she has so few years left to be prepared."

This was the prayer of a mother who was present in one of our seminars concerning the last days. It was September of 1989. Two days later, her nine-year-old daughter came running into her bedroom early in the morning. She said, "Mother, I had a dream last night. In the dream I was with three of my cousins on a highway. Suddenly the glory of the Lord appeared, along with lots of big angels. That glory shined on our way. We were all very excited. In the dream I was 16 years old."

Her mother was overwhelmed with joy and gratitude. She had prayed only two days earlier that God would somehow prepare the way for her to share with her daughter about Christ's soon return. The expression of His divine love and care toward a little life amazed her. She was able to interpret the dream for her daughter, explaining that the Lord had just shown her the year of His coming. When the girl had the dream, in September of 1989, she was nine years old, but in the dream, when she saw the Lord coming, she was 16 years old. The little girl understood that this meant His glory would come after seven more years, or in 1996.

A Concern for the Church

Thousands of Believers were stirred to seek God afresh in 1988 when a minister in the United States wrote a book predicting that the Rapture would take place in September of that year. His reasons seemed to carry some weight and seemed to be at least somewhat logical. When September passed many were disillusioned.

Then, the same author published another booklet explaining he had made an error due to a lack of understanding that there is no year zero ("0") in our calendar. Once again many prepared themselves for the Rapture in September of 1989. However, the disillusionment was probably less, because the doubts were far greater for the second date, and there were fewer people who believed the prediction.

I observed these things with sorrow in my heart for two reasons. First, I was concerned about the impact it would have on the Body of Christ. We *are* in the last days, and many are sleeping. However, when such a prediction awakens our spirits to the lateness of the hour, and nothing happens, we are even less likely to heed further warnings. Other voices will be ignored whether they are from God or not.

Second, I was concerned for the author of the booklets. He had invested many hours and years in his study. He was obviously sincere. What would ever happen to him after September of 1989? He would surely suffer a crushing humiliation. Sadly enough, his mistake was not that he had established a specific year. It wasn't the wrong year, but rather the wrong event. His mistake was in mixing "new wine" with "old wine" (new revelation with old doctrine and tradition). He declared in his booklets that September of 1989 would be the beginning of the last seven years of the Church Age. This is precisely what I am saying in this book also.

His mistake was to assume that the Rapture would take place seven years before the end of this Age. We have seen that the Rapture will actually take place about three and a half years after the Kingdom Age has begun. Nevertheless, the tremendous weight of evidence that was given to pinpoint September of 1989 cannot be ignored. Again, the error was not the year, but rather the interpretation of what would happen in that year. I believe that the last seven years of the Church Age did, in fact, begin in

September, 1989. It was God's purpose to reveal that year, and awaken us to the lateness of the hour, and also to show us some of the events that will accompany these last seven years. However, a study of those events is outside the scope of this book.

I declare to the Church, once again, that September of 1989 was the beginning of the last seven years of the Church Age. I further declare that Christ will come ***in*** His Church around September of 1996. He will later come ***for*** His Church around March of A.D. 2000 in what is known as the Rapture. Finally, He will come ***with*** His Church some time after that in what is known as the Second Coming.

What Should the Body of Christ Be Doing?

It is clear that the Lord is showing the time of His coming to the young and old alike in the Body of Christ. What should our reaction be to that wonderful revelation? One of the ministerial responsibilities God has given to us is a grade school and high school with hundreds of students. Many of the students understand that Christ is coming in A.D. 1996. Over the years, some have asked, "Since Christ is coming so soon, wouldn't it be better for me to drop out of school and seek the Lord?" My answer is that the best way for any of us to be ready for His coming is to continue doing His perfect will until He comes.

Is it possible that His will for some includes the study of reading, writing, arithmetic, chemistry, biology, and so on? The answer becomes clear if we ask a few simple questions that have obvious answers. What is God's perfect will for a baby of one year? Clearly God wants that little life to dedicate himself to learning to walk and play, thus developing physical coordination. It is God's perfect will for him to continue playing and also learn to talk. What is God's will for a child of five? He needs to learn to read and write. It is God's will for him to spend time studying, not preaching the gospel. After learning to read and write, should he discontinue his studies? Not if God wants to use him as a doctor. So when should a person discontinue studying? Only when he is finished with the course of study that God has chosen for his particular life.

The key to this Age is the same as to any Age—be led by the Spirit, hearing and obeying His voice. Why, then, do we need to know the end-time schedule if Believers of all ages simply need to be led by the Spirit? Those who have a vision that their lives will be cut short by His coming are more likely to seek the Lord's mercy with their whole heart than those who don't. Habbakuk 2:2 confirms this: "...Write the vision, and make it plain upon tables, that he may run that readeth it." This verse is a summary of the purpose of this book. I trust that those who read it will run after God and eternal values as never before. The young people of our congregations should know that they won't have seventy years in which to accomplish God's will as their forefathers had. In fact, it is doubtful that any of us will have enough time to accomplish *our* will, and then *His* will later. Let's hear and respond to His call on our lives *today*.

Chapter 46

The Feast of Tabernacles

During God's glorious visitation during the Feast of Tabernacles, the world will be reading headlines similar to the following:

"PLANE CRASH AND RESURRECTION." Today an airliner developed in-flight mechanical problems and crash landed. Two hundred and forty-three people died in the accident. But as rescue workers were beginning to remove the bodies, a group of so-called "Believers" arrived and began to pray. Eyewitnesses say that an astonishing thing happened, something they would have never believed had they not seen it themselves. All 243 people were raised from the dead. The final results are not known, but the initial impact was so awesome that hundreds more proclaimed that they would follow Christ without reservation for the rest of their lives.

"HOSPITAL EMPTIED." Today a group of fanatical "Believers" entered a hospital and began to go from room to room, praying for the sick. Within minutes every bed was emptied, and about 450 ex-patients who had been suffering from just about every imaginable ailment were ecstatic with not only their healing, but also their newfound faith in Christ. Since the hospital is located in the center of the city, by afternoon the group of 450 new Believers had turned into several thousand. The authorities are investigating to determine if any illegal practice of medicine by unqualified persons was involved in this amazing phenomenon.

These are the kinds of things that will soon be happening throughout the earth, as Christ begins to fulfill His promise that His disciples will do "greater works" than He did (Jn. 14:12). At the same time when darkness is covering the earth, and gross darkness is blinding the people, the glory of the Lord will be seen upon His Church, and all humanity shall see that glory, as Isaiah promises (Isa. 60:2; 40:5).

We are on the threshold of a new age. Men of faith throughout the ages have longed for this very hour. Since the day Adam lost his Paradise dwelling place, mankind has longed to live again in the presence of their God, and to know the fullness of His provision, communion, and approval. The last verses of the Bible reveal God again dwelling with man, the goal having been attained, and man being forever united with his God. John "heard a great voice out of heaven saying, Behold, the **tabernacle** of God is with men, and he will dwell with them" (Rev. 21:3). This is the **Feast of Tabernacles**: God making us, as human beings, His dwelling place. We are going to become His Tabernacle, or Body, to a degree we have never known before.

One of the principal purposes of this book is to declare that God will begin to visit His people during the time of that feast around September of the year A.D. 1996. Malachi 3:1 tells us that the Lord Whom we are seeking will suddenly come to His Temple. He will suddenly fill His Tabernacle with His glory, and this world will never be the same. The greatest revival and harvest of souls that humanity has ever witnessed will begin in that year. The gospel of the Kingdom will be preached in all the world for a witness to all nations, as Jesus promised (Mt. 24:14). The power, authority, and character of Heaven will be openly manifested in the earth to all humanity. In other words, the Kingdom Age will literally begin in the year A.D. 1996. Will we be among those found seeking Him in the day when "the Lord, whom ye seek, shall suddenly come to his temple?" (Mal. 3:1)

It will also be a time in which the greatest darkness ever known to man will be openly revealed on the earth, a time Jesus calls the "Great Tribulation." There will be glory and light, joy and beauty, but at the same time there will be wickedness, darkness, sorrow, and distress of nations. There will be a manifestation of the power of Christ, as well as a manifestation of the power of Satan and spiritism. Every man will be confronted with both. Multitudes, multitudes will be in the valley of decision, and every man will make his decision with a full awareness of what he is doing. Those who love the light will come to the light, but those who love darkness will resolutely choose that darkness more than ever before. "He that is unjust, let him be unjust still: and he which is filthy, let him be filthy still: and he that is righteous, let him be righteous still: and he that is holy, let him be holy still" (Rev. 22:11).

After three and a half years, or 1,260 days, the Church will leave this world in a glorious Exodus (Rapture), at the time of the Feast of Passover in the year A.D. 2000, just as Israel left Egypt many years ago. The Church will partake of the Marriage Supper of the Lamb, after which, the Lord will return to this earth with His saints and angels to physically establish His Kingdom. At that time He will finish the task of removing from His Kingdom everyone and everything that offends, a task that will have begun three and a half years before (Mt. 13:41 and 2 Thess. 1:7-10). This event is referred to in the Bible as the Battle of Armageddon.

Through the life of King David, we discover what type of dwelling place, or Tabernacle, will be chosen by the Lord. The Feast of Tabernacles will be a time when the Lord will make men His Tabernacle, a tent in which He will live, and through which He will reveal all that He is. In Acts 15:16-17 James declares that the Lord is building again the "Tabernacle of David," and when He does, all the Gentiles, upon whom His name is called, will seek the Lord. When there are many "Tabernacles," or dwelling places in the earth that are like David's Tabernacle, then the harvest will be reaped. The character, worship, and dedication of David, a man after God's own heart, will be revealed in many lives in these days. This will be the fulfillment of the "Feast of Tabernacles."

Will we be ready? Are we willing to wholly dedicate our lives, money, strength, and ambitions to the eternal purposes of God that are unfolding before our eyes? Will we pay the price to be among those who receive the fullness of His coming? Or will we be content to let the greatest opportunity ever given to mankind slip through our fingers?

The answers to these questions will depend primarily on two things. First, the mercy of God. Knowing that we can do nothing to merit a place in His plan, we need to see both our great need and His great kindness. And second, receiving truth changes us. Those who have a vision and understanding of these things are far more likely to totally surrender to Him than those who are not aware of the hour in which they live. As God's people, the purpose of this book is to help us to awaken from our sleep and to live in the light of this wonderful and tremendous hour. Are you willing to share this message with others so that they too may run in the light of the truth?

Chapter 47

1,260 Days

The letters of the Hebrew and Greek alphabets were used not only as letters, but also as numbers. Each letter has a number value.[1] The concept of using letters as **numbers** is found in Roman numerals also, where I is one, X is ten, L is fifty, C is one hundred, and M is a thousand. Therefore, when reading words in Greek or Hebrew, one can also consider the letters of each word to be a series of numbers. By adding the number values of the letters, one can arrive at the number value of the word. Those who have studied this matter in depth, and even written books on the subject, have discovered some very interesting number values. For example, the number value of the word "Jesus" in the Greek is 888.

Though I had never used these numerical studies, one day the Lord prompted me to find the number value of the word "sons" in Romans 8:19 (NAS). Paul says, "For the anxious longing of the creation waits eagerly for the revealing of the sons of God." So I researched the Greek alphabet and the respective number values of each letter. To my utter amazement, I found the number value of the word "sons" to be 1,260. So, when we read Romans 8:19, we can literally read the passage as, "the anxious longing of the creation waits eagerly for the revealing of the 1,260 of God."

Is this merely a coincidence, or has the Master Mathematician of the universe hidden a wonderful truth in that little word? In Revelation, the two witnesses minister for 1,260 days, and according to Romans the hope

---

1. Lucas, Jerry, and Del Washburn, *Theomatics*, Stein and Day Publishers, New York, New York, 1978, p. 31.

of the creation is the manifestation of the sons, or the 1,260 of God. Paul says that this is our "hope," and as we have seen, hope is related to the future, and something we do not yet possess (Rom. 8:24). So the Church has the hope that her mature sons will be revealed in the last days. It seems quite certain that they will minister for 1,260 days. Through these mature, prepared vessels, God will manifest His power, authority, and character as never before. The gospel of the Kingdom will be preached in all the world for a "witness" and "then shall the end come."

1,260 Days Are Found in the Feasts

Israel has always celebrated the Feasts of the Lord, and she will experience the total spiritual fulfillment of each one. As Deuteronomy 16:16 tells us, there are three principal feasts. They are the Feasts of Passover, Pentecost, and Tabernacles. We know that Christ is our Passover (1 Cor. 5:7). We also know that the Feast of Pentecost was partially fulfilled in Acts 2, and that the Feast of Tabernacles will soon begin in these last days.

It is important to note that God gave the spiritual fulfillment of these two feasts to the New Testament Israel on the very day they were being celebrated in the natural realm. For example, on the very day the Jews were celebrating their natural Passover, Jesus was crucified in fulfillment of the spiritual Passover. As the Lamb of God, He died on the cross on the fourteenth day of the first month, which is the day of the Passover. He rose again on the following Sunday morning, and ascended to His Father, and our Father, as He told Mary. As He did so, He became the firstfruits to God from among humanity (1 Cor. 15:20), and on that very morning, the Jews were offering up the firstfruits of barley harvest in the temple. Following His Resurrection He appeared to the disciples for a period of forty days. Then, after His Ascension, they waited in Jerusalem for ten more days, and "when the Day of Pentecost was fully come," the Lord poured out the Holy Spirit. In part, this fulfilled the Feast of Pentecost, and it happened on the very day the Jews were celebrating that Feast.

That leaves us with the third principal Feast to consider, the Feast of Tabernacles. This Feast, also called the Feast of Ingathering, will be fulfilled in the mighty harvest that comes at the end of the Church Age. Since the Lord began to fulfill the other two principal feasts on the very day Israel was literally celebrating those feasts, we can expect the same to happen with the Feast of Tabernacles. Once again, natural Israel gives a revelation of what is happening in spiritual Israel. This is yet another reason for declaring that the fulfillment of Tabernacles will begin at the time of that Feast in A.D. 1996.

When Israel first celebrated Passover under Moses in Egypt, several things were involved. First, they sacrificed the Passover lamb and applied the blood to the doorposts of their houses. Second, the Lord destroyed the firstborn of Egypt. Third, they were eating the supper while it happened. And finally, they came out of Egypt on that night. The Bible tells us that Christ, our Passover Lamb, was slain for us, and that His blood has been applied to our lives. However, this is not all that is included in the fulfillment of the Passover. They also came out of Egypt and were eating a supper when the final plague fell on the Egyptians. We will carefully consider these additional details.

Consider what Jesus says about the Passover in Luke 22:15-18. He tells the disciples that He will not eat the Passover with them again until it is fulfilled in the Kingdom of God. The Passover will become the "Marriage Supper of the Lamb." How do we know this? In Exodus 12:14 we are told concerning the Passover, "And this day shall be unto you for a memorial ...ye shall keep it a feast by an ordinance **for ever.**" Verses 17 and 24 contain similar statements. So when Jesus says that He will not eat it again until it is fulfilled in the Kingdom of God, He is making it clear that His death is only a partial fulfillment of the Passover. During the Passover, we will leave this world, "Egypt," behind. Therefore, the total fulfillment of the Passover will be the Rapture and that eternal Marriage Supper of the Lamb.

In summary, the beginning of the fulfillment of the Feast of Tabernacles should come when it is actually being celebrated in the natural, as happened with the first two principal feasts. The complete fulfillment of Passover will be the Rapture and the Marriage Supper of the Lamb when we leave "Egypt." This brings us to an exciting discovery. Between the date of the "great day" of the Feast of Tabernacles in any year and the date of the Feast of Passover, three and a half years later, there are always 1,260 days.[2]

2. The seventh day of the Feast of Tabernacles is referred to as the "great day" of the feast in John 7:37. On that day Christ promised the rivers of living water. On that day, in the last days, the mighty outpouring will begin. For more details on that "great day," see *Unger's Bible Dictionary*, p. 361.

1,260 Days Are Always Between Tabernacles and Passover

1062 days	(3 years x 12 months per year x 29.5 days per month)[3]
+30 days	(the month added every three years)
+176 days	(6 x 29.5 between Tab. and Pass. less 1 day for diff. between 7/15 and 1/14)
1268 days	(3 years later between 7/15 and 1/14)
-8 days	(from 7th day of Tab. on 7/21 to Passover on 1/14)
1260 days	(from 7th day of Feast of Tabernacles to Passover 3 and 1/2 years later)

Therefore, if the visitation of Tabernacles begins among the Believers in September of 1996 and continues for 1,260 days, we will arrive at the Feast of Passover in the year 2000. The Church will then be raptured out of "Egypt" at **the final victory** during the Passover as in the beginning.

3. For details on the biblical calendar, see Appendix D.

Chapter 48

His Presence, Our Need

"Lord, how does one end a book like this?" I prayerfully asked as I prepared to write this last chapter. The answer seemed to come in the form of heart-searching questions: "If you were permitted to speak to the Body of Christ today, what would you want to tell them? What counsel would you give them?"

I would encourage them to seek the Lord as never before because His presence alone can satisfy the heart. Every time I have truly entered the King's chambers, I have asked myself why I am so prone to allow the things of life to crowd in and take my attention from His fellowship. When I was a university student, many years ago, He made His presence very real to me. At the beginning of one semester, He gave me such a longing for His presence and the grace to seek His face, that for several weeks I spent entire days in prayer and fasting.[1] It was so wonderful that I couldn't imagine doing anything else for the rest of my life. I came to know by experience David's words "...in thy presence is fulness of joy; at thy right hand there are pleasures for evermore" (Ps. 16:11).

My favorite passage during those days was, "Oh, taste and see that the Lord is good...The young lions lack and suffer hunger; But those who seek the Lord shall not lack any good thing" (Ps. 34:8,10 NKJV). Day after day, I felt the urge to shout this message to all humanity, to all those who were engrossed in the cares, pleasures, and problems of this life, but who were ignoring the presence of the One who is called "the desire of all nations" (Hag. 2:7).

1. I actually dropped out of school for that semester.

However, I didn't shout it to the nations. Instead, I joined the crowd again in the daily rush to nowhere. I soon felt the attraction of this world and its ways once more. Oh, yes, I maintained my devotional life. I was still a "good Christian." But nothing was ever the same after experiencing a measure of the glory of His presence. Those encounters with Him had left an indelible mark on my heart that I could never forget. I soon came to realize that nothing in this world would ever again be able to satisfy the thirsting in my soul. Like David, I cried so many times, "As the hart panteth after the water brooks, so panteth my soul after thee, O God" (Ps. 42:1).

In spite of all that, once again I became deeply involved in living this life, and living it to the fullest. I went from a chemist to an ATP (airline transport pilot).[2] I became a missionary and a pastor, and also received training and experience in a few other fields as well. But what does all that matter without a deep love relationship with the Lamb of Calvary? Unless His presence means more to us than life itself, all else is "lying vanities," as Jonah declared (Jon. 2:8). Paul's deep love for the Lord caused him to count everything in this world as loss, in comparison to Christ and His presence (Phil. 3:8-10). Today, more than ever, my heart cries to Him the words of that little chorus:

> More of You, more of You,
> **I've had all, but what I need,**
> Just more of You.
> Of things I've had my fill, and yet I hunger still;
> Empty and bare, Lord, hear my prayer,
> For more of You.[3]

I long to end my walk as it began so many years ago—in His presence, in the secret place of the Most High. I want to deny myself and refuse to yield to the attraction of all that is around me. I want to build another altar on which to offer what is left of my life on this earth. The Shulamite in the Song of Solomon expresses the longing of my heart, "Until the day break, and the shadows flee away, I will get me to the mountain of myrrh, and to the hill of frankincense" (Song 4:6). The Lord was buried with myrrh in accordance to Jewish burial customs. In the Bible it symbolizes the sufferings and death of Christ—His cross. Until that new day comes, and Christ's millennial reign begins, He invites us to embrace the cross. He

2. I never flew for an airline. This is simply the license necessary to do so.
3. Copyright 1977 by Gaither Music Company and Christian Grit Music Press. All rights reserved. Used by permission.

invites us to offer to Him our bodies as a living sacrifice that the world may see the life of the crucified Savior in us and be drawn to Him (Jn. 12:32; Gal. 3:1).

The world will see Jesus only as the Church learns to spend time with Him, beholding the beauty of the Lord, as David desired to do daily (Ps. 27:4). From that secret place we will shout the message to the world with our lives *and* with our words. We will win their hearts, and evangelize this globe before He returns. We don't need more sermons or better sermons. We don't need to learn how to convince people to follow us through our own wisdom and words. We need more of His presence, which will break the hardest heart, convince the wisest skeptic, convict the most pious sinner of his need, and comfort the comfortless. Those who are bathed in His presence will do that without needing the strength and efforts of the flesh. They will manifest the strength and authority of the Lion, but they will do so with the mind and nature of the Lamb. They will win the war, and be part of **the final victory in the year 2000.**

Appendices

Index

Appendix A

Compared: Revelation 4–10 and Revelation 14–19

In the Chapter entitled, "The Chronology of Revelation" (Chapter 7), we state that the message concerning the last days that is given in the Book of Revelation is repeated in the mouth of two witnesses within the book itself. In other words, the entire message is given twice in Revelation. The book actually has six divisions that can be outlined as follows:

Chapter 1: A revelation of the Son of man and the Son of God.

Chapters 2–3: His message to the churches.

Chapters 4–10: The revelation of the end given by the messenger.

Chapters 11–13: The last three and a half years.

Chapters 14–19: The revelation of the end given by John.

Chapters 20–22: The Kingdom of God.

What we want to do in this appendix is compare what the angel reveals to John in chapters 4–10 with what John sees in chapters 14–19. These are the two parts of the above outline that are printed in bold letters. We will discover that there are at least forty-two similarities between the events revealed by the messenger and the events seen by John after eating the little book, confirming, of course, that the same message is indeed given twice in the book.

Simply stated, what we believe to be happening in the Book of Revelation is that God is confirming the Revelation of the events of the last days in the mouth of two witnesses. The Bible says that *every* word shall be established (or confirmed) in the mouth of two or three witnesses (2 Cor. 13:1). This certainly applies to the Book of Revelation also. Therefore, God has honored and fulfilled that principle of His Word by confirming the message of Revelation in the mouth of two witnesses. The first witness is the "angel" or "messenger" that is sent to John in Revelation 1:1. He is sent to reveal to John the events of the last days. And the second witness is John himself, who, after being shown all these things by the angel, then has an experience where he himself becomes a witness or messenger of these things. He then repeats them from his own perspective, using different words, but expressing the same concepts.

The Lord appears to John in chapter 1 and gives him a specific, personal message for each of the seven churches of Asia. He then begins to show John the future, starting in Revelation 4:1. In chapters 4 and 5, John sees the glory of the Lord and a "little book" that is sealed with seven seals. The events of the last days that are associated with the opening of those seven seals are the basis of the entire message from chapter 6 through chapter 10.

However, upon coming to chapter 10, John sees an angel descend from Heaven with a "little book" open. In Revelation 10:8 the "little book" is precisely the same Greek word that appears in Revelation 5:1 where there is a "little book" that is sealed with seven seals.[1] There is no reason to believe that the "little book" that was being opened, seal by seal, throughout these chapters, and that has been the theme and context of these chapters, suddenly has nothing to do with the "little book" that is now seen to be open. We are seeing the same little book. (See Chapter 7, footnote 9 of *The Final Victory*.) We know what the message of that little book is, because it has been unfolded and explained to us in chapters 6 through 10. That message involves seven seals and seven trumpets. But now John is commanded to eat the little book. The thought here, as in other places where the Word is eaten, is that it is assimilated and actually becomes a part of the one who is eating it.[2] After John has eaten that book, which contains a message of seven seals and seven trumpets, the messenger tells him, "**Thou must prophesy again...**" (Rev. 10:11).

Consider what this means. John eats the little book, giving us the clear impression that its message of seven seals and seven trumpets is literally

1. Refer to *The R.S.V. Interlinear Greek-English New Testament*, Zondervan, Alfred Marshall, D.Litt. Note that *Strong's Greek Dictionary* makes an error here. The word in Revelation 10:8 should be #975 and not #974.
2. Jeremiah 15:16 says, "Thy words were found, and I did eat them." Also, Jesus tells us in John 6:53-56 that we must eat His flesh to have life in us, but then in John 6:63 He explains that the "flesh" profits nothing, but that the words He speaks to us are spirit and life. So again the thought is of eating His Word so that His Word actually becomes a part of our own lives, walk, and message.

becoming a part of John. Then John is told that he must speak the Word of the Lord, prophetically. But what "word" is going to come out of his mouth? Obviously the same Word that went into his mouth, the Word of the little book that has just become a part of his own life. In light of this clear thought, that the message of the little book has become a part of John, it should not seem at all strange that later in the Revelation he speaks about **seven angels and seven vials**, since the message of the little book was **seven seals and seven trumpets**. We will see in the following comparison that these, as well as many other details and events, clearly link the message of the angel in chapters 4–10 with the message of John in chapters 14–19. Now let's compare these two passages to see that they are basically identical. We will consider each detail that is found in John's vision in chapters 14–19 and compare it, one by one, with the corresponding detail that is found in chapters 4–10, to see that each detail is actually a repeat and a confirmation of the first message. We have numbered these details consecutively from one through forty-two.

1. **Revelation 14:1**–He "looked" and saw Mount Zion. Not only is a mountain a "high place," but Hebrews 12:22 also tells us that Zion is a heavenly place.

   Revelation 4:1–He "looked" and received a revelation of Heaven, or a high place.

2. **Revelation 14:1**–There is a revelation of the Lamb in this vision.

   Revelation 5:6–There is a revelation of the Lamb in this vision.

3. **Revelation 14:1**–There is a revelation of 144,000 sealed ones in this vision.

   Revelation 7:1-8–There is a revelation of 144,000 sealed ones in this vision also.

4. **Revelation 14:1**–They are sealed in their foreheads.

   Revelation 7:3–They are sealed in their foreheads.

5. **Revelation 14:2**–A voice is heard from Heaven.

   Revelation 4:1–A voice is heard from Heaven.

6. **Revelation 14:2**–Thunder is heard.

   Revelation 4:5–Thunder is heard.

7. **Revelation 14:3**–A new song is heard.

   Revelation 5:9–A new song is heard.

8. **Revelation 14:3**–There is a revelation of the throne of God.

   Revelation 4:2-3–There is a revelation of the throne of God.

9. **Revelation 14:3**–Four "beasts," or four living creatures, are seen.

   Revelation 4:6–Four "beasts," or four living creatures, are seen.

10. **Revelation 14:3**–The elders are seen.

Revelation 4:4–The elders are seen.

11. **Revelation 14:4**–Purity is seen (typified by the word "virgins").

Revelation 4:4–Purity is seen (typified by white robes).

12. **Revelation 14:4**–They are with, and like, the Lamb (because if they follow His footsteps and life, then they end up where He is-in the throne).

Revelation 3:21–Those who live as He lived, and fully follow Him, will end up where He is-in the throne (Revelation 4–5 mention that throne 17 times).

13. **Revelation 14:5**–They have no guile; they are faultless.

Revelation 4:5-6–This is the nature of the Lamb.

Now We Come to Seven Seals and Seven Angels

The key to the following comparison is: The end of a thing is revealed, and declared from the very beginning of that thing (Isa. 46:9-10).[3] In the Book of Revelation the messenger shows John the beginning of each seal, but John, in his message, shows the ending or fruit of each seal.[4] We can clearly see the similarity between the seven angels and the seven seals if we understand that John's revelation of the seven angels in chapter 14 deals primarily with the **end** result of each seal, whereas Revelation 6-8 deals with the beginning of each seal.

14. **Revelation 6:1-2–Seal One**–For the meaning of this seal see Appendix B, where we compare the seals of Revelation with Ezekiel. There we give clear scriptural reasons why the first seal is the preaching of the gospel and is not the Antichrist.

Revelation 14:6-7–Angel One–The gospel is preached.

15. **Revelation 6:3-4–Seal Two**–The red horse reveals what the spirit of communism has done in the earth, taking peace from the earth. Communism has done this throughout the world. Wherever it has gone, terrorism has been its hallmark and byword. This seal is associated with a "great sword," and speaking of sheer numbers, the greatest military buildup in history is found in Russia. Note in Revelation 13:2 that the feet of the beast are the feet of a bear. The feet uphold or provide the

---

3. Part I, Chapter 3.
4. Although we cannot embark on a study of the seals in this book, it may help to understand that once a seal is opened, it continues to operate on the earth until the end. For example, when the sixth seal is opened, the consequences of all the first five will still be in effect on the earth.

foundation for the beast, or world system, later called "Babylon" in Revelation 17 and 18. The bear is a sign of Russian communism today, and in these last days will be involved with the founding or the upholding of the world system. So the red horse, or the spirit of communism, will be the beginning or root of Babylon, the world system of the Antichrist.

Revelation 14:8–Angel Two–As John sees the beginning of seal two and the world system it brings, he sees at the same time the end of that system. Here judgment is pronounced on Babylon.

16. **Revelation 6:5-6–Seal Three**–Here we find tremendous economic upheaval in the earth. The final result of this chaos will be the Antichrist imposing his world economic system on the nations. Those who choose to participate in that system will have to accept the mark of the beast. Economic upheaval will be a primary reason why otherwise sane people will accept a "mark."

Revelation 14:9-12–Angel Three–John specifies "the third angel" in verse 9, so angels one and two are in verses 6 and 8. Angel three gives a warning about accepting the mark of the beast related to the economics of buying and selling. As John sees seal three, he is also seeing the end result of that seal, which is revealed in the third angel.

17. **Revelation 6:7-8–Seal Four**–This seal brings death to one fourth of the earth.

Revelation 14:13–Angel Four–No wonder the voice of this fourth angel reveals death. Note that those who "die in the Lord" will be blessed. This gives the idea that some who die will not be "in the Lord." Regardless, we are seeing death in this fourth messenger or voice in Revelation 14.

18. **Revelation 6:9-11–Seal Five**–Here the martyrs are crying out to be avenged. But the Lord says that others of their brethren must yet die as they did, as martyrs. When a saint is martyred it is like planting a seed in the ground that will later give a wonderful harvest of souls and blessing. Jesus, referring to His death, says, "...Except a corn of wheat fall into the ground and die, it abideth alone: but if it die, it bringeth forth much fruit" (Jn. 12:24). No wonder the Psalmist says, "Precious in the sight of the Lord is the death of his saints" (Ps. 116:15). Imagine how precious Stephen's death was to the Lord (Acts 7). Saul was never the same after witnessing the glory that was upon that first martyr. Stephen's death was undoubtedly a key influence in Paul's life and ultimately in his conversion. Therefore, since Paul took the message to the Gentiles, we can say that Stephen's death also became a major factor in the conversion of most of us who are Gentiles! If many saints are

dying during the fifth seal, as Revelation 6:9-11 indicates, then the fruit of this seal will be a great harvest!

Revelation 14:14-16–Angel Five–Here we find that there will be a great harvest on the earth. (Christ's life and Stephen's life brought forth a great harvest for the same reason-the "seed" died and was planted.)

19. **Revelation 6:12-17–Seal Six**–This is simply an announcement of the wrath of God.

Revelation 14:17-20–Angel Six–Here the "vine of the earth" is cast into the "great winepress of the wrath of God." So the message of this angel is synonymous with the message of the sixth seal, which is God's wrath. Note that in verses 17 and 18 we find the sixth and seventh angels. One announces the coming of wrath, which is the same announcement that is made when the sixth seal is opened. The other angel, the seventh, seems to actually bring that wrath upon men as he casts the vine of the earth into the winepress of the wrath of God.

20. **Revelation 8:1-2–Seal Seven**–When the seventh seal is opened there is a revelation of seven angels with seven trumpets. The trumpets are seven plagues.

Revelation 15:1–Angel Seven–After the sixth angel announces that wrath is coming, the seventh angel actually brings that wrath (Rev. 14:19). One verse later, in Revelation 15:1, we are told what that wrath is. It is seven angels with seven vials. The vials are seven plagues.

21. **Revelation 7:9-17**–Note that after the announcement of wrath at the sixth seal in Revelation 6:12, 17, but before the seven angels with the seven trumpets in Revelation 8:1-2 actually bring that wrath on the earth, we are given a revelation of a great multitude that comes out of the Great Tribulation in Revelation 7:9,14. They are standing before the presence of God.

Revelation 15:2–Exactly the same thing happens here. After the wrath is announced in chapter 14, and before the seven angels actually pour out that wrath on the earth, we see a great multitude here who have clearly come out of the Great Tribulation because they have gotten the victory over the beast, his image, his mark, and over the number of his name. They, too, are standing before the presence of God.

22. **Revelation 7:10-12**–This multitude is worshipping the Lord.

Revelation 15:3-4–This multitude is also worshipping the Lord.

23. **Revelation 8:4**–In this context smoke fills the Temple.

Revelation 15:8–In this context smoke fills the Temple.

Now We Come to the Seven Trumpets and the Seven Vials

24. **Revelation 8:7**–TRUMPET One deals with the earth.
    Revelation 16:2–VIAL One deals with the earth.
25. **Revelation 8:8**–TRUMPET Two deals with the sea.
    Revelation 16:3–VIAL Two deals with the sea.
26. **Revelation 8:10**–TRUMPET Three deals with rivers.
    Revelation 16:4–VIAL Three deals with rivers.
27. **Revelation 8:12**–TRUMPET Four deals with the sun.
    Revelation 16:8–VIAL Four deals with the sun.
28. **Revelation 9:1-3,5**–TRUMPET Five deals with darkness and pain.
    Revelation 16:10–VIAL Five deals with darkness and pain.
29. **Revelation 9:14**–TRUMPET Six deals with the Euphrates River.
    Revelation 16:12–VIAL Six deals with the Euphrates River.
30. **Revelation 10:7; 11:15-19–TRUMPET Seven**–There are ten details given here that are related to this seventh trumpet:

The Ten Details Given Concerning the Seventh Trumpet

31. Revelation 10:7 and 11:15–The seventh angel is involved.
32. Revelation 11:15–There were great voices in Heaven.
33. Revelation 11:15–The kingdoms of the world are taken.
34. Revelation 11:18–Man's anger is seen.
35. Revelation 11:18–God's wrath comes upon man.
36. Revelation 11:19–There is a revelation of the Temple.
37. Revelation 11:19–Lightning accompanies the seventh trumpet.
38. Revelation 11:19–Thunder accompanies the seventh trumpet.
39. Revelation 11:19–An earthquake accompanies the seventh trumpet.
40. Revelation 11:19–A great hail accompanies the seventh trumpet.

Revelation 16:17-21–VIAL Seven–There are ten details given here that are related to this seventh vial. If exactly the same ten details are given for the seventh vial as were given for the seventh trumpet then we can conclude that, without a doubt, they are the same event.

The Ten Details Given Concerning the Seventh Vial

31. Revelation 16:17-The seventh angel is involved.

32. Revelation 16:17-18-There is a great voice and voices are in heaven.

33. Revelation 16:19-The kingdoms of the world are taken (as seen by the fall of the city, the capital city, Babylon, and the cities, which are governmental centers).

34. Revelation 16:21-Man's anger is seen.

35. Revelation 16:19-God's wrath comes upon man.

36. Revelation 16:17-There is a revelation of the Temple.

37. Revelation 16:18-Lightning accompanies the seventh vial.

38. Revelation 16:18-Thunder accompanies the seventh vial.

39. Revelation 16:18-An earthquake accompanies the seventh vial.

40. Revelation 16:21-A great hail accompanies the seventh vial.

If we add these ten details to our comparison between Revelation 4-10 and Revelation 14-19, we arrive at a total of forty similarities. We continue, then, with the last two, numbers forty-one and forty-two:

41. **Revelation 12:1**–Immediately after the seventh trumpet, and the ten things that are related to that trumpet, there is a revelation of a woman.

Revelation 17:1–Immediately after the seventh vial, and the ten things that are related to that vial, there is a revelation of a woman. The Holy Spirit makes twelve very clear contrasts between these two women. This is discussed in detail in this book. See Part II, Chapter 17, "Two Women: Two 'Jerusalems.' "

Note: Plagues are sent in the Book of Revelation because of these two women. In the case of the first woman they are sent to deliver her, as we learned through our father Abraham,[5] and in the case of the second woman they are sent to judge her.

42. **Revelation 10:7**–After the seventh trumpet we saw in Part II[6] of this book that the Church, His Bride, is raptured. She is carried to the Marriage Supper by the Rapture.

Revelation 19:7-9–We find that after the seventh vial the Bride is taken to the Marriage Supper, as clearly stated here.

5. See Part II, Chapter 12, concerning the plagues and why they were sent.
6. See Part II, Chapter 9, "Three Rapture Keys."

Appendix B

Compared: The Book of Revelation and the Book of Ezekiel

We observed in Part I of this book that the beginning and the ending are the same, and that Revelation is simply a summary of what God has spoken throughout the Bible. In light of this we want to compare the vision and experience of Ezekiel with the Revelation of John. Through this comparison we can see that these two books are parallel revelations. It is clear that Ezekiel had a message for the people of God living in his day, and we can find a partial fulfillment to many passages in Ezekiel in the history of that day. However, we want to see that a far more complete fulfillment of Ezekiel will come in the last days.

The Visions of John and Ezekiel Compared

1. **Revelation 4:1**–"A door was opened in heaven..."

   Ezekiel 1:1–"The heavens were opened..."

2. **Revelation 4:1**–"The first voice which I heard was as it were the voice of a trumpet talking with me..."

   Ezekiel 1:3–"The word of the Lord came expressly unto Ezekiel the priest..." (many scholars believe that John was a priest also).

3. **Revelation 4:2**–"And immediately I was in the spirit..."

   Ezekiel 1:3–"...and the hand of the Lord was there upon him." (this is an Old Testament expression for being "in the Spirit").

4. **Revelation 4:2**–"... and, behold, a throne was set in heaven and one sat upon the throne..."

Ezekiel 1:26–"And above the firmament... the likeness of a throne... and upon the likeness of the throne was the likeness as the appearance of a man above upon it."

5. **Revelation 4:3b**–"And there was a rainbow round about the throne..."

Ezekiel 1:28–"As the appearance of the bow that is in the cloud... round about."

6. **Revelation 4:5a**–"And out of the throne proceeded lightnings and thunderings and voices..."

Ezekiel 1:13-14–"...and out of the fire went forth lightning. And the living creatures ran and returned as the appearance of a flash of lightning."

7. **Revelation 4:6**–"And before the throne there was a sea of glass like unto crystal..."

Ezekiel 1:22–"And the likeness of the firmament... was as the color of the terrible crystal..."

8. **Revelation 4:6b**–"And in the midst of the throne, and round about the throne, were four beasts..."

Ezekiel 1:5–"Also out of the midst thereof came the likeness of four living creatures..."

9. **Revelation 4:6c**–"Four beasts full of eyes before and behind..."

Ezekiel 1:18–"And their rings were full of eyes round about them four."

10. **Revelation 4:7**–"And the first beast was like a lion, and the second beast like a calf, and the third beast had a face as a man, and the fourth beast was like a flying eagle..."

Ezekiel 1:10–"...they four had the face of a man, and the face of a lion... the face of an ox... the face of an eagle."

11. **Revelation 4:8-11; 5:9-14; 19:6**–John hears and sees the worship of Heaven.

Ezekiel 1:24; 3:12-13–Ezekiel hears and sees the worship of Heaven.

12. **Revelation 5:1**–John sees a book or roll.

Ezekiel 2:9–Ezekiel sees a book or roll.

13. **Revelation 10:9-10**–John is commanded to eat this book that was sweet in his mouth and bitter in his belly.

Ezekiel 3:1-3,14–Ezekiel must eat the book and it was sweet in his mouth and bitter (v. 14) in his spirit (belly).

14. **Revelation 10:11**–After eating the book, John is told that he must prophesy to many.

Ezekiel 3:4,27–After eating the book, Ezekiel must speak the Word of God to others.

15. **Revelation 6–11**–After seeing and hearing the worship of Heaven, John receives a revelation of the judgments of God poured out through the seals. Note that the message of Psalm 149 is that worshipers will bring judgments on the wicked.

Ezekiel 3–7–After hearing that same worship, Ezekiel sees the judgment of the seals that is poured out.

Compare Now the Seals of Revelation and Ezekiel

Seal One

Revelation 6:1-2–The Word of God goes forth to conquer. Some have said that this is the Antichrist. But without getting sidetracked, we should make one important observation. If the types or figures used in the context of the first seal refer to the Antichrist and something evil, then they are not consistent with the way they are used in other parts of Scripture. They are not used in a negative context anywhere else. For example, thunder is associated with the opening of the first seal. Thunder appears ten times in Revelation, and is always related to a voice from Heaven (4:5; 6:1; 10:3-4; 11:19; 14:2; 16:18; 19:6). Thunder appears in many other places, where it is also likened to His voice. The color "white" appears nineteen times in Revelation, and unless this is the only exception, it never refers to anything evil, but always to the righteous. The one who sits on this white horse has a bow, and Habakkuk 3:9 shows us that His bow and His Word are the same thing. We find the white horse later in Revelation 19 and the One Who sits on it is the Word of God. He will conquer the earth by the rod of iron that proceeds out of His mouth, according to Isaiah 11:4. In other words, He conquers through His Word.

To summarize, we have no scriptural grounds for assuming that all of the seals are negative. It seems clear from these types that the first seal is the Word of God going forth to judge and conquer. Christ Himself says that His Word will judge us (Jn. 12:48), so in that sense all of the seals will be judgments. But all of His judgments are not necessarily negative experiences.

Also, we find here another clear relationship between the beginning and the ending of the Church Age. In the beginning Herod imprisons

Peter, planning to kill him later (Acts 12). In verse 3 we are told, "Then were the days of unleavened bread." However, "bread" is a type of His Word (Jn. 6). And King Herod is clearly a type of the Antichrist who will slay saints in the end, according to Revelation 13:7. This history of Peter's imprisonment ends with the death of Herod and this statement: "But the word of God grew and multiplied." Herod dies, but the Word continues to conquer! They truly were days of "unleavened bread."

That Living Word is, I believe, the hope of the last days, and in Acts 12 we see how the enemy will be conquered. The first seal will be the hope of the Church. The Antichrist will indeed arise to destroy, but the One seated on the white horse will conquer the world through His Word.

Ezekiel 3:7-10,17,27–The Word of God goes forth. So this links with seal one, showing that the first seal is the proclamation of the Word of God.

Seal Two

Revelation 6:3-4–A sword comes (war).

Ezekiel 4:1-3–A sword or siege is revealed.

Seal Three

Revelation 6:5-6–Food is scarce and is measured.

Ezekiel 4:9-11, 16-17–Food is scarce and measured.

Seal Four

Revelation 6:7-8–The sword, famine, and pestilence come.

Ezekiel 5:12a–The sword, famine, and pestilence come.

Seal Five

Revelation 6:9-11; Matthew 24:9–Persecution and His people hated by the nations.

Ezekiel 5:12b-15–Persecution and His people suffer reproach among the nations.

Seal Six

Revelation 6:12-14–Consider the following details found here:

Verses 12-14-The heavenly bodies are touched, and the "stars" fall. (Rev. 1:20 tells us that stars are leaders in the Church).
Verse 15-This is related to "mountains."
Verses 16-17-His wrath will be manifested.

Ezekiel 6:1-14–Note now what is involved in Ezekiel's revelation:
Verses 1-3–God's Word against the "mountains." (Compare Revelation 17:9-10; Isaiah 2:14, 17; Psalm 83:14-15 to see that mountains are kings or leaders.) So we see the thought of mountains and leaders under judgment ("stars").
Verse 12b-His wrath is manifested here.

Seal Seven

Revelation 8:1–Consider these details:

1. The seventh seal is composed of seven trumpets of wrath. The end and Rapture occur at the seventh trump (there will be a short time of wrath after these seals and trumpets that take place during the Great Tribulation).
2. Revelation 7:1-This has to do with all four directions on the earth.
3. Revelation 16:5-7-He judges according to man's ways.
4. Revelation 6:16 and Matthew 24:30-There is lamentation.

Ezekiel 7–Compare details found in Ezekiel:
Verses 2,3,6,7,10,12,13-This is the end!
Verses 3,8,12,19-A time of the wrath of the Lord.
Verse 2b-Related to the four directions of the compass on earth.
Verses 3,8,9,27-He judges according to man's ways.
Verse 14-Here are trumpets because "they" (plural) blow the trumpet, but there is no one who will resist or fight against what God is doing in the earth!
Verse 16-Here is lamentation (cf. Zech. 12:10-14; 13:1; we see that this happens just before the end and the Second Coming).

Further Comparisons Between Ezekiel and Revelation

16. **Revelation 7:1-8**–In the context of the seals and in the midst of those seals He places a mark on the foreheads of His chosen ones.

Ezekiel 9:1-6–He places a mark on the foreheads of His chosen ones in the context of the seals.

17. **Revelation 7:9-17**–He reveals the multitudes of martyrs, and this is the reason His wrath falls.

Ezekiel 8–This is the reason for His wrath-wicked leadership (and in the end religious leaders will be drunk with the blood of the saints-Rev. 17:6).

18. **Revelation 8:2-5**–Immediately after the sealing and before the judgments begin we see a revelation of intercession.

Ezekiel 9:4–We find that in the context of people being sealed the key is intercession-these are the ones sealed, and because of intercessors the judgments are coming as Revelation 6:9-10 and 8:3 show us.

19. **Revelation 11:1**–The Temple is measured with a measuring rod.

Ezekiel 40:3–The Temple is measured with a measuring rod.

20. **Revelation 21**–John's vision ends with him seeing the glory of the eternal Temple.

Ezekiel 40–48–Ezekiel's vision ends with him seeing the glory of the eternal Temple.

Appendix C

Compared: Revelation and Matthew 22:41–24:35

The Book of Revelation is "the Revelation of Jesus Christ, which God gave unto him, to show unto his servants things which must shortly come to pass..." (Rev. 1:1). We do not know precisely when the Father gave the Lord Jesus this revelation and understanding of the last days, but it was before His discourse concerning the end found in Matthew 24. He wouldn't have given these details without first receiving them, since He only spoke what His Father gave Him to speak. We also know that there is only one true revelation concerning the last days. Therefore, the revelation in Matthew must be precisely the same as is found in the Book of Revelation. Matthew 22:41 to 24:35 is actually a miniature Book of Revelation. We will start in Matthew 22:41 and continue through to Matthew 24:35, comparing Scripture with Scripture.

1. **Revelation 1**–Christ is revealed here as the Son of God (v. 8,11,17), and also as the Son of man (v. 13).

   Matthew 22:41–46–The key to His question here is that He was both the Son of God and the Son of man. This is really the revelation of Himself. He is the Son of man because He came through David, but He is the Son of God because David called Him "Lord." The Pharisees had not received that revelation or understanding of Him, and therefore couldn't answer His question.

2. **Revelation 1:20**–There is a revelation of the leaders of God's people.

   Matthew 23:1-12–There is a revelation of the leaders of God's people.

3. **Revelation 2–3**–Seven messages to the angels (or leaders) of the seven churches. Note that each church has a problem to overcome, and therefore each one receives a promise to those who are part of that church and overcome their specific problem. These are actually seven problems that exist in the heart of all men; to be overcomers we must overcome in these areas. Even Smyrna and Philadelphia have a problem to overcome. Smyrna must overcome the problem of physical suffering and false brethren, and Philadelphia must overcome the fact that they have "little strength" to respond to an open door that God has set before them. And they, too, must overcome false brethren.

Matthew 23:13-39–Contained here are seven messages to the angels (or leaders) of the people of God. Seven times He pronounces this phrase: "Woe unto you, scribes and Pharisees, hypocrites!" Consider how they parallel the "problems" found in the seven churches:

The First Woe and First Church

Matthew 23:13–The Pharisees did not enter into His promises, because they had no love of the truth or of His presence.[1] These two things are seen to be the first love in Song of Solomon 1:2-3. At the beginning of that love relationship these are seen to be the first things that the Bride loves in Him.

Revelation 2:1-4–The first love was what was lacking in the church of Ephesus, the first of the seven churches.

The Second Woe and Second Church

Matthew 23:14–Here we find false prayers and false brethren with false motives. Note that His "house" is called the "house of prayer." So we also find here the thought of a "false house" of prayer.

Revelation 2:9–Speaking to the second church, Smyrna, He says, "I know the blasphemy of them which say they are Jews, and are not, but are the synagogue of Satan." So here we find false brethren also. But note that He says they are the synagogue of Satan, in other words, Satan's house. They have become Satan's dwelling place. We have here then a "false house," and Matthew gives us an idea of how that comes about - because of false prayers. If we pray as the Pharisees were praying there (pretentiously), we will soon find that other spirits enter.

1. In John 8:40-45 they had no love of the truth. In John 7:46-47 when He spoke, the anointing of His presence was overwhelming, but they cared nothing for that presence.

The Third Woe and Third Church

Matthew 23:15-22–They "compass land and sea" to make one convert, and then make him a worse "child of hell" than they are. They are "blind guides." Blind guides cause the people to stumble or fall into the ditch (Mt. 15:14).

Revelation 2:12-14–To the third church, Pergamos, He says, "Thou dwellest, even where Satan's seat is." This certainly sounds as if there are some in that Church who are children of hell. But in verse 14 we find Balaam and Balac. Balaam literally "compassed land" to make Balac his disciple and a believer in him and his spiritual powers. He ended up making him "twofold more the child of hell" than he was, because he taught Balac to cause the people of God to stumble through fornication.

The Fourth Woe and Fourth Church

Matthew 23:23-24–They gave the appearance of righteousness. They were very religious, but knew nothing of judgment, mercy, or faith.

Revelation 2:18-29–The fourth church, Thyatira, had within it Jezebel, who called herself a prophetess. Jezebel was indeed very religious. She was a Baal worshipper, and even had hundreds of prophets. She gave the appearance of being very righteous as she killed Naboth and many others, but she knew nothing of righteous judgment, mercy, or true faith in God.

The Fifth Woe and Fifth Church

Matthew 23:25-26–They project a very good outward appearance, but within they are defiled and filthy.

Revelation 3:1-6–Sardis has a name or reputation that it lives, it gives that outward impression, but it is dead. She has within her only a few who have not defiled themselves (v. 4).

The Sixth Woe and Sixth Church

Matthew 23:27-28–They appear to be something they are not. They appear to be righteous, but they are hypocrites and living a lie.

Revelation 3:7-13–"Behold, I will make them of the synagogue of Satan, which say they are Jews, and are not, but do lie." This was a problem that the church of Philadelphia had to overcome. They had to overcome those who were living a lie, whited sepulchers, appearing to be something they weren't.

The Seventh Woe and Seventh Church

Matthew 23:29-39–They say, "If we had been in the days of our fathers, we would not have been partakers with them in the blood of the prophets." They don't see their own need and depravity. They think they are quite righteous, and not at all like the men their fathers were.

Revelation 3:14-22–The Laodicean church is the "rich" church, not necessarily in material goods, but rich in spirit, and has need of nothing. They don't see their own need and depravity. Because they are not poor in spirit, they are in fact spiritual beggars. They don't understand that they are "wretched, and miserable, and poor, and blind, and naked."

Continuing now with the comparison between Revelation and Matthew:

4. **Revelation 4–5**–The glory of His dwelling place.

   Matthew 24:1-2–The disciples want to show Him the "glory" of the temple.

5. **Revelation 6–10**–The seals are revealed here, and then we are brought to the end in Revelation 10:7, when the last trumpet is blown and the Rapture occurs.

   Matthew 24:5-14–The seals are revealed here, and then we are brought to the end in verse 14.

The Seals in Matthew (compare Revelation 6 here)

Matthew 24:5–Seal One-Tremendous anointed preaching, so much so that some will do the opposite of what John did, and they will say that they are the "anointed one" ("Christ"). John's preaching caused people to think that he was the Christ, but he made it very clear that he wasn't. Some will fail that test!

Matthew 24:6–Seal Two-Peace is taken from the earth (wars, rumors of wars).

Matthew 24:7a–Seal Three-Because the nations of the earth beat their plowshares into swords there will be rationing and economic upheaval. Rationing is common when there is war.

Matthew 24:7b–Seal Four–Hunger and pestilence are two of the aspects of seal four seen in Revelation 6:8.

Matthew 24:9-12–Seal Five–The Great Tribulation and martyrdom.

Matthew 24:29–Seal Six–The same nine things mentioned here are found in the context of the sixth seal in Revelation 6:12-17. It announces the wrath of the trumpets, and there is lamentation among the nations.

Matthew 24:31–Seal Seven–The seventh seal consists of seven trumpets. They are plagues that will fall over **a very short period of time,** just as happened during the plagues of Egypt. The final trumpet is seen here in verse 31, and the Rapture occurs at this point. Therefore, we understand that the first six trumpets, or plagues, come between the sixth seal mentioned above and this final trumpet and Rapture revealed here.

6. **Revelation 11–13**–After bringing us up to a revelation of the very end in Revelation 10:7, with the seventh trumpet, He then goes back and gives us further details about the last three and a half years from three different perspectives:

   Revelation 11–The last three and a half years from *Israel's* perspective.

   Revelation 12–The last three and a half years from the *Church's* perspective.

   Revelation 13–The last three and a half years from the *world's* perspective.

   Matthew 24:15-30–After bringing us up to a revelation of the very end in verse 14, He then goes back and gives us further details about the last three and a half years from three different perspectives:

   Matthew 24:15-21–The last three and a half years from *Israel's* perspective.

   Matthew 24:22-25–The last three and a half years from the *Church's* perspective.

   Matthew 24:26-30–The last three and a half years from the *world's* perspective.

7. **Revelation 14–18**–The message of Revelation is repeated.

   Matthew–He does not repeat the message in Matthew.

8. **Revelation 19–20**–The call to the Marriage Supper.

   Matthew 24:30-34–The call to the Marriage Supper.

9. **Revelation 21–22**–The new Heaven and new earth.

   Matthew 24:35–The new Heaven and new earth.

Appendix D

Christ's Birth Date

Our goal in this Appendix is to first determine, through biblical and historical facts, the year in which Christ was born. Then, in the same way, we will establish the approximate month of His birth.

The Year of His Birth

To determine the year in which He was born we will show the **latest** possible year for His birth, and then the **earliest** possible year.

1. **The latest possible year:** Josephus, the Jewish historian, states that a few days before the death of Herod there was a complete lunar eclipse. He also tells us that Herod died just before the Feast of Passover of that year.[1] So we can determine almost the exact date of Herod's death. It has been astronomically determined that this eclipse took place on the night of March 13 of 4 B.C.[2] The Passover of that year came during the month of April. Therefore, Herod died between March and April of the year 4 B.C.[3] We know that Herod was alive when Christ was born, so He had to have been born **before March of 4 B.C.**

2. **The earliest possible year:** Luke 3:1, 21, 23 shows that the Lord started His ministry in the "fifteenth year of the reign of Tiberius Caesar." (See Chapter 29 for more details here.) There is disagreement among historians regarding the year to which Luke is referring in this passage. This is because Tiberius began to reign over the provinces of the Roman

---

1. Josephus, XVII.VI. 4, p. 365.
2. Ibid.
3. *Encyclopaedia Brittanica,* see "Herod."

Empire in A.D. 12, when he was appointed to "equal authority with Augustus (Caesar) **in the provinces.**"[4] However, he did not begin to reign over all the empire until the death of Augustus Caesar in A.D. 14.[5] Therefore, the "fifteenth year" refers to either A.D. 26 or A.D. 28.[6]

However, Luke 3:23 says Jesus was approximately thirty years old at that time.[7] If we use the latter date for the fifteenth year of Tiberius (A.D. 28), this means Christ was born in 2 or 3 B.C. We already know this is impossible. Therefore, Luke had to have been referring to A.D. 26 for the year in which Christ began His ministry.[8] Thus, Christ was born between the 5 B.C. and 4 B.C.

Many knowledgeable history books, encyclopedias, and studies confirm this timing for His birth, as well as the year A.D. 26 for the beginning of His ministry.[9]

The Month of His Birth

There is no evidence that He was born in the month of December, much less on December 25. However, there is sufficient biblical evidence to establish the approximate month of His birth. To do so, we must be aware of several details regarding (1) the biblical calendar and (2) the twenty-four divisions of the priesthood in Bible times.

1. The Bible Calendar

a. The biblical month was determined by the first sighting of the new moon. A lunar month is 29.5 days, which means Israel's months had 29 and 30 days, alternately.[10]

b. The normal biblical year was composed of twelve lunar months. Therefore, the normal year contained 354 days (12 x 29.5 = 354).[11]

---

4. Bromiley, Vol. I, p. 674, "The Baptism of Jesus."
5. Ibid.
6. The "fifteenth year" means Tiberius had reigned fourteen full years, and was in his fifteenth at the time. Therefore, we add fourteen years to either A.D. 12 or else to A.D. 14, to arrive at the two possible dates for the "fifteenth year."
7. See Chapter 29, footnote 14, for our comment on the age of Jesus when He began His ministry.
8. This would be the logical conclusion for a Jew anyway because Palestine was one of the Roman Provinces. Therefore, as far as Luke and the Jews were concerned, Tiberius began to reign over them in A.D. 12.
9. E.g., *Encyclopaedia Brittanica*, see "Herod."
   E.g., Alexander, p. 256.
   E.g., Halley, pp. 459-460.
10. Spier, p. 13.
11. Ibid.

c. **The biblical leap year** added a thirteenth month every three years.[12] By this means, the lunar year was adjusted regularly to the solar year of 365 days. So the Bible uses both the moon and the sun to determine the year, as Genesis 1:14 confirms. The biblical year is therefore called a "luni-solar year."

2. The Twenty Four Divisions of the Priesthood

a. **First Chronicles 24:7-18** lists the divisions of the priesthood, giving the name of each. The thousands of priests in Israel were divided into these twenty-four smaller groups. There were sufficient priests in each group to meet the needs of the temple at any given moment, so only one group at a time would be in Jerusalem. Verse 19 also states that those divisions went to Jerusalem according to the "schedule" given there.[13]

b. **Each division ministered two weeks per year in Jerusalem.** However, they ministered only one week at a time, thus making two trips each year to Jerusalem.[14]

c. **The yearly schedule** began on the first day of the seventh month (Rosh Ha-shanah), with the first division. This was the first day of the civic year. The schedule did not begin on the first day of the first month, which was the first day of the religious year. Rosh Ha-shanah was the day of the Feast of Trumpets.[15] God's calendar was such that each division began and ended its ministry on precisely the same dates every year.

d. **The additional days of the year were covered by all the priests.** The divisions only provided temple ministry for forty-eight weeks each year (24 x 2 = 48). However, all priests were present in Jerusalem during the three principal feasts, or "pilgrim festivals."[16]

e. **Therefore, we can determine the precise days on which each of these divisions ministered during the year.** The twenty-four

12. Ibid., p. 14. Actually an extra month was added seven times in the course of nineteen years, in a predetermined fashion.
13. NKJV.
14. *Judaic Encyclopedia*, Keter Publishing House Ltd., Jerusalem, Israel, 1973, p. 91 ("Mishmar").
15. A complete schedule for these divisions, covering six full years, was discovered in the Qumran caves, confirming these details. This was one more key to establish the dates necessary for correctly interpreting Daniel's Seventy Weeks, a key providentially given in the "time of the end." See Bromiley, Vol. I, p. 688.
16. *Judaic Encyclopedia*, p. 91 ("Mishmar").

divisions ministered according to the schedule on the following page during every normal year:

Schedule for Twenty-Four Divisions of Priests

DIV:	MO/DY - MO/DY	DIV:	MO/DY - MO/DY	DIV:	MO/DY - MO/DY
1:	7/1 - 7/7	17:	11/3 - 11/9	**all**	3/6 (Pentecost)
2:	7/8 - 7/14	18:	11/10 - 11/16	9:	3/7 - 3/13
all	7/15 - 7/22 (Tabernacles)	19:	11/17 - 11/23	10:	3/14 - 3/20
3:	7/23 - 7/29	20:	11/24 - 11/30	11:	3/21 - 3/27
4:	7/30 - 8/6	21:	12/1 - 12/7	12:	3/28 - 4/4
5:	8/7 - 8/13	22:	12/8 - 12/14	13:	4/5 - 4/11
6:	8/14 - 8/20	23:	12/15 - 12/21	14:	4/12 - 4/18
7:	8/21 - 8/27	24:	12/22 - 12/28	15:	4/19 - 4/25
8:	**8/28 - 9/5**	1:	12/29 - 1/6	16:	4/26 - 5/3
9:	9/6 - 9/12	2:	1/7 - 1/13	17:	5/4 - 5/10
10:	9/13 - 9/19	**all**	1/14 - 1/21 (Passover)	18:	5/11 - 5/17
11:	9/20 - 9/26	3:	1/22 - 1/28	19:	5/18 - 5/24
12:	9/27 - 10/3	4:	1/29 - 2/5	20:	5/25 - 6/1
13:	10/4 - 10/10	5:	2/6 - 2/13	21:	6/2 - 6/8
14:	10/11 - 10/17	6:	2/14 - 2/20	22:	6/9 - 6/15
15:	10/18 - 10/24	7:	2/21 - 2/27	23:	6/16 - 6/22
16:	10/25 - 11/2	**8:**	**2/28 - 3/5**	24:	6/23 - 6/29

Explanation of Chart: This is the schedule by which the twenty-four divisions, or groups, of priests went to Jerusalem each year. It covers a full year, and begins with the seventh month because the first group of priests started on the first day of the seventh month.[17] According to the Bible, this was the beginning of the year for Israel. (We will see why later in this Appendix.) Each of the twenty-four division appears twice on the list, because they ministered in the Temple two different times each year, for a week each time. The number of each division, or group, of priests is the first number on each line. The week in which each of those divisions ministered is given alongside that number (month and day). For example, 5: 8/7 - 8/13 means division five ministered in the eighth month from the seventh to the thirteenth day. There were three times when all priests ministered together. That was during the three principal feasts. These times are indicated by the word "all" in place of a division number.

The Division of Abijah

The approximate month of Christ's birth can be determined by using the above chart, along with several details given in Luke 1. Zacharias, the

17. Bromiley, Vol. I, p. 688.

father of John the Baptist, was ministering in Jerusalem, with the division of Abijah, when Gabriel appeared to him (Lk. 1:5,8,11). Abijah was the eighth division to go to Jerusalem each year, according to First Chronicles 24:10. Referring to the above chart, we are able to find the two weeks in which the eighth division ministered in Jerusalem yearly. Those dates are 8/28 to 9/5, and 2/28 to 3/5 (the weeks of the eighth division are highlighted.) Therefore, Zacharias was in the temple ministering during one of those two weeks when he received the heavenly visitation.

There are two reasons why we conclude that Gabriel appeared to Zacharias during the second week (2/28 to 3/5). First, there is other biblical evidence for placing Christ's birth in the month of September. (We will consider it below.) However, if Gabriel appeared during the first week (8/28 to 9/5), then He could not have been born in September. Second, it will be noted in the chart that the second week of the eighth division brought Israel up to the time of the Feast of Pentecost. It is significant that the announcement of John the Baptist came at that very time, because he was the forerunner of the One who would baptize Israel in the Holy Spirit. That baptism in Acts 2 was going to bring Israel into a spiritual fulfillment of the Feast of Pentecost, just as the ministry of Zacharias and the division of Abijah were doing in the natural at that time. (That is, the ministry of Abijah ended at the Feast of Pentecost each year.)

Returning to Luke 1 we find that immediately after his days of ministry had ended two things happened. One, Zacharias returned immediately to his home (v. 23). Two, Elizabeth conceived immediately after his days of ministry were fulfilled (v. 23-24).[18] Therefore, since Zacharias arrived home a few days after the Feast of Pentecost (which was on 3/6), Elizabeth conceived around the middle or end of the third month.

Luke 1:36 states that the angel Gabriel visited Mary during Elizabeth's sixth month of pregnancy. **Immediately after** that visitation, Mary went to Elizabeth's house (v. 39). However, by the time Mary arrived there, the **Son of God had already been conceived in her womb**. This is evident from the words of Elizabeth (v. 42-43), and also from the reaction of John in Elizabeth's womb. According to John the Baptist, Christ was the One who brought him joy (Jn. 3:29). The first time John experienced that joy

18. It was the heavenly visitation that caused her to conceive. From several other biblical examples of barren women conceiving supernaturally, we are shown that the woman conceives as soon as the Word of the Lord comes. See Second Kings 4:16-18 and Genesis 18:10; 21:2. The "time of life" in Hebrew is an expression referring to the nine months between conception and birth, as seen in the first reference. In Luke 1 the same thing happened to Mary. She conceived at most within days after the heavenly visitation, as shown in the text above.

was when Mary, carrying His presence in her womb, visited Elizabeth that day. John leaped for joy in the womb of Elizabeth, because Christ was already there (v. 44). Therefore, Mary conceived shortly after Gabriel visited her, at most a few days later.

We now have sufficient facts to establish the month of Christ's birth. Elizabeth conceived around the middle or end of the third month. Then, approximately six months later, Gabriel visited Mary, and she conceived within days of that visitation. Therefore, Mary conceived around the end of the ninth or beginning of the tenth calendar month (about six months after Elizabeth conceived, in other words, six months after the third or fourth calendar month). Mary's nine months of pregnancy bring us to the sixth or seventh calendar month. The seventh month in the Bible corresponds to our month of September. So here is simple biblical evidence that Christ was born sometime around September.

Adam Was Created in the Seventh Month

According to Jewish calculations based on their calendar, the creation of the world took place on the first day of the month Tishri.[19] Tishri is the seventh month of their civic calendar and the first month of their religious calendar.[20] The Jews call this day Rosh Ha-shanah. In addition to this Jewish calculation, there is evidence supporting this concept in the Bible. In Exodus 23:16 the seventh month is referred to as "the end of the year." In other words, according to God's way of counting time, He declares that the seventh month is the end of the year. Therefore, His year ends in the seventh month of the civic year, which is the first month of the religious year.[21] Why does God do this?

At the moment a year ends, the new year begins. Therefore, the seventh month is not only the end of the year, but also the beginning of the year. God gave man six days, or 6,000 years, to do all his works (see Chapter 44). He started to count those years with the creation of Adam.[22] Since God calls the seventh month the "end of the year," it is evident that His years began with the creation of Adam. That event occurred, then, on the

19. Spier, p. 13.
20. Tenney, *Bible Dictionary*, p. 139.
21. Ibid.
22. It is evident that Adam and Eve did not spend even one year in the Garden together because God made them to be fruitful, and the first child was born outside the Garden of Eden.

first month of the religious calendar, which was the seventh month of the civic calendar.

We mentioned in Chapter 43 that the Church Age is exactly 2,000 years long. God is a Mathematician who does everything with precision. Since man is going to have precisely 6,000 years of history, and since the Church Age will be precisely 2,000 years long, then there were precisely 4,000 years between the "first Adam" and the "last Adam." So if time began with the seventh month, then the "last Adam" had to have been born in the seventh month also, exactly 4,000 years after the "first Adam." Again, this is the month of September.

Daniel's Seventy Weeks

In Part III we learned that there were exactly 62 weeks (434 years) plus 2,300 days between the command to restore Israel and the birth of Christ. This is possible only if He was born in either August or September. Therefore, Daniel gives us further evidence that He was born around that time.

The Ministry of Christ and Daniel 9:27

Chapters 36 and 37 of this book show that Christ will confirm His covenant for one week, or seven years. Daniel also states that those seven years have been divided into two halves of three and a half years each. Christ fulfilled the first half of that "week" during His earthly ministry, 2,000 years ago. We are able to determine the approximate month of His birth from these facts also. First, the Gospels tell us that Christ ended His ministry at the Passover, which is around March. Counting back three and half years from March brings us to September. He therefore began His ministry in September. Second, that was also around the time He was turning thirty years of age.[23] So His birthday must have been around September.

1,260 Days

The Feast of Tabernacles, to the Jewish mind, as well as to the mind of Christians who understand its significance, represents the Kingdom. Christ partially fulfilled that feast in His First Coming, when He came preaching and manifesting that Kingdom. Based on the way He linked

23. See footnote 12 in Chapter 31 concerning Luke 3:23.

His earthly ministry with the feasts of Israel,[24] it is **reasonable to suspect** that Christ began to manifest the fulfillment of that feast on, or around, the very time when Israel was celebrating it. It is usually celebrated in September. However, since we said it is "reasonable to **suspect**" that He began to minister around the time of that feast, we cannot draw any firm conclusions from this. We will only say that this is an "indication" that His ministry began in September. However, there is another "indication" that He began His ministry at the Feast of Tabernacles, and therefore in September. That indication is even stronger.

In Chapter 49 of this book we saw that there are always 1,260 days between the "great day" of the Feast of Tabernacles and the Feast of Passover, three and a half years later. The Word was made flesh in Christ. He experienced what is written, and He was also made to be like His "brethren" (Heb. 2:17). Since the two witnesses found in the last days will give a testimony of the gospel of the Kingdom for 1,260 days, it is likely that He too did the same in the beginning. And since He died on the Passover, the only way He could have had a ministry of 1,260 days was if He began that ministry on the Feast of Tabernacles, in September. Therefore, we have another very strong indication here that He was born around September, because He was either turning thirty or had just turned thirty at the time He began His ministry.

---

24. Examples: In John 6, He used the occasion of the Feast of Passover to feed the multitude and to teach on the Bread of Heaven. In John 7, He used the occasion of the Feast of Tabernacles to teach on the Water of Life (a concept directly related to the celebration of the feast). He died on the Passover, showing that He was the Passover Lamb. He rose from the dead and ascended to Heaven as the Firstfruits of God on the day Israel was celebrating the Feast of Firstfruits. Fifty days later, on the very day Israel was celebrating Pentecost, He sent its spiritual fulfillment to His disciples in Acts 2. In light of this pattern, which He established throughout His ministry and even afterward, we could say that it is "unreasonable" to believe He did not begin His ministry at the time of the Feast of Tabernacles, the feast His ministry actually fulfilled!

Appendix E

Answers to Commonly Asked Questions

In this Appendix we will present many of the questions that have been presented over the years during our seminars on the last days. Immediately following each question we will give a short answer.

1. Question: Don't all Christians go in the Rapture and participate in the wedding? Why will there be Christians on earth after the Rapture, watching and waiting for Him to return from the wedding?

Answer: Jesus answers that for us very clearly in Matthew 25:1-13 where He compares the Kingdom to ten virgins. Though all ten are part of the Kingdom, not all enter the wedding, because five do not have sufficient oil.

Perhaps there is a false hope in many immature Christians of participating in the Resurrection and Rapture. Paul had a longing to participate in the Resurrection, which will occur at the time of the Rapture (Phil. 3:11). But while writing the epistle to the Philippians, approximately six years before his death, Paul said that he had not yet attained that blessing in his life (Phil. 3:12-13). He had not finished his race or the fight. As seen, then, Jesus and Paul indicated that there are certain requirements that must be met to participate in the Rapture and the wedding.

Revelation 20:6 tells us that those who participate in the First Resurrection (which takes place at the Rapture of the Church)[1] are "blessed and holy." Those people will "reign with him a thousand years." Over whom will they reign? Some have said that the Church will reign over those who

---

1. 1 Thessalonians 4:16-18.

did not accept the Lord during the last days. However, Second Thessalonians 1:7-10 and Matthew 13 (the parable of the tares) tell us the wicked won't be here after His coming. When He comes He is going to send forth His angels to gather out of the Kingdom all who offend and do iniquity. Paul says that when He comes all those who "know not God, and that obey not the gospel of our Lord Jesus Christ" will be destroyed (2 Thess. 1:8-10). No one who has followed the beast or received his mark shall remain in the Kingdom after the Second Coming and the Battle of Armageddon.[2] Therefore, only Christians will remain in the Kingdom when He comes.

Zechariah 13:8-9 tells us that this will involve one-third of the world who have turned to the Lord during the tremendous outpouring of the Spirit, and the harvest, of the last days. But because they will be newborns they will not be ready to reign as kings with Christ. They will not go in the Rapture, but they will be watching and waiting for Him to return from the wedding!

2. Question: Is the great harvest at the same time as the Great Tribulation?

Answer: We have observed this throughout our study. When "darkness shall cover the earth, and gross darkness the people," then the "Lord shall arise upon thee [Jerusalem, the Church], and his glory shall be seen upon thee" (Isa. 60:1-3). The Great Tribulation will be a time of the greatest darkness the earth has ever seen, and at the same time it will be the time of the greatest light and visitation the world has ever seen.

Isaiah also tells us why this will be so. "When thy judgments are in the earth, the inhabitants of the world will learn righteousness" (Isa. 26:9). The greatest judgments of God ever witnessed by man will fall during the Great Tribulation. Therefore, it will also be a time when men learn righteousness more than at any other time in history!

3. Question: Since there are qualifications to participate in the Rapture, what will happen to the natural children of those who go in the Rapture, if they are not mature enough themselves to go to the wedding and reign with Christ?

Answer: This question is asked in most seminars, and is a concern of any normal parent. We saw in Exodus 19 a revelation of the Rapture, where the Church is brought up into Mount Zion at the sound of the trumpet. Note that the "elders" of Israel, those who were mature, went up into

2. Revelation 14:10-11 makes it clear what will happen to anyone who receives the mark of the beast. The end of that way, as revealed there, is anything but a wonderful time of blessing in the millennial Kingdom!

the mount, but the rest of Israel did not (Ex. 24:9-11). The Church goes up the same way into the Mount Zion of Revelation 14:1.

I will give the answer I give in every seminar where this question comes up. I do not know! However, there is one thing I do know, and of which my wife and I are **very** sure, having traveled around this world as missionaries with four small children. God loves our little children more than we do! He cares for them in loving and tender ways far beyond our abilities. Over and over we have seen Him provide for them in ways we would not even have considered or imagined! Not one little detail escapes Him. He is so loving and kind that whatever His plan for the little children is, it will be wonderful! It will reveal that same love He manifested toward them when He was on earth, and will bring great joy to all of us!

4. Question: I understand that the coming of the Lord involves three aspects. He first comes **in** His people in 1996, in a spiritual birth, or spiritual coming, then **for** His people in the Rapture in the year 2000, but when will He come physically **with** His people, once the wedding has taken place?

Answer: Jesus says no one knows the day or the hour of this event, as we mentioned above. I do not have the precise answer to that question, but from Daniel 12:11-12 we are given the impression that His coming, after the Rapture, will take place in a matter of **days**, not months or years.

5. Question: What will happen to Christians who are in the "outer court" of the Temple after Christ manifests Himself in the Temple in the year 1996? (That is, the Christians who are in the outer court that is mentioned in Revelation 11:2 rather than being in the Holy Place, or the Holy of Holies).

Answer : With these Satan makes war, according to Revelation 12:17 and 13:7. He is unable to conquer the "man child" of Revelation 12; rather he himself is conquered by that man child. He can do nothing against the woman, because she is protected by the Lord. So, just as any bully would, he picks on someone who is small and weaker. This is actually a revelation of Satan's weakness, and this brings further glory to God. Satan did the same thing when Israel came out of Egypt. He attacked those who were the weakest and furthest behind in the journey (Deut. 25:17-18). But those who are martyred in this way receive an eternal reward and inheritance in the Lord.

6. Question: This study states that the thousand-year reign of Christ will begin in A.D. 1996, when Christ comes in His Temple. During that time there will be both harvest and also Great Tribulation, as Satan and the Antichrist war against the people of God. However, the Bible says that Satan will be bound a thousand years and placed in the bottomless pit.

How can a three-and-a-half-year period (where Satan is still loose) fit into the thousand year reign of Christ if it begins in A.D. 1996, because, at that time, Satan will not yet be in the pit?

Answer: First, we note that Jesus bound Satan before He began His earthly ministry. For that reason He was able to enter his house, and spoil him.[3] However, the fact that Satan was "bound" during that period did not mean that he was already in the bottomless pit. Being bound and being in the bottomless pit are clearly two different things.

In Revelation 20:1-2 an angel comes and **binds Satan for a thousand years.** Then, in verse 3, he casts him into the bottomless pit. It is important to note that the Bible says he will be bound a thousand years. It does not say he will be in the pit for a thousand years. Then in verses 3 and 7 we are told that "when the thousand years are expired" Satan will be loosed. But the "thousand years" refers to the time in which he is "bound," not the length of time he spends in the pit.

So then, the Church will be able to spoil Satan's house during the last three and a half years of the Church Age, just as Christ did for that length of time in the beginning. This will happen because Satan will first be bound. We see this happening in Revelation 12, followed by a period of three and a half years. The angel that fights against him there is Michael. The result is that Satan is bound, in the sense that he can no longer occupy the heavenly realm (v. 8,9,13). All his activities will be limited to the earth at that time. When the principalities and powers in heavenly places no longer occupy that position, revival will come to the nations of the earth. The Church will be able to spoil, and take, the kingdoms of this world, which have been controlled by Satan. For that reason Revelation 12:10 states, "Now is come...the kingdom of our God, and the power of his Christ."

In conclusion, Satan will be bound for a thousand years, beginning in A.D. 1996. Three and a half years afterward he will be cast into the bottomless pit. He will remain there until the thousand years have expired. Therefore, he will actually spend about 997 years in the pit, but will be bound for a thousand years.

7. Question: The Bible says that we should obey the authorities that are placed over us. If the Church is here during the Great Tribulation, when the Antichrist will be ruling, won't we have to disobey God's command to submit?

---

3. Matthew 12:28-29.

Answer: The beginning of the Church Age gives us the answer. The recognized governmental authority over Judea and the Jews was the council in Jerusalem. However, Peter made it clear to that council that the apostles were going to obey God and not man (Acts 4:19). Several examples in the Bible show us that our first responsibility is to obey the Lord. Afterward, if we can obey the Lord and the earthly authority at the same time, we should do so. The Bible never teaches us to obey man first and the Lord second. If this were the case, the Christians who are currently living in countries that oppress the Church would have to renounce the Lord, because that is what the authorities demand in some of those places. This question would not even be asked in a country such as China or Russia today. The Christians there already face the problem, and know what to do—they obey the Lord!

8. Question: Understanding that the Church Age will last 2,000 years, when did those years begin? With the birth of Christ, or with the outpouring of the Holy Spirit on the Day of Pentecost?

Answer: Colossians 1:18 declares that Jesus Christ is the "head of the body, the church." It would be a little presumptuous on our part to believe that the Church began when we entered, and not when the Head of the Body came! The Church Age began, therefore, with the birth, or coming, of Christ, the Head. It did not begin when the first members of the Body entered the Church on the Day of Pentecost!

9. Question: Does the millennium begin in A.D. 1996 according to our calendar, the Gregorian calendar?

Answer: Yes. Our calendar has an error of about four years. Therefore, the end of 1996 on our calendar is, in reality, the end of 2,000 years since the birth of Christ, which was the beginning of the Church Age.

10. Question: When will Armaggedon take place?

Answer: The Battle will be fought at the Second Coming, when Christ comes with His people, after the Rapture (Rev. 19:8-21). Therefore, it will be fought shortly after the Rapture in the year 2000.

11. Question: When does the Battle of Gog and Magog occur?

Answer: That Battle occurs at the end of the thousand-year reign of Christ (Rev. 20:7-9).

12. Question: The millennial reign of Christ is called a "reign of peace." How then can it start with the Great Tribulation and the Battle of Armageddon?

Answer: Solomon's reign was also called a "reign of peace." However, he began that reign with a time of tremendous judgments on the wicked. That reign and throne, inherited by the earthly son of David, are a revelation of

Christ's reign and throne, and the heavenly Son of David. Jesus Himself said that when He comes He will first send His angels to gather out of the Kingdom all that offend and do iniquity (Mt. 13:30, 41). They have to first be in the Kingdom for the angels to be able to take them out of the Kingdom! So the Kingdom begins with wicked people still present on the earth.

13. Question: In Revelation 12 the woman, which is the Church, flees into a desert. Is this a physical desert?

Answer: All the other symbols and terms used there in relation to the woman clearly have a spiritual meaning. Therefore, it is safe to say that the desert is a spiritual condition also. Furthermore, preparing for the Tribulation through natural means would go contrary to one of the things the Lord wants to teach man in the end. He will show that the arm of flesh cannot save us, but that He can do so through a supernatural deliverance. If we were to try to save ourselves by storing up food, etc., then we would disprove the very thing He is trying to prove!

14. Question: Why are we sanctifying ourselves today, if we are going to be in the Great Tribulation anyway?

Answer: The Lord commands us to sanctify ourselves and be holy because He is holy (Lev. 11:44). We do so because we want to walk with a Holy God, and experience His presence, not because we want to escape a time of purification that will make us even more holy!

15. Question: How many Raptures will there be?

Answer: Some have taught that the mature Christians will be raptured before the rest of the Church. God always gave His people the very best leadership in the time of greatest affliction and trial. That is the nature of our Father's heart. Moses in Egypt is an example, as are the judges found in the Book of Judges.

16. Question: In this study you say that the leaders of the Church will not be raptured before the rest of the Church. However, the study also declares that not all Christians will participate in the Rapture. Won't the leaders be leaving the others behind at that time?

Answer: It is true that there are qualifications for participating in the Rapture, as we have considered. It is also true that some Christians will remain on earth when the leaders of the Church, and all who have been prepared for the wedding, depart in the Rapture. However, we are talking here about a matter of days, not years. The leaders will leave and then return with Christ a short time later (after the wedding), when He comes to establish His Kingdom on the earth. The Second Coming will be a few days after the Rapture, not a few years! It will be much the same as when

Moses went up into Mount Sinai for forty days in Exodus, leaving the children of Israel behind in the valley. Let's remember that Exodus 19 and Hebrews 12:18-29 link that experience of Moses and Mount Sinai with the Second Coming and Rapture.

17. Question: What about the "historicists" who say that all of the Seventy Weeks of Daniel have already been fulfilled by the events of history, long before Israel returned to Palestine through the command of 1947? The historicists believe that the "futurists" interpret Daniel incorrectly when they say that at least part of the Seventy Weeks has not yet been fulfilled.

Answer: The historicists believe that Daniel's Seventy Weeks should be interpreted using the "year-day" principle, where each of the 490 days represent a year. If this is the case, then all Scriptures in Daniel and Revelation that speak about a certain number of days must be interpreted using the same principle. Therefore, the 2,300 days of Daniel 8 are supposedly 2,300 years, and the 1260 days of Revelation 11 are 1,260 years. They argue that futurists have no right to use the "year-day" principle for Daniel's Seventy Weeks, but not for other Scriptures. One example of historicist theology says that the 2,300 days found in Daniel 8:14, during which the sanctuary would be "trodden under foot," are the 2300 years from 334 B.C. when Alexander the Great conquered the East and A.D. 1967 when the Jews regained Jerusalem.[4]

What is incorrect about this theology? First, it is possible that their concepts have **some** validity. The prophecies of the Bible often have more than one fulfillment, but saying that this is *the* interpretation is, I believe, an error. There may well have been a measure of historical fulfillment to many prophecies found in Daniel and Revelation, but it can be shown that they are not the *primary* fulfillment God had in mind. It seems that all the prophetic messages in the Bible point to the end, and not only to history. Remember, history repeats itself over and over, and especially in the end.

Without question, it is interesting that 2,300 years fit between Alexander the Great and A.D. 1967, but to say that this is *the* fulfillment of those 2,300 days presents major problems. First, a careful reading of the vision of Daniel 8 and of its interpretation, given by the angel, shows that it was a "little horn" that came out of the great Conqueror from Greece who took away the daily sacrifice and trod under foot the sanctuary. It was not Alexander the Great who did this, but rather Antiochus Epiphanes. In so many words, the question posed in verse 13 is, "How

4. Caringola, Robert, *Seventy Weeks: The Historical Alternative*, Companion Press, Shippensburg, Pennsylvania, 1991, p. 69.

long will the vision concerning the work of the little horn last?" The answer is 2,300 days. So we can't use Alexander here, or the date of his conquest.

Furthermore, the sanctuary was not trodden under foot, nor the daily sacrifice taken away, during all of the 2,300 years between Alexander and A.D. 1967. In fact, during most of the years from Alexander until Christ's day the Jews offered the daily sacrifice, and had a temple that was ritually clean and free from Gentile presence or defilement. Not only this, but A.D. 1967 was not the end of their problems, because they were not able to return to the daily sacrifice after regaining control of Jerusalem, nor is there even a temple on Mount Moriah to be trodden under foot. Far from their temple being free again from the Gentiles, the Gentiles continue to tread under foot the temple mount, where a Gentile temple continues to exist! This is just one of many problems that are not answered by the historicists' interpretation of prophecy.

In conclusion, the historicists say that the futurists have no right to use the "year-day" principle to interpret Daniel's Seventy Weeks, and ignore it in other Scriptures. The grave fault in that reasoning is that the word "week" in Hebrew actually means a "week of seven years," as we have already learned. It's not an issue of "right," but rather that no one has any "right" to interpret Daniel's Weeks otherwise! To carry that clear biblical principle over to every other Scripture in the Bible that speaks about days could be called a giant leap of faith if it weren't presumption.

Bibliography

Alexander, David and Patricia Alexander, eds., *Eerdmans' Concise Bible Handbook,* William B. Eerdmans Publishing Co., Grand Rapids, Michigan, 1980.

Barrett, David, *World Christian Encyclopedia,* Oxford University Press, Nairobi, Kenya, 1982.

Blaiklock, E.M. and R.K. Harrison, eds., *The New International Dictionary of Biblical Archaeology,* Zondervan Publishing House, Grand Rapids, Michigan, 1983.

Bromiley, Geoffrey W., *The International Standard Bible Encyclopedia,* Vol. I., William B. Eerdmans Publishing Co., Grand Rapids, Michigan, 1979.

Caringola, Robert, *Seventy Weeks: The Historical Alternative,* Companion Press, Shippensburg, Pennsylvania, 1991.

Collier's Encyclopedia, Halsey, William D., editorial director, Johnston, Bernard, ed.-in-chief, Macmillan Educational Company, New York, P.F. Collier, Inc., New York, Vol. 17, 1988.

Dake, Finis, Jennings, *Revelation Expounded,* Dake Bible Sales, Inc., Lawrenceville, Georgia, 1977.

Dubnov, Simon, *History of the Jews,* A.S. Barnes and Company, Inc., Thomas Yoseloff, Publisher, Cranbury, New Jersey, Vol. I, 1967.

Edersheim, Alfred, *The Life and Times of Jesus the Messiah,* Eerdmans Publishing Co., Grand Rapids, Michigan, 1969.

Egan, Jack, *A Genuine Common Market?,* U.S. News and World Report, November 7, 1988.

Encyclopaedia Brittanica, Encyclopaedia Brittanica, Inc., William Benton, Publisher, Chicago, Illinois, Vol. 11, 1973.

Green, Jay, ed., *The Interlinear Hebrew/Greek English Bible,* Associated Publishers and Authors, Inc., Evansville, Indiana, 1978.

Halley, Henry H., *Halley's Bible Handbook,* Zondervan Publishing House, Grand Rapids, Michigan, 1965.

Hartom, A.S., *The Book of Daniel Explained,* "Yavneh" Publishing House, Tel Aviv, Israel, 1966.

Hicks, Laurel, ed., *The History of the World in Christian Perspective,* A Beka Book Publications, Pensacola, Florida, Vol. I.

Illustrated Bible Dictionary, The, Inter-varsity Press, Tyndale House Publishers, Wheaton, Illinois, 1986.

Josephus, Flavius, *The Antiquities of the Jews,* Kregel Publications, Grand Rapids, Michigan, 1981.

Judaic Encyclopedia, Keter Publishing House Ltd., Jerusalem, Israel, 1973.

Lucas, Jerry, and Del Washburn, *Theomatics,* Stein and Day Publishers, New York, New York, 1978.

MacPherson, Dave, *The Great Rapture Hoax,* New Puritan Library, Fletcher, North Carolina, 1983.

Marshall, Alfred, *The R.S.V. Interlinear Greek-English New Testament,* Zondervan Publishing House, Grand Rapids, Michigan, 1970.

Morris, William, ed., *The American Heritage Dictionary of the English Language,* Houghton Mifflin Company, Boston, Massachusetts, 1981.

Nelson, Thomas, The Open Bible Expanded Edition, The New King James Version, Thomas Nelson Publishers, Nashville, Tennessee, 1983.

New International Version, The Holy Bible, Zondervan Bible Publishers, Grand Rapids, Michigan, 1978.

Packer, James I., Merrill C. Tenney, William White, Jr., eds., *The Bible Almanac,* Thomas Nelson Publishers, Nashville, Tennessee, 1980.

Spier, Arthur, *The Comprehensive Hebrew Calendar,* Feldheim Publishers Ltd., Jerusalem, Israel, 1986.

Strong, James, *Strong's Exhaustive Concordance,* Baker Book House, Grand Rapids, Michigan, 1977.

Sullivan, Scott, "The Czar of Brussels," *Newsweek,* February 6, 1989.

Tenney, Merrill C., *The Zondervan Pictorial Bible Dictionary,* Zondervan Publishing House, Grand Rapids, Michigan, 1967.

Tenney, Merrill C., ed., *The Zondervan Pictorial Encyclopedia of the Bible,* Zondervan Publishing House, Grand Rapids, Michigan, 1975.

The Lockman Foundation, *New American Standard Bible,* A.J. Holman Company, Philadelphia, Pennsylvania, 1973.

Thompson, Frank Charles, *The Thompson Chain-Reference Bible,* B.B. Kirkbride Bible Co., Inc., Indianapolis, Indiana, 1964.

Unger, Merrill F., *Unger's Bible Dictionary,* Moody Press, Chicago, 1978.

Vine, W.E., *An Expository Dictionary of New Testament Words,* Fleming H. Revell Company, Old Tappan, New Jersey, 1966.

Hebron Ministerial Institute

Does your heart long to know the Lord in a deeper, more intimate way? The purpose, calling, and ministry of Hebron Ministerial Institute in the United States and Guatemala, Central America is to share vital keys from God's Word that will help hungry hearts experience the joy of His presence. Our vision is to share revelation on God's Word that ministers to the heart, not only impart academic information about His Word.

The program consists of a completé two-year course. All the courses listed below are already available in Spanish by either video or audio cassette. Many of the courses are also being made available in English on both video and audio cassette. For those who are able to dedicate two full years to the study of God's Word, Hebron offers a complete bi-lingual Ministerial Institute in Guatemala, Central America. The modern facilities include housing for both single and married students.

The curriculum includes a complete study of the books of the Bible, along with many other related subjects needed for effectual and victorious Christian living. Some of those related subjects covered in the two year course are listed below:

The Tabernacle of Moses
The Journey of Israel
The Priesthood
The Offerings
The Feasts
Foundational Doctrines
The Tabernacle of David
and Praise

Customs of Bible Times
The Hope of the Christian
Christian Ethics
Prayer
Homiletics
Hermeneutics
Church Government
The Local Church

Women of the Bible
The Holy Spirit and His Gifts
Doctrine of God
Doctrine of Man, Sin, and Salvation
The Names of God
Life of the Pastor and Practical Ministry
The Principles of the Kingdom
The Fruit of the Spirit
Marriage and the Family
Bible Geography
Divine Guidance
Apostolic Principles for a Ministry
Numerology
Typology
The Relation Between the Beginning and Ending
The Cross
Evangelism
The Fear of God
How to Give Counsel
Evolution and the Bible

For more information write to either of the following addresses:

Hebron Ministries
Section 0374 P.O. Box 02-5289
Miami, FL 33102-5289

Hebron Ministries
P.O. Box 765
Mount Clemens, MI 48046-0765

Hebron Ministries
2203 E. 11 Mile Rd.
Royal Oak, MI 48067

Or call:
1-800-LAST-DAY (1-800-527-8329) in the U.S.
or
33-26-15 in Guatemala City, Central America